Acclaim for

CAN'T IS NOT AN OPTION

"In the 1980s, the founder and director of ArtExpo, Gerald Leberfeld, did more then anyone to introduce art and artists to the American public. Through ArtExpo he created a giant canvas for all people to feel comfortable in a place many felt intimidated. Leo Castelli, perhaps the greatest art dealer of the twentieth century, said he couldn't believe that Jerry could get so many new people interested in art. I will never forget the '80s and this special time that we worked together."

—PETER MAX

"When I was young, a wise man I trusted told me that when you choose a business partner, look for three important qualities: intelligence, integrity, and industry. My former FunExpo partner, Jerry Leberfeld, earned a perfect score in all three. And thanks, Jerry, for never letting me settle for giving less than 100 percent effort. It's a lesson that has served me well throughout my professional life. Told in his unique voice, this book is the "refresher course: that we all need in how to work smart and beat the odds."

—BAILEY BEEKEN
VICE PRESIDENT AND EXECUTIVE DIRECTOR,
LINCOLN HEALTHCARE EVENTS

"Gerald Leberfeld, founder and director of ArtExpo, has transformed the business of art, changing it from a business conducted in hushed whispers behind closed doors to an open forum, stimulating in its diversity and scope and accessible to all. We have ordered a case of books to share with our employees, our clients, and anyone who seeks and appreciates an honest American success story."

—PAUL BAKER AND LARRY WINOKUR,
CEOS, B | W | R PUBLIC RELATIONS

"Partnering with Jerry Leberfeld in reopening the New York Coliseum and building a fabulous Antique Show together were great achievements as well as an amazing adventure. A rare partner and a brilliant businessman. Jerry's book is sure to be a true collectible!"

IRENE STELLA, PRESIDENT,
STELLA SHOW MANAGEMENT

CAN'T IS NOT AN OPTION

Benny the Book's Book

GERALD LEBERFELD

Aviva Publishing
New York, NY

ISBN: 978-0-6158018-4-1

Cover and Interior Design: Gary A. Rosenberg

Printed in the United States of America

10   9   8   7   6   5   4   3   2   1

Contents

To my only siblings, Maxine and Freya,
who left me—and this world—much too soon.
I miss them terribly.

To my children, Michelle and Daniel,
and to my son-in-law, Scott Whitney,
who kept encouraging me to do this book.

And of course to my darling wife, Aviva,
who has been all things to me:
supporter, mother of my children,
lover, listener, and critic,
and thus the foundation for everything good in my life.

Introduction

In November 2011, I decided to write my memoirs, but it was, in fact, the 75th year of my life that the process started that brought me to this point. At that stage of our lives, we begin to question our mortality or immortality—in other words, how much time we have left, and we reflect on these realities.

In 2008, Aviva and I went to Charlotte, North Carolina to visit our friends, Claude and Ree Stone, at Christmastime. These visits always include long family conversations about anything and everything. Claude Stone's brother Jim was a retired president of a major American corporation, who always loves to engage me in new and different business ideas. In 2008, Jim suggested that we start a new business called Death-A-Sketch, which would involve finding methods of engraving a photo of the deceased on their tombstone. It was an impractical, unprofitable, and somewhat ridiculous idea, but we spent that Christmas evening laughing our way through the different ways we might develop this business.

It just wasn't a good enough idea. Funeral homes wouldn't be able to make any money on it. It's too much trouble to pursue, for its limited potential. So nothing came of it, but it put in my mind the idea that once you die, your whole life story and experiences totally die with you. When you reach the later years of your life, most of us start losing good friends and acquaintances. If these people are fortunate, they might receive six or eight lines in their obituary in the local newspaper, but most people—including prominent actors, artists, business executives, scientists, etc.—are quickly forgotten.

To me, it seems unimaginable and inappropriate that the great stories of almost all human beings are relegated to only a brief obituary and are not passed on to any other members of our society. Personally, I love to read biographies of important, successful people. Much of my motivation in life was enhanced by the biographies of three special heroes in my life, namely Abraham Lincoln, Winston Churchill, and Ronald Reagan. They all had many things in common: for example, they were multifaceted human beings. Their political lives were all complemented by their ability in other endeavors, such as painting, writing, poetry, acting, and much more.

They were all personally attacked in their political lives, and they were called such things as stupid, unpatriotic, just to name a few. They had a great talent to succeed in the most difficult periods in the history of the world. One of their major assets was to admit that they were human, sometimes wrong to the point that they were able to change their worldly point of view as circumstances dictated, even changing their political parties.

My love to dwell on the personal lives of so many accomplished individuals made me hunger for the idea of keeping people's life stories in perpetuity. So I developed a business idea that goes like this: Starting a website called myobituary.com. I would retain a group of professional writers: God knows there are plenty of good ones available, who can assist people in writing what they want to remember about their lives. It could be one page, or it could be an entire book, whatever suits each person. You can write your own obituary, or you can hire a professional writer to work with you. And the information you provide would be a permanent part of this website that any person could access in the future. Or you could restrict it to certain family members by establishing an access code or leave it open to anybody's interest by categories. There are many people in my somewhat small circle who are either Holocaust survivors or in science and business who would make one last investment in their own life's experiences.

Then I would take it a step further. I would develop an electronic chip in which their story, or part of their history, would be permanently recorded in this chip and would be placed on the tombstone or in a bank vault or any other place that family and friends desired. That way, you could go to the cemetery, or even your computer, and you can access the story of one of your ancestors or someone whom you were interested in. Again, you could limit accessibility to access codes or not. Everybody I discussed this idea with loved it, and, of course, it needs development, which takes time, energy, and some investment. The greatest part is you never run out of customers.

Secondly, this is a great new income stream for funeral homes and cemeteries. At my age, I need somebody to run with this idea, but as I discovered with my many prior ventures, there are very few who are willing to take on new ideas and give it the appropriate time and effort. So if you like the idea, it's yours to run with, and if it's a big success, just remember to credit me in your own obituary!

Then in 2011, I decided to write my own memoirs Perhaps it's an ego trip, but really, I simply wanted to explain to others how one child of immigrants and his Holocaust-surviving wife could start with nothing but desire and ambition and reach the American Dream. This would be "Benny the Book's book."

It's been a very difficult and long process, especially now that I'm one year into the project and still anticipating another few months before it's complete. Remember the name of the book, though: *Can't Is Not an Option*. I hope that after reading this preface, you'll read on, and if you do, I think you'll find it entertaining, humorous, and perhaps instructive.

More than anything, people ask why, at my age, would I spend all this time and money on such a project? To me, it was a no-brainer. I'm proud of what I've done with my life, and I want to share this story with my family, and especially my grandchildren, and anybody else who might be interested. As for the money, publishing my memoir will probably cost me over $10,000. To me, that's a small investment—if it can positively affect one person's life with the story of my life, it will be well worth the cost. This effort, for me, will have much greater lasting value than an expensive vacation or a bad stock investment.

In reflecting on this idea, a second motivation appeared to finally close the deal. In the spring of 1951, I was in my senior year at Far Rockaway High School and scheduled to graduate that June. I had already been accepted to a small college in Plattsburgh, New York, called Champlain, and I was the first person in my family to go to college.

Then my English teacher, Mr. Traeger, told me he was going to give me a failing grade of 62, which meant I could not graduate with my friends and classmates. He told me I was a wise guy, and I didn't take English seriously, and he was going to teach me a lesson. He said I would never make it in this world, that my grammar and my writing skills were awful, etc. So this book is for Mr. Traeger. I'm sending him a free autographed copy, and I would appreciate if he would take time to read it, wherever he may be.

P.S. My parents went to our principal, Mrs. Riley, who superseded on my behalf and persuaded my English teacher that there were no grounds for this extreme action. This experience probably helped me become a stronger person, and encouraged me to work even harder to make something of myself.

So please, travel along with me in GL's life adventure in reading *Benny the Book's Book.*

Following the Laws

In considering my best way to write this book I utilized some parameters and ideals that I followed in my life calling them "Jerry's Law's." They consist of rules that motivated me in making the proper decisions in all aspects of my life both business and personal. These guidelines came together from 3 sources: My own words, actions and words of people I most respected and my children's interpretations of how I lived my life.

Jerry's Laws are interwoven into my memoirs where specific circumstances required specific actions. Those laws have given me strength and direction in making the right decisions, and I believe will help you understand the mindset that has influenced my life.

—*Jerry Leberfeld*

JERRY'S LAWS

1. If anything goes wrong, fix it. (To hell with Murphy!)
2. When given a choice, take both.
3. Multiple projects lead to multiple successes.
4. Start at the top and work your way up.
5. Do it by the book, but be the author.
6. When forced to compromise, ask for more.
7. If you can't beat them, join them, *then* beat them.
8. If it's worth doing, do it right.
9. If you can't win, change the rules.
10. If you can't change the rules, ignore them.
11. Perfection is not optional.
12. You learn much more by listening than by talking.
13. "No" simply means begin again at a level higher. Deal direct and always qualify.
14. Inspect what you expect.
15. Bureaucracy is a challenge to be conquered with a righteous attitude, a tolerance for stupidity, and a bulldozer when necessary.
16. Patience is a virtue, but persistence to the point of success is a blessing.
17. The faster you move, the slower time passes, the longer you live.
18. You cannot do the minimum and reach the maximum.
19. Verify to clarify.
20. Winston Churchill said, "Never give up." I say, "Never, never give in."

1

Growing Up
in Rockaway Beach

I was born in Brooklyn, New York, on September 18, 1933. My father, Harry, and my mother, Esther, had my sister, Maxine, five years earlier. This was during the middle of the Great Depression, although I was too young to have any personal recollections. I had no awareness of where we lived; all I know is it was somewhere in Brooklyn. Because of my family's financial situation, my parents moved every year: in those difficult days, if you signed a one-year lease, you would get one month free and a new paint job for the apartment, so that's what my parents did to survive.

My first recollection of the neighborhood in which we lived was when I was five years old, at 3099 6th Street in Brighton Beach, Brooklyn, which is close to Coney Island. We lived one block from the boardwalk and ocean in a very nice apartment building with an elevator; two of my father's sisters, Pearl and Hannah, each had their own apartments in the building. The subway in that part of Brooklyn is elevated, and I believe we were the last stop on the D line.

I was greatly affected by a dramatic incident that happened when I was about 5 years old. I remember playing on the sidewalk outside my building where one of the older children, who was maybe 8 years old, was playing ball with a friend. The ball accidentally rolled into the middle of the street, and this child ran between two parked cars and was struck and killed instantly by a motorcycle. The image of that child's body parts all over the street was so traumatic and is still engraved on my mind. To this day, I'm very nervous whenever I see young children playing in the street.

Around that same time, my family faced real tragedy, when my ten-year-old sister Maxine died. I only vaguely remember her, since I was only five years old, but every relative in my family said she was the happiest, most fun-loving child. I was told she was climbing up on a heavy dresser to reach something, and the dresser tipped over and fell on her, and after that, she became ill and died. Some called it cancer, but my family didn't really know what happened: whatever her cause of death was never specifically diagnosed, at least not to my knowledge.

My parents were understandably devastated and grieved over the loss of their very young, wonderful first child. Seven years after Maxine's death, my parents decided to have another child as a way to fill the void in their lives; my sister Freya was born. Her name came from a German war movie that my father's wealthy sister, my Aunt Jean had loved. Apparently she suggested this name strongly, and perhaps there was even a gift involved; I'm not sure. Freya was a very unusual and interesting name, so nobody ever forgot it.

I have another strong memory of Brighton Beach from about 1940, when the Second World War was on in Europe, and the U.S. was preparing our military for potential involvement against the Germans. Our military assembled on the beach in Brighton to pitch tents and train for possible war; they even brought tanks and artillery. I was around 7 years old, and I walked all by myself to the boardwalk to observe the excitement of what was happening, and I got lost. My parents had no idea where I was, which created quite a panic, but eventually the police found me. This experience sent patriotic juices through my system, which have stayed with me my entire life. I can't quite explain why, but it's a good feeling.

In 1940, we moved to Rockaway Beach in Queens, New York, to be closer to where my mother's sister, Ronnie, lived with her husband, Al

Miller. They owned a small grocery store and worked seven days a week. That's what people did in those days to survive; there was no welfare, just hard work. We lived with them in their house for about a year, and then we rented an apartment in a two-family house around the corner on Swan Road in Arverne; it was between 68th and 69th Streets, one block from the beach.

In 1942, when I was 9 years old, we moved to 216 Beach 69th Street, which was only two blocks from Swan Road and one block from the Millers' grocery store. This was between Rockaway Beach Boulevard and the railroad, which at that time was not an underground subway or elevated but at street level. My parents bought a ten-room house for $2,500, and we lived there until I went into the military in 1954. My life changed dramatically when we bought our own house, and that's where most of my childhood memories are from.

Our house became the social center for my friends. At the time we bought that house in 1942, Rockaway was booming: it was the place where everybody from all over the city of New York came during the summer. The beach was beautiful, and the rentals were reasonable. The boardwalk was filled with food concessions and clothing stores and a penny arcade, which was a little amusement center. It was a great place for families to go to get away from the hot, scalding city (that lacked air-conditioning) and enjoy the cooler community at the beach. People were trying to get away from the horrors of the war, and Rockaway Beach became even more popular in 1945 and 1946 when the war was winding down.

There were probably 20,000 people living year-round on the 10-mile Rockaway peninsula, which goes from Neponset to Far Rockaway, yet during the summer season, this increased to a population of more than a million. There were cottages along the beach that were used only during the summer (they weren't winterized), and there were some larger rooming houses that people rented a room at a time. Almost everyone who owned a house in Rockaway rented out part of their home to summer tenants. In the 1940s, there was very little affordable long-distance transportation, so people vacationed locally, not like they do today.

As mentioned, our house had ten rooms, and my father rented every room that was available: in fact, he even asked my sister and me to move out of our rooms during the summer and to sleep either on the porch or in some other place in the house. Our attic had three rooms, which we usually rented to one family of four or five people. And we had a few more people renting my sister's room and my room. In total, we had anywhere from seven to ten people living with us every summer. The rooms were rented out only in the summer from the time we bought the house in 1942 until 1950.

By renting out rooms in the summer, my father was able to supplement his income substantially. My room was rented for around $300, so my father probably made more than $1,000 for the whole house every summer, which was a tremendous amount of money compared to his regular income at that time.

I suppose we all wished we could have our rooms to ourselves, instead of renting them out, but we didn't resent the situation. We knew this was what we had to do, and we knew it was helping us financially. And most of my friends had the same situation: it was very customary in those days.

We interacted with the tenants, but we didn't become friends. Essentially, everybody tried to stay out of each other's way since we were living in such close quarters. People find that hard to do today, and most houses were smaller then. We were polite to our tenants, and once in a while I made a friend, but the friendship typically didn't last since the summer tenants would come and go quickly.

There is one thing I'll never forget about living in Rockaway Beach. In those days, there were no air-conditioners, and we didn't even have very many fans. So when the nights were very hot and humid, when the temperature was in the 90s, almost everybody in Rockaway took blankets, towels, and pillows and slept on the beach. Beaches are usually 10 degrees cooler than inland, and if you're right beside the water, it's even cooler. Nobody was concerned about being robbed or mugged or harmed in any way; we just slept there. I'll never forget those days: sleeping on the beach was great fun.

Around 1950, things began to change as air travel became less expensive and more common, so people began to take vacations to more exotic places, like Florida or the Caribbean—which were exotic back then! In fact, in all the years when I was growing up, my parents took us on only one vacation to Florida, and a couple of times we went to the

Catskill Mountains. That was our travel experience. And who did we meet in those places? The same people we were growing up with: middle-class Jewish people. We all called ourselves middle-class in those days. Many times, it was more of a dream than a reality.

From the time we moved into that house, many things happened. My father bought an early television set. We couldn't really afford it, but he wanted a television, and maybe the money he got from the summer tenants helped pay for it. I remember it was an Andrea television, which in those days was one of the best sets made, and I think the company still exists, although it doesn't make television sets anymore.

That TV gave my father real power. He used to sit in front of it all day long (when he wasn't working), but he'd let us bring our friends, though he would be selective about how many could come and at what time. Everybody wanted to be at our house since hardly anybody else had a television set with such a large screen—it must have been 12 inches—so we always had visitors. The first television set I ever saw was at my friend Gary's house: his parents had a seven-inch television set, and Gary invited a few of his closest friends to watch. Some of us sat on the stoop outside his house by the window, and we found a space to peep in. We couldn't hear anything, but we were fascinated by just the *idea* that there was a television set, something speaking or singing to us. It was amazing. Today, of course, every one of my grandchildren has access to television as well as a computer, an iPad, an iPod, and any other new gadget that comes on the market. But back in the 1940s, when I was a kid, the family shared a radio.

I was a very happy child. I had so many friends growing up. Our toys were things like chemistry sets or Erector sets, which were fun and also taught us something. Most of the time, though, we played stickball with Spaldeens—those pink hollow balls made by the Spalding Company. Spaldeens were great since you could use them for a lot of different games. In fact, we often used them to play punchball; our parents didn't let us use their sticks all the time, since our sticks were broom handles. In punchball, you use your fist to punch the ball (hence the name); other than that, it's the same idea as baseball, because there's a first, second, third, and home base—although when we played, first base was usually a fire hydrant, second base was a manhole cover, third base was probably somebody's sewer drain or car, and home base was something we threw on the ground. We made do with what we had available. We also had people out in the field, just like in a baseball or softball game, but we just ran around in the street. We didn't even go to the schoolyard for that; we stayed close to home.

Another great game was stoopball. Most of our houses had brick staircases with six to eight steps leading up to the front door. Stoopball involved simply trying to hit the ball against the highest stoop, with the goal being to make the ball bounce back as far as possible without letting the guy behind you catch it. We had quite a variety of these games; they cost nothing to play, and they were good, healthy fun.

We did go to the schoolyard to play softball. We'd write our names down on the ground with a piece of chalk, and then captains were chosen and they would pick teams. Everybody played, but of course some guys were better than others, which meant that some of us—myself included—would only get to play in the worst positions. Right field was the worst spot, since nobody ever hit the ball there; most people were right-handed hitters and would therefore hit the ball into left field. Most times I had to play right field. I wasn't very good, but I was always *very* competitive.

At some point—I don't recall how old I was—all the kids started coming to my house because my parents set up a basketball court in our backyard. It wasn't fancy, but it was all we needed to play. The court was on dirt, and we had a big wooden board for the backboard and a metal rim(which my parents bought), and they put it up on a tree in our backyard. They called it Leberfeld Square Garden.

After that, everybody congregated at my house. There were so many kids that we couldn't all play at the same time, so the guys who weren't playing would sneak next door into a detached garage that belonged to my doctor, Dr. Langer, where they played cards or dice, anything to keep them busy until they could play basketball again. When they won, they kept playing; if they lost, they got off the court. It was just three people on each side at a time since the backyard wasn't that big, so the loser had to move out, put his name back on the list, and again wait his turn to play.

The neighborhood kids came even if it rained. Of course the yard was full of puddles and mud . . . but we played anyway! We loved playing basketball, and we were kids, so we'd say, "Oh, it's pretty dry," and we would play on.

One thing the other kids really disliked was that I was always winning. I wasn't even that good, but I had a great hook shot. You don't really see it a lot in basketball today, but a hook shot is when you have your back to the basket and somebody's covering you, and then you swing your arm around from behind and hook the ball into the basket. I was very good at that, so the other kids all claimed there was one dead spot on the wooden backboard, and I was the only one who knew where it was. If I hit that dead spot, the ball would go through the basket. To this day, those guys are convinced that I knew where that spot was. Even today, I still deny it.

I had many good friends, but unfortunately, I was still bullied a lot when I was around 11 years old. First, my breasts were oversized, so some kids made of fun of me about that. Also, I wore glasses, so some kids made fun of that. Then somebody decided to give me a nickname that I couldn't stand and that made me cry: they called me Fish Face.

Why? I still don't exactly know: maybe they thought something about my jaw or my head looked like a fish head. But some stupid kid came up with this name, and it stuck for quite a while, and nothing upset me more than that. It made me feel really inferior.

Even my close friends called me this. When you get a group of kids together—particularly boys—there's bullying and harassment. But I got past it. Just recently, I looked at pictures of myself to see what I looked like then, and I was a pretty nice-looking kid. There was no real reason to call me that. Unfortunately, some people have real deformities and real problems; I didn't have anything like that, but, for some sad reason, kids like to make fun of others, especially at a certain age. Eventually, it stopped. We all grew up.

When I was 12 or 13 years old, my friends and I started a social and athletic club called the Hawks. We collected a little bit of money for dues, and we got beautiful black jackets with the word "Hawks" on them. We started the Hawks because we weren't accepted into another club, the Arverne Demons, who were middle-class elitist: they thought they were better than the rest of us. Arverne was the name of our neighborhood: it's in the middle of the Rockaway peninsula, which has many small neighborhoods: in only about 10 miles, there might be 6 different local communities with different names.

I was always a leader, and I was the first president of the Hawks. There were about ten kids in the Hawks and probably another ten or so in the Demons. My closest friends in that group were Marty Holzberg and Norman Zipkin, both still my friends.

Within a year of forming the Hawks as a separate group, we had a big business venture: we merged. We decided we were all friends anyway, so the Hawks merged into the Arverne Demons. That was good for everybody, because when you have 20-plus members, you have enough for a baseball, football, or basketball team. We could also host a community dance, which we did in the synagogue in a little basement room that they let us use. It made real sense to merge, and we were able to do so much more. It was my first good business decision.

I knew all these kids from my neighborhood, since everybody went to the same schools. We went to PS 42 for elementary school, which was on 67th Street, toward the bay. Rockaway Peninsula is between the Atlantic Ocean and Jamaica Bay, but it's only 10 blocks at the widest part, so it wasn't that far to walk to elementary school, which we all did. There was no middle school then, so after PS 42, we all went to Far Rockaway High School, which was on the east end of the Rockaway peninsula. We took the bus to get there. Most of our families didn't have cars, so instead of driving everywhere, we walked to the corner or to Rockaway Beach Boulevard (which was the main avenue), where the shoemaker, the bakery, the grocery store, and the laundromat were located. Everything was within a couple of blocks of where we lived, so everyone always saw each other in the street since we walked everywhere.

Getting back to the Arverne Demons: we were about 13 years old, and we decided to give each other nicknames—but not nicknames that would make each other feel bad. We came up with Singing Sam, Pierre, Benny the Book, Rock, Goofus, Willy the Weep, Skup, Pussyfoot, and Banana Nose, etc.

"Pierre" got his name one cold winter day when he met us at the candy store. His aunt had bought him a hat to keep his head warm; our parents and aunts and uncles were always telling us to put on a scarf, gloves, and a hat, so we wouldn't catch a cold. He showed up at the candy store wearing this French beret, so we called him Pierre. And he's still called Pierre, even though his real name is Marty and he doesn't speak a word of French.

Another friend was nicknamed "Rock." His real name was Herb, and he was a big guy. One day, we were playing basketball at my house and some of the kids were playing cards while they waited to get into the basketball game. On this particular day, Herb decided (for some stupid reason) that he wanted to climb to the top of the garage. Maybe there was something up there that he went to retrieve; I don't really remember. But he climbed up, and then he fell off. He landed on his head, yet he got up as though nothing had happened. So we called him "Rock," because he had a rock-hard head. That nickname stuck with him for the rest of his life: in fact, when he went into business, in the garment industry, he often traveled to the Orient and many other places, and everywhere he went, people called him Rock.

"Skup" was an unbelievable nickname: "Skup" is "pukes" backward (sort of). His real name was Milty, and I think he used to throw up a lot, or he might have thrown up only once for all I know. But somebody started calling him Skup. I don't know if he's still called that, since I didn't keep up with him . . . maybe because of his nickname.

I think "Willy the Weep" got his nickname because he cried a few times when somebody wouldn't let him get in some game. His real name was Larry, but he was very sensitive. Larry became a professor at City College in New York, and he's now very well known. He's a historian, among other things: he even wrote an acclaimed book on the Rockaways. But at 13, we thought he cried a lot, so we called him "Willy the Weep."

Then we had "Singing Sam," who for some reason broke out in a song one day when we were together. His real name was Mickey, but we couldn't call him "Singing Mickey," and since his father's name was Sam, we called him "Singing Sam."

My friend Paul was "Banana Nose." Paul was the best-looking guy of any of us. He was probably my best friend. He recently passed away, and I choke up just thinking about him. Why did we call him "Banana Nose"? He was beautiful. He played shortstop. He batted fourth, and he played on the high school baseball team. He was like a professional athlete. He was good at anything he did, without any effort. I guess we were mad at him because he was good at everything, so we called him "Banana Nose." There was no real reason for it. I guess it was just the thing to do.

My name was "Benny the Book," and I got it in a very interesting way, although it's a bit of a convoluted story. It started with my Aunt Jean, one of my father's sisters, who was a little crazy. She was afraid to fly; she was even afraid of traveling in a car: when her husband drove, she would be in the back seat on the floor. She was very nervous about everything. But she was also the richest aunt we had, and even though WWII was winding down, and even though I was only 13 years old, she was worried I would be drafted. So she said to my father, "Look, I want Jerry to learn a musical instrument, so when he goes into the Army he won't be in the infantry. He'll survive the war, because if he plays a musical instrument, he'll get into the Army band."

I didn't want to take music lessons, but she bought me a clarinet and paid for the lessons, so I went. I used to sit on the screened-in porch and practice the clarinet. Also, I wore black horn-rimmed glasses. So when my friends came by and heard me tooting on my clarinet, wearing my black glasses, they called me "Benny," for Benny Goodman. They would holler, "Benny, come out and play." So that was how I got the Benny part of my nickname.

I also learned to play cards, as a lot of young boys did at that age. My parents didn't like it, so we played down at the beach locker club behind the last handball court, and I was lucky: I won all the time. So my friends started calling me "Benny the Book" because of the gambling aspect. They used to call my house and ask my mother, "Can The Book come out to play?" That made my mother cringe; hearing that was her worst nightmare. My mother was a lovely, soft-spoken woman, so she didn't overreact to it, but that used to really, really upset her.

That name caught on, and everyone—and I mean *everyone*—called me "Benny the Book." I don't know why; it just caught on. To this day, some people still call me "The Book." In fact, after we were married for maybe 20 years, my wife got me a vanity license plate that reads "B the B." You cannot imagine how many people ask me what that means, because people are really fascinated by license plates. Even strangers ask me what it stands for, but I don't want to tell them "Benny the Book," so instead, I give them a long explanation. Sometimes I tell people it means "Benny the Butcher"; sometimes I tell them it stands for "Bozo the Brave." But the best one I tell them is "Be the Best." I still have that license plate.

So we all had our nicknames, and we all called each other only by these names, which our parents didn't like. As we got older, we went into the military, we got married, we had kids. We didn't see each other all the time, but when we did, we still called each other by our nicknames.

In fact, a funny thing happened at my son's bar mitzvah. We weren't wealthy, but we had a very nice party at a German restaurant with our son's friends and all of our closest friends, including my childhood buddies with the nicknames. When I got up to make a toast to my son to tell him how proud I was of him, I said, "What I'm most happy about today is that I have my friends here who were at *my* bar mitzvah party many years ago. They're still my friends, and they're in this room. I want to introduce them to *your* friends," I said to my son. And I started introducing them: "this is Pierre, this is Singing Sam, this is Willy the Weep . . ." As I said all these funny nicknames, the kids' mouths fell open, I suppose because they had never heard adults with such crazy names for each other.

The next morning, my son got together with *his* group of friends, and they all gave each other nicknames! I don't remember what my son's nickname was, but I was tickled that my son was inspired to follow in his old man's footsteps.

My generation grew up differently from his generation. We didn't have such organized lives as kids do today: we weren't carpooled everywhere. We didn't have anything except our friends. We didn't go anywhere, except outside, to play whatever games we could: punchball or stickball or basketball with a homemade backboard, or cards or dice in the garage next door or on the boardwalk. When we weren't doing our homework, we listened to the radio. I was fascinated by the radio— I still am, since your imagination really works when you listen to the radio. We listened to *The Green Hornet*, *The Shadow*, and all these famous radio programs, and my mind would wonder, *What is really happening? What are the real images of these people who are in these radio soap dramas that young people listen to?* We spent a lot of time just lying on the floor listening to those radio dramas.

But we didn't miss out on anything; we didn't need all the things kids have today. I don't begrudge kids having things today—video games and Playstations and Xboxes and Wiis and everything else they're into today—but I think since they have so many *things*, they miss out on a lot that *we* had. Necessity really is the mother of invention, so my friends and I became close since we had to talk to each other, and we had to find imaginative ways to safely enjoy ourselves without spending money, since none of us had much.

My parents didn't even have an automobile until they were in their early fifties and I was $18^1/_2$ years old. My parents didn't drive, and I didn't drive. But I wanted a car, like most 18-year-olds do, so we chipped in and bought a new 1952 green Chevy; Chevrolet was the most popular car of my era. It was a wonderful car. My parents and I took driving lessons together, and we shared the car. Can you imagine sharing a car with anybody today? No way: kids today want their own cars. Once they learn to drive, they want a car all to themselves. But when I was growing up, it was no big deal to share; in fact, it was important to share.

Another important thing in my family was that we had dinner together every night. My father was a man of strict routine: he came home from work at 6:00, and he would walk in the door and start asking, "Where's my food? Where's my food?" So we ate as soon as he got home. Also, my father ate very fast. My mother made five courses: soup, salad, a main course, dessert, and coffee, and my father would eat it all within 15 minutes. My mother was a wonderful cook, so her meals were great. The rest of us couldn't keep up with how fast my father ate, plus my mother couldn't serve us all at the same time, so we would linger at the table well after my father finished eating.

Also, we had many family dinners with either my mother's family or my father's family. Everybody cooked in those days, and I loved those family dinners. I would keep my mouth shut and listen to whatever the adults were talking about. I was never allowed to leave the table before the meal was over; I wasn't allowed to say—like today's generation does—"Oh, I have to do my homework," or "I have to make a phone call," or "Can I leave the room?" Kids today, as soon as they can leave, they leave. But my generation sat at the table for hours and we listened to the adults. And I think that's important. Not everything we heard was good; but it was important to listen.

JERRY'S LAW #12::
"You learn much more by listening than by talking."

My Father's Family

My father had four sisters—from oldest to youngest, they were Hannah, Jean, Gus (for Augusta), and Pearl. My father was the only son. He was born in 1902, in Austria, but we don't know exactly since they lived there during the Prussian Empire, when the boundaries in that part of Europe kept shifting.

In those days, man was king, so if a family had five kids and one of them is a boy, he's the one who gets priority over everything. And the mother took greater care of her son: whatever my father wanted, his mother made, and all of his sisters were obviously resentful.

My father's family came to the United States in 1904 when my father was only two years old. They came to New York, probably since there were other family members here. I believe they left Europe because they were persecuted: Anti-Semitism and the pogroms were prevalent in Eastern Europe. There was little opportunity for Jewish people in Europe. That's why America was such a great place for them to come: there were opportunities here no matter what your economic or educational level.

I know my father had some family in America. My grandfather's brother had a department store in Maspeth, Queens: it was called Leberfeld's Department Store, and it just closed maybe 10 years ago. One of his sons was Alfred Leberfeld, a somewhat famous Broadway actor. But that part of the family never spoke to my family, either because they thought they were more elite, more cultured, or more successful, or because my father was insulted about something. I don't know. We went to that store once or twice since I wanted to see who they were.

My father's father came here alone at first; he left his family in Europe, and then he went back once a year or so and impregnated his wife. This is true! My mother's father did the same thing. The men sent money back to Europe until they had enough money to bring their families to America.

I don't know exactly when my father's father first came to America; in fact, I don't even know what his first name was. My paternal grandparents died when they were only in their fifties, so I was a very young child. I didn't really know my father's parents at all, and I only know a little bit about them. I knew who they were, of course, because when I was young, we visited them in their apartment. In those days, parents did not talk to their children in the same way we do today. They didn't tell children about themselves or about their history. Parents weren't friends with their kids like parents are today. They loved us, but they weren't our friends.

My paternal grandfather's life was very hard. As with most Eastern European Jews, he came to this country to make enough money to bring over his wife and kids. He started a little pillowcase factory on Canal Street, on New York City's Lower East side. The building is still there, but the company, The Madewell Company, is long gone.

Interestingly, there's another company today with the same name as my grandfather's company. I don't know why he chose Madewell as his company's name, though I suppose it was because he wanted his customers to know that his pillowcases were good quality.

Before my grandfather Leberfeld started Madewell, he did what a lot of people did back then: he was a traveling scrap-metal salesman. In the early 1900s, many Jewish immigrant men became scrap-metal dealers. They traveled all over the country, mainly in Texas. After scrap metal, he still traveled as a dry-goods salesman. At the time, there were dry-goods salesmen who sold mainly to Jewish-owned small department stores in midsized towns across America, and my grandfather was one of those salesmen. My father told me one tale—a terrible, almost unbelievable story—about what happened to his father once on his travels, sometime in the 1920s.

My grandfather had traveled to a town somewhere in the Deep South for many years. Every year, he went at the same time and stayed at the same hotel and ate at the same restaurants. Over the years, he got to know some local people who lived there. My father's father was Jewish, of course, and he had a Jewish name: Leberfeld. But there weren't many Jewish people in the Deep South (if there were any at all). One night he went out to eat, and he got into an argument with somebody; they started pushing and shoving each other, and the other guy pulled a gun. My grandfather grabbed the gun to stop the guy from shooting him, and the gun went off and shot the other man. The sheriff came, and he put my grandfather in jail: he said my grandfather had killed the other person.

A couple of weeks later, there was a trial, and, at the end of the trial, the man my grandfather had supposedly killed showed up! The arrest, the weeks spent in jail, and the trial were all just a prank on my grandfather. Everybody in the town was in on it. That's what some people did in those days: a lot of small southern towns were controlled by only a few people, and there were a lot of prejudices. This was a form of humor in this town. I'm sure my grandfather didn't think it was so funny. My grandfather thought the sheriff had put him in jail forever and he was going to die in that small town without even being able to defend himself. He survived this experience by immediately making a career change to the Canal Street pillowcase factory.

My paternal grandparents died within six months of each other, which was interesting to me since they fought like hell; every minute of their lives, they bitched at each other (at least, that's what I was told). Yet within months of my grandfather's death, my grandmother died of a broken heart, probably because my grandparents were so connected to each other. When my grandfather died, my father took over the pillowcase factory.

My Mother's Family

My mother's parents had four daughters: the girls were Eleanor, Esther, Rose, and Ethel. My mother's family name was Beldner; my maternal grandfather's first name was Max, and my maternal grandmother's first name was Anna. I never met either of them.

My mother, Esther, was the second-oldest daughter. The four girls were close in age; they were born two years apart. My mother was born in 1907 in Poland, although (again, like my father's family), my mother's family frequently moved due to the European pogroms.

Like my father's family, my maternal grandmother stayed in Europe with her four daughters while my maternal grandfather left to work in America. He came here because America was the place to make some money: people used to say, "The streets are lined with gold." And for many immigrants, the streets *were* lined with gold.

I don't know why my mother's family came to New York; I presume they came because the Lower East Side was a place where Jewish immigrants from Europe felt comfortable, and they lived in overcrowded tenement buildings. There's a wonderful Tenement Museum on Manhattan's Orchard Street that shows how those immigrant families lived in the early 1900s.

My mother's father had a variety of different jobs here, but the job where he made the most money was as a window cleaner on New York City skyscrapers. He must have accumulated some money, since he was able to bring his family here. Only six months after his wife and daughters arrived in 1918, my mother's father was working one day on Broadway and 42nd Street; the rope tying him to the building broke free of the bricks, and he fell 40 stories to the ground to his death.

My mother, Esther, was only about 14 years old at the time. I think the girls were only 19, 17, 14, and 12 years old when their father died. Their mother, Anna, didn't speak any English, and she like many immigrant women of that day, she didn't know how to be self-reliant, how to take care of anything. All she knew how to do was cook, clean the house, and raise her children.

My grandmother Anna had no money: her husband had probably used all his savings to bring over her and the four girls. Somebody (I don't know who) recommended she get an attorney to see if he could get some money from the building owner. Maybe this person even found the attorney for her. As the story was told to me, the attorney visited Anna a few weeks later and told her, "The insurance company is offering you $500. I think you should take it." And, of course, he took one-third of that $500. But Anna didn't know any better, she didn't realize the attorney might be cheating her or lying to her, so she took the money, which was only about $300. Later on, someone in my family found out that the lawyer actually received many thousands of dollars from the insurance company. I don't know how we found that out; I think somebody in the family investigated this guy.

After her husband died, Anna had what I would call a nervous breakdown, and in those days, when you had a breakdown, you were sent to a sanitarium; Anna was sent to a sanitarium on Long Island. Who placed her there, I don't know, but she lived the rest of her life in that facility. She was alive when I was growing up, but my parents didn't tell me (or anyone else) this fact. In those days, anyone who was living in a sanitarium was considered crazy. And if you were crazy, then your children and even your grandchildren might be crazy. Nobody wanted that stigma attached to their family, so my parents kept Anna a secret. It was a few years after her death that I found out about her.

After their father died and their mother was sent to the sanitarium, my mother and her sisters were all alone. There was no one to raise them, nobody at all. To my knowledge, my mother and her sisters had no aunts or uncles or other family. And there was no welfare. So they raised themselves. I don't know how they survived, but they did. They lived somewhere in Brooklyn.

The oldest, Eleanor, was only 19 years old when her mother was institutionalized. She was also the smartest one—smart in the sense that she was worldlier than her sisters. She became a hat maker. She went to work for a milliner, then later went into business for herself as a hat designer. She even became famous for a hat she designed; it was a beret-style hat called the Duchess that became very popular. She made some money, and she got some very nice job offers. But instead she decided to open her own store, a women's boutique specializing in hats, in Manhattan on 72nd Street between West End Avenue and Broadway. She was there for years. But then the millinery industry went kaput: women's hats went out of fashion, so the store closed. Today, it's a dry cleaners (what else?). Today it seems that New York's retail stores are mainly composed of drug and clothing chains, Starbuck's, banks, and restaurants. What we New Yorkers miss the most is the personal relationship with our neighborhood shop owners.

Eleanor never married. Her three sisters eventually got married and had children, but Eleanor was the career woman in the family. Of all my aunts I always loved her best, and I think she might have been the inspiration for me to go into business for myself, even though that was probably subconscious. I was always proud of my Aunt Eleanor: after all, in those days—in the 1920s, '30s, '40s, and '50s—there were very few women who were working professionally, and there were even fewer who were making a good living in their own business.

Neither my mother nor her sisters ever talked about how they felt when their father suddenly died and their mother lived in a sanitarium. They didn't talk about their feelings or how devastated and affected they were. They never said anything to me.

How My Parents Met

My mother was only 14 years old when she got her first job, which was in my grandfather's pillowcase factory. That's how my parents met. My mother was very attractive (as were her sisters), and when she was 16, my father asked her to marry him. I don't even know if they even went out on a date anyplace. He was 21, and she was 16 when they got married in City Hall, in 1923.

But they didn't live together at first. After the wedding ceremony, my mother went home that night to her sisters in Brooklyn, and my father went home to his parents' apartment in Brighton Beach. They lived separately for about six months. My mother kept asking my father, "When are we going to talk to your mother about everything? When are we going to move in together?" My father hadn't even told his mother that he had gotten married!

Her three sisters probably egged her on to keep after him. They probably wondered, "When is he going to tell his mother?" To my mother and her sisters, my father was a rich guy: after all, he had a lit-tle factory, and that contrasted starkly with how they were living as teenagers raising themselves. By that time, Eleanor must have been 21, and the youngest sister, Ethel, must have been 14, and they were all working at some kind of job. Since my father had his own business, he must have been rich in comparison to them.

My mother wasn't a strong person, but eventually, she got the cour-age to say to my father, "Look, you've got to tell your mother that we're married." So he finally did. I don't know what his mother's reaction was, but she invited my parents to live in a room in their apartment.

My father loved his mother's cooking, so this was a great chance for his mother to teach my mother how to cook. In those days, they ate wonderful, tasty (but unhealthy) food like liver and kidney since they were cheap organ meats. I can't even name all the things they ate; I only know they went to the butcher's and bought any part of an animal that was inexpensive. And they made it taste good: they put potatoes around it and made gravy, and it tasted great. My mother learned to cook from her mother-in-law, and she continued to cook that way when she was raising my sister and me. People don't cook that way today; you can't even get those foods at a butcher or in a restaurant anymore.

At first my mother wasn't close to my father's mother or sisters. They treated her like a stepsister. Eventually, they grew to love my mother, once they got to know her. My mother was terrific: she never argued with anyone. I'm not like that, and I always admired my mother for that quality. There were times, though, when I got mad at her because she didn't stand up for herself enough; my father was sort of a tyrant, and he always had to have his way. My father was a very difficult man. I might call him abusive, but she loved him very much. But my mother found the good side of anything and anybody. That is a special quality that most of us don't have.

I don't hate my father, though, and I never held him accountable for anything that went wrong in my life. I can't stand when people of all ages still blame their parents for what they didn't accomplish or what they are today, so much so that those people can't move on with their own lives. It's their parents' fault that they're unhappy, or it's their parents' fault that they got divorced. Everything bad that happened in their lives is their parents' fault. I never believed in that. We must rise above it and become our own person.

After about a year of living with my father's family, my parents got their own apartment and started living their own independent lives. My father made some extra money. One way he do this was by doing some work for Bugsy Siegel, the gangster, and his crowd. He met Bugsy through one of his sisters, my Aunt Gus, who had a girlfriend who was dating Bugsy himself, and my Aunt Gus dated one of Bugsy's friends. She was quite a fun-loving character.

This was "The Roaring Twenties" after all, and Aunt Gus and her girlfriends were flappers. They were living the life where you knock on a door and you get a drink. Everything was illegal because it was Prohibition. When you don't have anything and you're attractive, doing something illegal often appeals to you. I don't know what happened in my father's sisters' lives; my parents didn't tell me the details. All I know is that Aunt Gus used to call my father and ask him, "Would you take this car and drive it to another part of Brooklyn?" He didn't even have his driver's license but that didn't matter in those days. He drove the cars to wherever they wanted. He didn't know why he was doing it, he just did what he was asked to do, and they paid him. I don't know if there was something in the trunk; there could have been dead bodies. Or perhaps the cars were stolen. Whatever it was, it obviously wasn't legal, but my father didn't ask any questions. He did it until one time he hit a fire hydrant; he just left the car, and he never did that job again. I don't believe my father was ever a criminal or part of the Jewish Mafia, as they called it in those days. He was just another high school dropout innocently making extra bucks to help support his immigrant family.

My Bar Mitzvah,
1946.

Arverne Demons at my Bar Mitzvah, 1946.

Leberfeld family
(Harry, me, Freya,
and Esther) at my
Bar Mitzvah, 1946.

My sister, Freya,
and me at Beach
69th St. House,
1946.

A happy Boy
Scout, 1945.

Our baseball
team, early
1950s.

Singin' Sam,
Pierre, Benny
the Book, and
Willy the Weep.
Arverne by the
Sea, 1950.

Prom date at Copacabana with Dean Martin. "That's Amore"! 1951.

2

Growing Through Work

I started working in 1942 during World War II, when I was 9 years old. I was too young to get a regular job, so most of my friends and I worked for the war effort. We didn't get paid for it. We did it because all of us were highly motivated and patriotic: it was *the* war, the *just* war, and it probably is still considered just today. We were very young; most of us were between the ages of 9 and 11, but we all pitched in.

During the Second World War, resources were in short supply, so the government asked everyone to recycle a large number of items for use in the war effort. In our neighborhood, every family saved their newspapers, piled them into big bundles, and tied them up. They also collected tin cans. At least once a week, my friends and I went around to every house in the neighborhood, picked up the bundled newspapers, bagged the cans, and brought everything to a designated collection site, which I think was at the Sanitation Department. We did this for a couple of years.

My First Paycheck

I got my first paying jobs when I was somewhere between the ages of 12 and 14. They were the kinds of jobs most kids my age did. My first job was delivering groceries after school—I carried them in a basket I attached to the front of my bicycle.

I loved getting my first tip and my first paycheck. I think minimum wage was 25 cents, but I doubt if I got paid that much. I also delivered newspapers and shoveled snow.

The first real job I remember having was in a laundromat, which was right next door to the food store I had been delivering groceries for. It was 1947, and I was 14 years old. I got the job the way many of people get new jobs: I got to know the owner, Tom, while I was delivering groceries. One day, Tom asked me to come to work for him: he said, "You'll make more money!" And I thought, "Why not make more money?"

The laundromat did a huge business during the summers in Rockaway Beach, which (as mentioned earlier) was a booming seasonal community. After the war ended, everybody wanted to get away and do something special, and Rockaway was a place New Yorkers could afford. Every single unit, every summer bungalow, every boardinghouse, every private house, and every room available was rented for the summer. Of course, the summer renters needed to have their laundry done outside since none of the units had washing machines. So every Monday morning from Memorial Day to Labor Day, everybody brought their laundry to Tom's Laundromat, and I can say without exaggeration, that the whole laundromat, every inch of it from the floor to the ceiling, was filled with bags of laundry. We washed it and returned it to the customers by Tuesday morning. There must have been four or five of us working there, and we worked all night long: we just kept piling the laundry into the washers. When a load was done, we put it into the dryer, which meant we put our heads and hands into hot dryers for 24 hours, which wasn't easy. It was summer and hot, and, of course, the laundromat had no air conditioning.

Still, it was a great experience; I don't know why, maybe since, like any youngster, I was excited about my first real job, and about getting probably the biggest paycheck of my life (up until then, of course). I don't remember how much it was, but I was thrilled.

What I didn't much like was that we found lots of things in the laundry that weren't so nice. The very worst, which I'll never forget, were the diapers. In those days, people used cloth diapers, not disposables like they do today. The diapers had to be washed, and many people left everything in the diapers (a shitty proposition). Some people were responsible and cleaned them up a bit before sending them to the laundry. But other people couldn't care less; they just tossed the dirty diapers in with their laundry. Washing those was an experience, but I survived, and the machines cleaned up the mess.

Tom, the owner, was a character. He was married, but he was also very flirtatious: he flirted with every decent-looking woman who entered the store. I was only 14 years old, so his behavior astonished me: I liked girls, but I had not yet discovered what to do with them. Tom was in his forties—which seemed quite old to me then, though it's very young today—which was about the same age as my parents. That he flirted with my friends' mothers and aunts made quite an impression on me.

I worked at the laundromat for two-and-a-half years. My next job was for a place called the Curtain Factory, which was a pretty big company. I got the job because friends of mine worked there, and they said they could always use part-time help after school.

My job was to pack curtain sizes into boxes, stack them in numeric order in the back where the inventory was kept, and then fill orders that were to be delivered. That was a little better paying than the laundromat. I was 17 when I got that job; it was right before I began to think about whether or not to go to college.

I worked in the Curtain Factory for a while, even though it was a boring job. Things are different today. Most of my grandchildren's generation don't take jobs like these for many reasons: first, because their parents give them allowances; also, their parents are over-protective. Today's parents are more security conscious than my parents or my wife and I were. We didn't worry about anybody hitting us over the head or doing something bad. Whatever the reason, by not working on minimal jobs, they're not learning important life lessons.

The jobs I had, as simple as they were, helped build my character. They laid the groundwork and provided experience that helped me later in my working life. Unfortunately, young people and their parents are missing the boat. There's nothing wrong with working in McDonald's or similar places, because you meet people, you build character, and you may learn what you *don't* want to do for the rest of your life.

Working for My Father

The summer after I graduated from high school, I worked for my father. He had a small factory on Canal Street where he took what you call remnants from blankets and pillowcases and used them to make sheets, pillows, pillowcases, and blankets for dolls. In the '30s, my father's father had actually made real sheets and pillowcases there, but my father converted the factory, since by the 1950s, he couldn't compete with the big textile mills. He packaged the doll bedding in little plastic bags, and he sold them to 5-and-10-cent stores—Woolworth's, Kresge's, Grant's were the biggest. My father sold to about six of these large chain stores, and the packages were to be retailed for 69 cents each, and he struggled since his margin was only pennies a package.

The summer I helped him was quite an experience. My father left the house for work at the same time every morning, and he arrived in the city at about 20 minutes before 9:00. He'd stop at a coffee shop for five minutes where he would have a cup of coffee and a buttered roll. The coffee was boiling hot, which is how he liked it, and the counterman knew it. My father ordered the same breakfast for me, but the coffee was so hot that I couldn't drink it, which made him yell at me, "Let's go! We've got to get to work!" As a result, I very rarely drank my coffee; I just grabbed my roll, and we went to work.

My job was to flip the pillowcases inside out after they were sewn in order to hide the stitches. I'd put them on two little metal bars and flip them. I would do thousands of them every day. My dad's older sister Hannah also worked there, along with about four other people.

Working for my father was horrible. First of all, there were his work habits, and, second, he was totally inflexible. I'll never forget this incident: I said, "Dad, it's very hard to make a living selling the packages for only 69 cents." The item was very saleable, so I suggested he import a doll from Korea, which was at that time the place to buy inexpensive merchandise. I said, "You could get a doll for about 20 cents, add it to the package, and raise the price by a dollar to $1.69."

It was a great idea, but he screamed at me, because he didn't want to try something new. After all, he must have thought, what could I possibly I know? Later, he admitted to me that I might have had a good idea. It was very frustrating. Whenever I tried to make any changes or suggest anything, my father's response was, "What do I need it for?" It was a generational thing. He needed money, but he had no vision for how he could make more money by trying something different.

I knew how hard my father worked. He took the same train every night and arrived home every evening at six. When he arrived home, my mother had his food on the table. There was no lost time; it was all very efficient. Too bad he couldn't utilize that efficiency in a more productive way—smart and stubborn is not a winning formula.

I Wanted to Go to College

While I was working in my father's factory, I began to think, "What am I doing here?" I saw what my father was going through, and I learned how hard it was to make a living. So after a while, I decided I wanted to go to college. My mother encouraged me, but my mother had no control over the family finances. She didn't even know how much money my father had. He gave her money: I remember it was $100 a week. He probably gave her the same amount of money forever. With that, she took care of everything, buying all the food, and paying all the bills. We never knew what my father earned. Later, we found out he didn't make much more than that, not ever really profiting from his hard work.

I wanted to go to an out-of-town college since I was 18 years old, anxious to get away from home, move out, do the things I dreamed of. I found a college in Plattsburgh, New York, which is close to the Canadian border, one hour from Montreal. It had opened fairly recently (for veterans of World War II), and it was relatively inexpensive.

I went off to Champlain College. I had saved some of the money I had earned working in the Curtain Factory and for my father and doing other jobs, and, of course, my parents chipped in some. But once I was at college, I had to survive on my own, since my father wasn't very supportive. He wanted me to go to work, like he did; formal education was not very important to him. He had gone to work when he was 14 years old; he had never even graduated from high school.

I went to Champlain College along with two other guys from Far Rockaway High School. One of them had a car, which was great, since we drove up together. We had wheels, as they say.

Champlain was really a very nice place. It had been an Air Force barracks during the war and then was converted into a college. It was located right off Lake Champlain, which is beautiful country. Winters

Can't Is Not an Option

are very cold, but special. The lake froze during the winter months, so you could walk across from New York State to Vermont.

Many good things happened during my brief stay at Champlain, even though I was there for only one semester. I met my first serious girlfriend there: her name was Gerri. I remember because of its unusual spelling. Also, she told me she was American-Indian (Native American today), which fascinated me. She fell in love with me, though I still don't understand why, but, in those days, it was different. It was an age of innocence, and relationships were less complex.

While I was at Champlain College, I also lost my virginity, although not to Gerri. Remember, my friend had a car, so on weekends four or five of us would pile into it (the three of us from Far Rockaway and two friends) and we would go to the French section of Montreal, to St. Catherine's Street, which was a street that had (and probably still has) a lot of music and bars. We had heard that the French women were loose and wild—I never experienced that firsthand, but I always did have a good time dancing and drinking.

One day, we saw an ad in the *PennySaver* in Plattsburgh from a prostitute from Montreal, offering special discounts for Champlain College freshman. You know how guys go *Animal House*. So five of us piled into our car, and we went to the address listed. I still remember, for whatever reason, that the woman's name was Odette. She was French-Canadian.

I have no idea how old she was, probably in her thirties. She was a young, attractive woman. And there we were sitting in this waiting room, all of us probably virgins, eager for this worldly experience. I can't imagine that many 18-year-old men are still virgins today. Odette asked, "Who wants to go first?" None of us answered. We were all afraid to go first. Finally, one guy volunteered. Another guy lost his nerve, and never went at all. A third got so excited in the waiting room, he had nothing left by the time it was his turn. So only two of us—me and one other friend—went into the room. It was an intimidating experience. She was kind and sensitive, but I doubt that either of us had the greatest time of our lives that night. We were all so inexperienced and so innocent; still, I'll never forget it.

I don't remember what she charged, but it couldn't have been much, since none of us had money. My father sent me $20 a month to pay for weekend meals (the food plan covered only weekday meals) and laundry. Thank God, after working for Tom, I knew how to do my own laundry, and I earned extra money doing other people's laundry. So my experience came in handy: my laundry cost me almost nothing. The rest of the money my father gave me was spent on snacks and such. Most of us didn't eat much. In fact, many of my friends subsisted on cigarettes and cola, although I didn't do that. I smoked, but I also ate real food.

I also picked up some extra cash playing cards. Remember, I had earned the nickname Benny the Book because I learned to play cards when I was quite young, and by some miracle, I won most of the time. I used my winnings to help me get by during the semester I spent at Champlain College.

My college career abruptly ended, though, on a snowy, sleety day in December 1951, when I was going home for Christmas break. My friends and I were heading home along Route 9 (which was the main road in those days), and as we drove through a town called Schroon Lake, we got into an accident. I was sitting next to him in the passenger seat, and our other friend, Burt, was in the back. A city snowplow was backing up over a little hill, so we couldn't see it from a distance. The plow was supposed to have backup lights, and if it had, we might have seen it coming. Mike hit the brakes but skidded into it, and the car was totaled. I was tossed at least 20 feet from the car and landed on my head, but luckily on a snow bank, which must have been at least five feet high. In those days, some cars didn't have seatbelts. One friend broke his arm, the other had bruises all over his body, and I had hurt my head.

We all survived, but the police, probably fearing the town would be sued, accused us of driving recklessly, which wasn't true. Mike really was driving slowly and cautiously. They were trying to intimidate us, just to get us away. They did let us go to the emergency room, where we were bandaged up, and then the police told us they wanted us on the next bus out of town. They even threatened to arrest us! So we did what they said and took the bus to the Port Authority in Manhattan; from there, I took a train and a bus to Far Rockaway, where my parents still lived.

When I eventually arrived, I banged on the door: obviously, my parents weren't expecting me, and there were no cell phones in those days. When my mother opened the door, she screamed. I didn't realize it, but my head had swelled to twice its normal size. As far as I know, I didn't have a concussion or any brain damage, and eventually, the swelling went down. We must have gone to a local doctor, but I never went to the hospital, nor do I remember anything specific being done for it. I was young, and I guess I had a hard head. Most of all, I was lucky.

None of us went back to Champlain College, in Plattsburgh NY. I don't remember why. I assume our parents wanted us closer to home.

Later, when people heard the story, they immediately asked, "How much money did you get?" It never once crossed my mind to sue my friend, who hadn't done anything wrong: suing him, even if he had insurance, was tantamount to falsely blaming somebody. I suppose my friends and I could have sued the town of Schroon Lake, but by the time we collected, I'd probably be writing this memoir. The deck was stacked against us. The town would have denied everything, the judges were local, and we would have had to travel back up there. Suing them was not practical. I'm sure we discussed it with an attorney. If I had sued Mike, his insurance company would have settled and sued the town. But I never did it, and I don't feel bad about it. Today, everybody sues everybody—their closest friends, their wives, their sisters, their mothers. It doesn't matter since some insurance company pays for it. Times have definitely changed—and not for the better, as far as I'm concerned.

Moving on to State Tech

It didn't take long to recuperate. The accident occurred in December, and in January 1952, I enrolled in The New York State Institute of Applied Arts & Sciences in downtown Brooklyn, which I attended until I graduated in January 1954. It's now called New York City College of Technology and is a four-year engineering college, but in those days, it was a new concept to have two-year colleges intended for kids who weren't ready for, or who couldn't afford, a four-year college. It was a great idea to have programs like that; in fact, it's still a good idea. To give young people an opportunity to learn a practical skill is wonderful. After all, a Bachelor of Arts degree, even a Bachelor of Science degree, doesn't exactly prepare someone for a job.

State Tech offered a new type of degree, the Associate's Degree, in various specialties. I chose to major in "industrial sales," and when I graduated, I received an Associate's Degree in Applied Science. To this day, I don't know exactly what industrial sales means, and at the time, all I knew was that it was sales.

Many of my friends, maybe eight of us, went to this school, because we all came from the same background, and none of our parents went to college. We called ourselves middle class, but we had very little money. You had to be extremely bright to get into a city college, needing 90+ marks, and none of us got grades like that. Any other choices were obviously out of our financial sphere, so we started with this two-year college. It worked out well to go to State Tech first, as we all went on and obtained four-year degrees.

We drove from Rockaway to State Tech, which was on Jay Street in downtown Brooklyn. That area was all industrial then, and the school was located in an old factory building that had been converted into classrooms. There was nothing fancy about it; no campus, no sororities or fraternities, and very few extracurricular activities. Still, we had a good experience traveling together every day to and from school.

One day, our friend Milty was driving, and my friend Smokey was sitting in the back seat. Milty was a very serious type, and Smokey was one of the funniest people I have ever met. Also, Smokey could mimic anything, including the sound of a police siren. He was so clever. That day, he made the sound of the siren, opened the back seat window, tapped his hand on the top of the car, and said, "Pull over." It sounded just like the police, so Milty pulled right over. We laughed for hours. You had to be there, but it was really funny. That was what it was like traveling back and forth to college: we had a great time. Everything was funny. I look around today and I see young kids and my grandchildren laughing, and think, "What are they laughing at?" I could have said the same thing about us back then: what were we laughing at? Everything we said to each other was considered funny. We were young, and those were fun times. It would be great if we could transfer this continuous laughter to our later years.

Double-Dating in the Chicken Truck

In those days (1952-53), the father of my friend Rock (one of the nicknames I mentioned) owned what we called a "chicken factory": live chickens were taken from farms in New Jersey (which had the best chickens in those days) and were killed just before they were sold, so they would be as fresh as possible. Rock's job was to help his father slaughter the chickens for market. He did this every day, before he went to school, at 4 or 5:00 in the morning.

Rock's father had what we called a chicken truck, which he used to transport the crates of chickens from New Jersey to the factory and to deliver the freshly killed chickens to the local butchers. Of course, the truck was always filled with feathers.

One day, Rock and I met two beautiful girls, on the Long Island Railroad from Rego Park. We started talking, and made a date. To us, Rego Park, with its fancy new high-rise apartment buildings, was like Park Avenue. Rich girls lived in Rego Park.

We had no car, and we couldn't take girls like that out in the chicken truck, so Rock parked it about three or four blocks away from the girls' apartment building. We told them that we came by train because our car had broken down. The father of one of the girls let us use his beautiful new car. Not thinking, Rock drove the car up the block where the chicken truck was parked. Of course, the girls recognized the name on the truck and asked about it. Rock tried to cover by claiming it belonged to a relative who lived in the area, but I don't think they believed him. Needless to say, we only went out with those girls that one time.

Look, Mom, I'm a Fuller Brush Man

In the summer between my first and second year at State Tech, I decided I wanted to get a job with the Fuller Brush Company. I went for an interview, and I quickly realized they weren't hiring summer help; they had only full-time positions, so I lied and told them I wanted a permanent job. And in May 1953, at 20 years old, I became a Fuller Brush man.

In those days, Fuller Brush was a great American company. They made the best hairbrushes, mops, and cleaning materials ever. It's no longer in business, but, in those days, it was a very well-respected company. I received one week of training, during which I was accompanied by the district sales manager to learn from what he did. The whole idea was very sound, from a business perspective.

The next week, I was assigned to Middle Village, Queens, which was a middle- class, attached-house community in New York. I was assigned a territory of a couple of miles of houses, and I went from house to house to house. The company's sales technique followed a multi-day process: on the first day, I left a brochure under the doors of as many houses as I thought I could cover the following day; on the second day, I knocked on each of those doors, and when the person asked who it was, the prescribed answer was "Fuller Brush." Often, the person would then say, "I don't need anything today," but my job was to make sure that whoever answered opened the door, which gave me a chance to talk to them. Then I kept talking, and I offered them a free sample. Fuller Brush had cleaning fluids, sachets—any number of things that we gave away to potential customers, since most people would open the door to get something for nothing.

Once I got my foot in the door, I was trained to put my sample case in the open space, so the person couldn't close the door on me. And I started talking immediately. Often the person repeated, "Well, I don't know if I want anything today"; sometimes they even added, "I don't even want a sample." My response to that was something like, "How can I tell my boss that I can't even *give* this stuff away?" That little bit of humor helped open people up, and then I could sell them something—wet mops, hair brushes, brooms, cosmetics, whatever. Fuller Brush had a pretty extensive line.

A week later, I delivered the orders. The key thing I learned from this experience was to *never waste a sales opportunity*. When I made a delivery, I always tried to sell them something else, usually something inexpensive. I often chose spot remover: 75% of the people to whom I delivered their new product also purchased this spot remover, which cost only a dollar. I did great. I made $300 in the first week, which was amazing in those days. The district manager thought I was fabulous.

I was good at it because I listened to the company. *I did exactly what they told me to do.* Fuller Brush salesmen had to pay the company for the samples and brochures: the brochures cost 8 cents apiece, and the samples cost 6 cents each. Then, about a month into the job, I asked myself, "Why waste my money giving out so many?" So instead of leaving brochures under *every* door in a particular neighborhood, I began selecting which doors I would leave a brochure under: I thought, "this one looks good, that one hasn't been painted, I don't like this house," whatever struck me. I invented reasons for not approaching certain houses, and I began leaving brochures only at selected houses, and I called only on those houses the next day.

Of course, my income went down by 50%, and I learned that I wasn't smarter than the Fuller Brush Company! Growing up, we all think we're smarter than those who came before us. That's not true: if it ain't broke, don't fix it, just paint it over once in a while and make it look better.

Working as a Fuller Brush man was a wonderful learning experience. I made a lot of money for someone my age, but, of course, I had to quit in September. The district manager was mad at me; after all, I made him good money since he got a commission on everything I sold. But I returned to school, and I graduated from State Tech in January 1954.

JERRY'S LAW #18:
"You cannot do the minimum and reach the maximum."

3

Military Service: From Boy to Man

n April of 1954, I was drafted into the United States Army. The Korean War was still going on, although it was winding down. But every one of us, to a man (since women were not drafted) knew we had to serve our country. There was a program called "push up your draft number" where you could serve early, before you were drafted. My friends and I did that, since we had just finished two-year college, and we wanted to get our military responsibility over with. It was part of our commitment to our country.

At that time, nobody had any ideas about going to Canada or getting additional exemptions for something they didn't really need, or saying they had no brothers or sisters—all of which went on during the Vietnam War. This was a different time and a different place. We were all proud to serve.

Basic Training

I was assigned to basic training in Fort Dix, New Jersey. The first eight weeks of basic training is always pure military training. We all lived in barracks with bunk beds, and we were all treated in a way we had never before been treated in our lives, focusing on discipline and getting in condition. I got into the best condition of my life. I loved basic training: after 8 weeks I was 169 pounds of pure muscle, and I had never seen myself look this way in my life!

The first day, everyone gets called out by what is called the *cadre*. Those are the people who trained us. Our cadre was all hard-nosed Korean War veterans—"regular Army" guys. They were battle-tough and combat-ready, and they made us reach goals never imagined.

Once we were assigned, bunked, called out, and lined up, the cadre worked us over a little bit. On my first day, the guy looked at me and said, "What are you wearing glasses for?" I said, "I've been wearing glasses since I'm two years old. I've got a crossed eye, and I'm far-sighted. I can't live without glasses." He said, "There's nothing on your record. Get those glasses off right now."

So he took my glasses, and I walked around for about a week until I got an appointment at the medical center in Fort Dix for an ophthal-mologist/eye doctor to see me, and, of course, the doctor rewrote the prescription for my glasses. So I got my glasses back, but it was quite an experience to be without glasses when you can't see for a week!

And in those days, if you did anything wrong, or if they didn't like the way you looked at them, they would tell you to get on all fours and give them 50 pushups, or maybe 100 pushups. When we first started, that was torturous, but by the time we were in great condition at the end of the 16 weeks, we were able to do it without much difficulty.

So I went through my basic training, where we did everything. We learned to use a weapon, an M1 at the time, we crawled under barbed wire on our bellies, we slept in tents, we carried 80 pounds on our backs as we marched 20 miles, and we did all those things that we never thought we would be able to do.

I remember that I met a young man from rural Kansas, which was my first experience meeting people from other parts of the country, and we got friendly. We had only a few weekends off during the first eight weeks, so I took him to my parents' house and got him a nice meal and showed him where and how this Jewish boy from Rockaway lived.

We took the bus from Fort Dix to the Port Authority, in Manhattan on 40th Street. There was a place nearby with a blinking sign that adver-tised "a dime a dance." So I said to my friend, "You want to go?" and he said "yes." The women dancers were not dressed like they would dress today, but they were dressed in long gowns, like in an old movie, showing some cleavage. For 10 cents, they danced with us for five or six minutes. As soon as those five or six minutes were over, they would stop, and then we gave them another 10 cents. This was a heck of an experience, because we had never seen anything like this before. These were beautiful women (in our eyes anyway), and they didn't get close-close, but they got close enough to make us want to give them another dime. I'll never forget that, since it's something I would never have done in my life. It was the age of innocents.

My Military Specialty: Typing

I got through the first eight weeks of basic training, then for the second eight weeks, they assigned everyone to a specialty. In my case, I was assigned for the next eight weeks again to Fort Dix; others went elsewhere. I got into something called clerk-typist school, which was a place where they sent guys who they deemed intelligent. Apparently, I was (though I didn't know it at the time), because when I took my IQ test, I scored very high. I didn't know how smart I was, since during my basic schooling, I was kind of a wise guy and never took my schoolwork seriously.

They wanted me to go to officer's candidate school, which meant I had to stay in the military for at least four years. So I never went through that. (Interestingly, most of the people in typist school were attorneys, all well-educated, but the military didn't really know what to do with them. After all, how many attorneys do you need in the Army?) Maybe, in hindsight, they should have assigned them to the Infantry. Just kidding! An apology to my lawyer friends.

So I went to this clerk-typist school, where they taught me how to be an administrator, and I would be reassigned to some post to take care of the paperwork. Since it was the second eight weeks, we could go home most weekends, but a weekend pass was required for anyone who wanted to leave the base. Unfortunately, the captain in charge of our group left the assignment of the weekend passes to some sergeant who was a miserable SOB: he would make us stay as long as possible, unless we gave him money: if we gave him five or ten dollars, he'd let us go earlier.

He was also an anti-Semite—there's no question about it, since he said some things to me directly. He called me "a Jew bastard" and said, "You guys are all the same: you're money grubbers," and other terrible things people say about Jews. It was not subtle. One afternoon on the weekend, I still hadn't gotten my pass. We bumped into each other in the latrine, and he started making some anti-Semitic remarks. I knew everything he was doing was so wrong, so I said to him, "Take your shirt off and let's do battle," because if you're an officer, even a non-commissioned officer, if you take your shirt off and there's no stripes or bars on your uniform and you get into a fight, it's okay; but if you fight an officer when he still has his shirt on, you get thrown into jail. This guy and I never got into a fistfight, but we got into a screaming match. He was a little bit of a coward, I guess. Eventually, I got my pass.

From Typewriters to Machine Guns

When I finished this clerk-typist school, I checked the board where they posted our next assignments. I wanted to go to Germany, even Korea, anyplace, just to travel. But I was the only guy in the whole class who got reassigned to Fort Dix to do my permanent duty! And I got reassigned as the company clerk at the stockade, which is the military prison.

A nice Jewish boy from Rockaway doesn't know about prisons.

That experience was unbelievable. All the guys who worked there were regular Army Military Police. They wore light-blue cadre helmets, and when you saw someone in a light-blue helmet, you got out of that person's way: it was a power thing.

Those MPs taught me how things work in prisons. There is a system (which you might read about as a civilian) where everybody knows what they're supposed to do. There's leadership amongst the prisoners. They know where not to cross the line. They know where they can get extra favors, etc. So I learned all about how that stuff works—you know, the real world.

On Friday of every week, a new batch of prisoners came through the gate, and we all stood in front, at attention, to (for lack of a better word) "welcome" them. They saw us all as Military Police, since I wore one of those blue helmets, even though I was just an administrator.

So who do you think was the first guy to walk through that gate? That's right, the one who was selling the passes, the real anti-Semite. Apparently, he had a history of being a bad guy, and he got busted down in rank, which was a term for losing your stripes. They don't always throw you out of the military, but you get busted down from, let's say, a sergeant to a corporal or a private, and you serve time.

He looked at me, I looked at him, and he instantly knew he was in deep shit. After I told the guys I worked with about everything he had done, they made his life miserable. I've always said (although a lot of people don't agree) that if you live long enough, justice will prevail.

I continued in the military police for quite a number of months. We had a commanding officer—I remember his name: Captain Allen—who was very angry with headquarters, since they hadn't sent him enough real military policeman. They were trained much differently than I was. They were trained to use machine guns and other automatic weapons. So one day, the Captain said to me, "I don't care that you don't have the right training. I have two company clerks, so Jerry, you're going to be a real military policeman," and he sent me up to the tower, where the searchlight goes around the prison grounds, to make sure nobody escapes.

Well, if you could name the most boring job in the world, that's it. In those days, no radios were allowed, no nothing. You couldn't even go to the bathroom for two hours until you got relieved for 10 minutes. So I lived under that circumstance for about six weeks, and the boredom was really getting to me. Then somebody told me, "You know, you don't have the credentials to be a military policeman, because they gave you an automatic weapon. You wouldn't know how to properly use it." Which was true: I wouldn't know what to do if there was an escape. I probably would have shot myself!

It was suggested that I go down to the administrative headquarters in Fort Dix and say something like, "Look, I don't know if I'm qualified to do this type of work..." Sure enough, within one day, I was transferred out of there, and I went to the central administrative office, and one of the things I did next was a very important job: I stamped shot records, for vaccinations. Everyone had to get certain shots when they left Fort Dix basic training—we all got many different vaccinations in those days. I found out, to my dismay, that a couple of the guys were actually selling shot verifications, and then stamping on their shot cards that they had gotten them. That disturbed me since I realized these guys could get very sick. But they were afraid to get the shots. I didn't do anything like that, but I learned that things go on in your life that you can't imagine. I guess people will do anything for money. I still had a simplistic morality.

I continued on this assignment for almost a year. My tour of duty was two years, and I got very bored with all this paperwork. We periodically received orders for what was called TDY, for temporary duty, which meant that for 30 days, up to 120 days, someone would be reassigned to a special project. So one TDY order was for making movies in Long Island City at the old Paramount studios, and that sounded great for me. They really needed background people. Of course, these were not regular movies; they were training films.

So I asked my commanding officer if I could do that. He didn't want me to leave, because nobody wanted anybody to leave since they had such a hard time getting headquarters to replace people. But I insisted, "No, I really want to go." And he said, "Well, if you go, when you come back in 60 days, you'll be assigned as a company clerk for a basic training unit and be on bivouac all the time," which meant I would have to sleep in tents and eat rationed food and be in a miserable environment that they created for the trainees, to simulate a war zone. But I took a calculated risk and I said, "Okay, I agree."

You Oughta Be in Pictures

But what happened was that the civilian directors at Paramount movie studios also never let anyone go once they got them, because they couldn't get replacements from headquarters, either! It took forever. So they wanted to keep the men they had. They didn't use me every day, but I actively performed in two films. We still had to report in every day, and eventually they let me go home—in my case, to my parents' apartment. Since they paid a per diem for this assignment, which covered food and hotel, I was able to save some money by living with my folks.

I ended up staying in this assignment until I got mustered out of the Army. It was about six months. Many days were not that productive, since the civilian director or somebody didn't show up, so they cancelled the shoot. Perhaps it was this experience making these training films that led me to take up acting later in life (as I cover in another chapter).

I made two training films. One was on first aid: we needed to show how to apply serious first aid to wounded buddies using bandages and stopping the bleeding, plus other basic stuff. So I was in that training film lying on the ground as a wounded soldier, and other guys were taking care of my wounds. It trained me for later in life of proper usage of a Band-aid.

The second film was the one that everybody seems to enjoy hearing about, since it was about VD—venereal disease. This was important because, in those days, diseases like syphilis and gonorrhea were very common. We didn't have AIDS or anything like that, then.

The film was called *Don't Let This Happen to You*. And it showed us the different kinds of venereal diseases you can get, and what you should do if you get them, and what you should do to protect yourself from getting them. That information was very important in those days, since a lot of guys got VD. I never had it, but I was one of the young men who had it in the film, which was probably 30 minutes long.

After I finished these training films, I got out of the service early. Of course, my commanding officer back at Fort Dix was very annoyed at me, since he figured I had gotten one over on him. I got discharged early and honorably, I might add. I served $21^1/_2$ months, so I got out $2^1/_2$ months early. I knew that I could get out of the Army up to 3 months early, if I were accepted into a college.

It *Is* for Everyone

The thing about my Army experience was that I came out a much better person than I was when I went in. Before my Army service, I was not a student who would concentrate; school wasn't important to me. I was an excellent student when I went back to college after my discharge.

Also, after my Army service, I was no longer a shy and nerdy guy; I had a tremendous amount of self assurance, and women started chasing *me*! Since I was now in shape and I knew I looked better, I had a newfound confidence.

In fact, everything about me was different. The Army just changed everything about me and about the way I thought about the world. I wish that the young people today—men and women—would get a chance to serve their country for at least a year. It wouldn't have to be during wartime. But I think it's important to get young people out of their protective environments to learn more about people who are different from them, to understand that people grow up differently. Some have less; some have more; some have everything. To me, there was nothing like being in the Army. I always say it was one of the best things that happened in my life.

Even though I didn't serve overseas, I got the benefit of the GI bill, which helped me get through college. My parents had no money at all, and in fact, my father didn't even want me to go to college. Neither of my parents finished high school; they came here as immigrants from Eastern Europe, and they had nothing. They worked when they were very young. They got married when they were very young. Although *my* generation encouraged our kids to continue school for higher education at any cost, our parents, by and large, did not. None of them went to college, so they didn't quite understand the importance of it.

I would say virtually every one of my friends graduated from college through the GI bill. A two-year college degree was a wonderful new idea then, just perfect for us average students. One other thing I remember about this time was that when I got out of the Army and got into Hofstra, there were three weeks until school started, and I received the only unemployment check that I ever collected in my life for those three weeks. In those days, there was what people called "the 52/52 club," which meant that if you were honorably discharged, you were eligible to receive $52 a week for up to 52 weeks.

That's pretty much my story of the Army. It was a learning experience, but it was, for me, very unusual. Can you imagine spending two years in New Jersey?

I didn't keep up with any of the people I met in the military, not even the guy from Kansas, who I took to my parents' home for dinner and who went with me to the "ten-cents-a-dance" place. He disappeared. He was very much a country boy, but we really got very friendly. He had never seen a Jew before in his life. But he wasn't anti-Semitic, he just hadn't met any Jewish people in Kansas. Except for the jerk who got busted, who tried to sell us our weekend passes: he was the only anti-Semite I encountered. Most of the people I met in the Army were just regular people who loved their country.

When I left the Army, I never saw any of them again, since, in those days, we didn't travel that much. I didn't have money to go to another state to visit anyone I had met in the Army. We just went home.

I spent 21 months in the army, and it was a great experience because it taught me so much about life. I went in a boy and came out a young man.

Going to College and Working Part-Time

As mentioned, I got out of the army in January 1956, a few months before my two years was up, because the army let us leave early if we were going to college, and I wanted to get a four-year college degree. I chose Hofstra University since it was in Hempstead, only 20 minutes from Far Rockaway. By then, I had a car that I shared with my parents, where I was living, so it was easy for me to get there.

Almost immediately, I got a part-time job at a place called Korvette's. It became very famous. It was started in 1948 by a World War II veteran and his friend (although there's a popular urban legend that says it was founded by eight Jewish Korean War veterans, which isn't true). The store offered steeply discounted merchandise, and in some ways, it was somewhat similar to today's warehouse stores: Korvette's put its merchandise on the selling floor in stacks of giant boxes; if you wanted to buy something, men on forklifts would take it down for you, and they'd put it in your car. The stores kept their prices down, and they were successful.

One day, I was restocking merchandise and checking inventory when a woman approached me asking questions about something she wanted to purchase. Of course, I helped her. I later found out she was Dorothy Shaver, the first female president of a multi-million-dollar corporation. In 1946, she was named president of Lord & Taylor. Only recently, I learned that Dorothy was not only one of the first women executives with a major U.S. corporation, but that her career began with her own small business she founded with her sister. They designed a line of dolls called the Five Little Shavers. Encouraged by representatives at Lord & Taylor, they developed the line, which they sold to Lord & Taylor and elsewhere. Eventually, they opened their own stores. As a result of this success, the president of Lord & Taylor offered Dorothy a management position. Starting a small business and working your way up is something I firmly believe in. It is something most of us who accomplished the American Dream have in common.

Back then, Dorothy befriended me. She was much older than I was, so it was not that she was romantically interested in me or anything like that; she simply liked me because she knew I went out of my way to help her. I did it naturally. I didn't know who she was, but since I helped her, she said, "You're the kind of young person I want working for me." She offered me a job, which I accepted, at Lord & Taylor in Garden City, which was the first major suburban department store.

When Dorothy opened the suburban stores, she also started what is called a one-on-one policy, which meant that if a customer needed help, the sales executive stayed with the customer until they were taken care of. Not many department stores had a policy like that. Small stores may have done it, but not department stores. She brought this one-on-one personal concept to the department store, which is what made Lord & Taylor so successful. At the time, these were upscale stores, and people wanted this kind of service; we're coming back to this policy now. You go into a large store now, and a salesperson asks, "Good morning. How are you? Can I help you? Let me take you to that department." For many years, that wasn't true. Dorothy was the person who initiated the concept of service in department stores. Perhaps because I responded to her as I did, she saw in me something that she saw in herself.

Other department stores began expanding into the suburbs. Until then, department stores were only in cities. There were no malls in those days. These were standalone stores. The Lord & Taylor store I worked in was on Franklin Avenue in Garden City, which was a very beautiful street. After Dorothy opened it, a couple of other stores, Bloomingdale's and others, moved in, and the area became a major suburban shopping area.

My job was still in the stockroom, but Dorothy would come and talk to me periodically when she visited the store. At twenty-some years old, I didn't realize what a visit from the store's president meant, but now when I think about it, I realize maybe I did something right. I probably would have gone back to her for a job after I graduated from college, but she died suddenly two years later. She left my life, but I'll never forget her.

My life was moving quickly. While I was still in the Army, I had met Aviva, the woman who would become my wife. By the time I was working at Lord & Taylor, Aviva and I were getting serious, and I knew that if we got married, I couldn't go to school fulltime. I couldn't afford it. My responsibility was to support our family. But I'm getting ahead of my story.

Protecting our country, 1954.

Me kneeling, far left, U.S. Army training film, 1955.

4

Meeting Aviva
and Getting Married

On November 5, 1955, my life changed forever. I was a few months away from being honorably discharged from the Army. One of my best friends, Paul Rozansky, married his lifetime sweetheart, Lilly Weissman, on that day. I was an usher and wore my first tuxedo, and Aviva was a bridesmaid and wore her first beautiful gown. Aviva lived in the same building as Lilly, although she was a few years younger, and she and Lilly were good friends. Aviva called herself "Vivian" in those days, because when she came to America as a 10-year-old survivor from Europe's Holocaust, she wanted American kids to accept her, so she wanted to have an American-sounding name. She learned English within six months. Later, she changed her name back to Aviva, a name everyone loves. But she was Vivian for 10 years, until she realized that she was Aviva, the wonderful young Holocaust survivor who was so full of life and who we all loved and admired.

Paul and Lilly's wedding was at the Avalon Ballroom, on Burnside Avenue in the Bronx. It was one of those beautiful catering halls where, no matter how much (or how little) money you had, you had to have your daughter's wedding there. All the ushers and bridesmaids got together before the wedding to rehearse, and that's when I first met Aviva, when she was 18 years old. I took one look at her, in this beautiful gown, and I thought she was so gorgeous, innocent, and sweet, and I felt something special. This may sound corny, but something made me say to myself, "oh, my God, this is a young lady I really want to spend my life with!" And as we all chatted with each other, in my inimitable style, I announced to everybody, "I'm in love again." I probably meant it as a joke, but obviously, it ended up as reality!

So when we lined up to figure out how we were going to pair off to walk down the aisle, I noticed that Aviva and I were not walking together. In those days, couples were matched not because of who they knew or liked, but simply based on both of their heights. My height and Aviva's were not exactly matched, and I was supposed to be one person behind her. So I gave my friend two dollars and said, "Let's switch," and we did. And from that moment on, Aviva and I have been walking together for 55 years and counting.

Aviva's parents and some of their Polish friends were also invited to this wedding. So of course, they kept their eyes on Aviva and me all night. We both love to dance and were excellent dancers. When you first dance with somebody, there's an instant reaction: you either dance beautifully together, or not. With us, there was no struggling, we were in perfect synch, so we danced all night, and, of course, her parents and their Polish Holocaust-survivor friends couldn't take their eyes off us. After all, she was only 18 years old and innocent, and they were wondering, *who is this guy?*

What they were really interested in was whether I had the prerequisites to be a potential husband. In those days, the two most important prerequisites were, *Is he Jewish?* and *Does he have a job?* So I qualified, which made that evening even more special for her parents, because maybe Aviva had met the guy she would marry.

So we danced all night. Toward the end of the evening, there was a custom where the lights would go out, and there would be a dessert presentation called *the flaming jubilee*. This was a dessert set on fire, and the only thing people could see was the flames, and then the lights would go back on, and everyone would cheer, and the Viennese-style desserts were served from a large table in the center of the room.

When this happened, I decided to be humorous, and take advantage of the darkness. I was standing next to Aviva, and I had a handkerchief (because, in those days, if you wore a tuxedo, you had to have a handkerchief), and as soon as the house lights went on, I wiped my lips as though I had been kissing her. That created quite a buzz at her parents' table: in those days, kissing somebody even on a first date was considered outrageous. But that was how we started our relationship.

Within a few weeks, we started dating. I lived in Rockaway, Aviva lived in the Bronx, and I had no car: I think my parents had sold our joint car, because I was in the Army, they didn't really need it that much, and they were very practical, always remembering the Depression they grew up in. There was no direct subway from the Rockaways to the Bronx. So what did I do? I took a bus to the subway to the Bronx, and then walked from that subway station to her house. On a good day, I would say that took about two to two-and-a-half hours. Today, young people would call that geographically undesirable, or geographically inconvenient, and they would never do it. But I did it on a regular basis, so I could see my Aviva.

We didn't do much; mostly, we went to the movies and perhaps for some ice cream. Then, at the end of the evening, I took the long jog home. I couldn't afford to stay in a hotel, and Aviva's parents didn't have any place to put me up for the night, so I got back on the subway, and I got back on the bus and got home late at night. And I did this many times. After a while, I had a few friends who had cars, and Aviva fixed them up with her girlfriends, so we could double-date and I wouldn't have to take public transportation. Double-dating was very common in those days.

Aviva and her parents lived in the East Bronx, at 743 East 180th Street, in a very nice six-story building. They lived only one flight up, so I could easily walk up (there was no elevator anyway). The building is no longer there: it was demolished. I thought it was a lovely building at that time: it had a big red lobby door and marble staircases: when those apartment buildings were built, the architects tried to decorate them in a special way. They didn't want all the buildings to look the same. It was a new concept in apartment living, where high-rise buildings were changing the face of New York City.

After I was discharged from the Army in January 1956 and I had enrolled at Hofstra and bought a used car, so it was much easier for me to date Aviva, so we started dating very frequently, almost every week. In those days, there were rules of dating about when a guy was supposed to call a girl (and a rule that a girl *never* called a guy). The rule was that you had to call a girl before Wednesday, because if you called her after Wednesday, she would say she was busy. Girls then were too proud to go out with someone on the spur of the moment—which is no problem in today's world. This was especially true for Saturday night, which was the prime night. Friday nights or Sunday nights were also important, but if you went out on a Saturday night, that was special: you meant something to each other. And Aviva and I went out on many Saturday nights.

Then one day, a friend of mine asked me to go with some other friends to a dude ranch. I hadn't really traveled a lot in those days, and I hadn't really even sown any wild oats. I thought going to a dude ranch would be exciting. So I told Aviva I would miss a weekend, and I went to this dude ranch.

But we were stupid: we went to a dude ranch in the middle of the winter, and it snowed! We couldn't use the horses, and very few people showed up, and there were very few women.

To my surprise, though, there was a very attractive waitress working there, who apparently fell for me. She was also a bit aggressive with me, which I didn't mind, and we made out that weekend. After all, I wasn't engaged or even going steady; I was just seeing Aviva. And it was really nice to know I was attractive to someone else, and this young woman was a very interesting person. She was a struggling young actress who came from Redwood, California to New York to be in the theater—she was a kind of person I had never met before in my life, so I was infatuated.

At the end of the weekend, she said, "We've got to see each other. You've got to meet my friends." So we continued to see each other, and I did meet her friends, and I was living my infatuation. Then I went back to Aviva and said, "Aviva, things are great with us, but I think we should slow things down. We're going too fast." This is a guy's way of saying, *I want to break up.*

At the time, Aviva was only 18$^1/_2$ and I was 22. Even so, when I said to her that I wanted to slow down, she was very unhappy about that. I still saw her every other week, but after a few weeks, she did something brilliant: she said to me, "Look, if you want to keep Saturday night, and you want to be special in my life, you have to commit to me. If not, that's it. You have one week to decide."

I had known her only about six months, but she knew she loved me and didn't want to lose me. Aviva had the courage to do the right thing, since I was forced to make a decision. Unfortunately, today, young people who are living together never get married because they *don't* have to make a decision: girls today don't have the courage to say anything like what Aviva said to me. She called my bluff, so to speak. I had to decide whether I wanted to live on this little wild side, which I was enjoying, with this girl who took me to a new world? Or did I want to be with Aviva? Obviously, I decided to go the Aviva way, and within six months, we got engaged, and I never looked back. The best decision in my life.

I think my experience is a lesson for any girl: don't be afraid to stand up for yourself and force your boyfriend to make a decision. The longer you put it off, the less chance you have of getting what you think you want.

JERRY'S LAW #19: "Verify to clarify."

Aviva's Unbelievable Parents

So we got engaged, and Aviva's parents planned an engagement party for us. Aviva's parents were Abraham and Lucy Gotteiner (*Gotteiner* means "one God.") They were born and lived in Czestochowa, Poland, a religiously important city and the home of the Catholic shrine, the Black Madonna. Aviva was also born there and lived in Czestochowa until she was two-and-a-half, when the war broke out. Abraham was a dentist, and in Europe, dentists were considered regular doctors: they had to go to medical school for seven years, so becoming a dentist was quite an accomplishment. Lucy was his nurse. She was about 10 years younger than Abraham, who had never been married until he was in his forties, and then he married Lucy; soon after, Aviva was born.

When Aviva was about two-and-a-half, the family took a vacation to a Polish resort on the Black Sea, on the border between Poland and the Soviet Union (which is what it was called then). In 1939, the war had broken out, and the Soviets and Germans had made a treaty that they would both invade Poland on the same day: the Germans said they were only interested in the German side where they had German-speaking people, and the Soviets said they were only interested in their side where they had Russian-speaking people, so the two countries agreed to split the country in half. When the attack started, in September 1939, Aviva and her parents were stuck in this vacation place, not knowing what to do. Lucy sneaked back into Czestochowa to see if she could get some possessions or even go back, but the town was surrounded by German soldiers. So she returned to the vacation resort, where they were taken by the Soviets: everyone was gathered up and put in railroad cattle cars and sent to Siberia to what the Soviets called "work camps." The Germans worked their prisoners and eventually killed them in the gas chambers in concentration camps, but the Soviets worked and starved their prisoners to death.

Yet Aviva and her parents survived that ordeal in Siberia! They were there for approximately four years. They probably survived because Abraham was a dentist: periodically, he was sent to the Russian front, to take care of the military officers who had dental problems. After all, if you have a toothache, you're not going to kill a dentist, which there was a shortage of anyway. So that kept the family alive, although they had little to eat and were worked very hard. Aviva was tiny for her age, mainly due to malnutrition.

In 1944, they were liberated from that camp. We don't know who liberated them, because the Allied forces did not go into the Soviet Union, but there was great pressure from around the world to repatriate the concentration and work camps, to set all people free, letting them return to their original homes. The Soviets didn't do that, not right away, since the Nazis and the Soviets were trying to hide the fact that they had such camps. They were in denial. They denied everything. Dictatorships still do it today, and people still believe such denials.

Eventually, they were pressured to set everyone free, and Aviva's family went back to Czestochowa. Abraham had property there, and he had been a successful dentist, so he tried to renew his life and his practice. That was all he knew. The family stayed for two years, and it was awful, because most people who suffered from the war blamed the Jews for the war, and then they blamed the Jews for the destruction because of the war. The only school Aviva could go to was a Catholic school, because that's all they had in Poland, but people knew she was Jewish, and she was very small from the malnutrition suffered in the Siberian work camp. Aviva was abused and beat up often by the other kids.

So her parents realized they couldn't stay in Poland. So they went to Zeilsheim, Germany, to a DP camp, where "displaced persons" went and were then sent on to a permanent resettlement. They made applications to go to Palestine, where they had relatives, and America, where they also had relatives, and they decided their fate would determine where they would go, to whichever country allowed them to come in first.

For some strange reason, the person at the American Embassy put their application on the top rather than on the bottom: it wasn't intentional; it happened just because the person was probably new and got confused where the applications go (bureaucracy at work). So very quickly, Aviva and her parents were called to go to America. Abraham would have been much better off in Palestine (not yet Israel), because he could have practiced dentistry and Lucy could have practiced nursing, whereas in America, they couldn't do that; they would have had to go back to school. Most of the American medical personnel were returning home from the military, and the country was protecting these jobs of American servicemen.

So in America, Aviva's parents had to struggle to make ends meet, whereas if they had been in Palestine—which became Israel—they could have had a normal life almost immediately. But they went to America because they wanted their daughter—who at that time was almost 10 years old—to have a normal life and some sort of childhood.

In the United States, Abraham had an older brother who lived in the Bronx, in a one-bedroom apartment, which was the same apartment where, years later, I would pick up Aviva for our dates. In those times, a family couldn't just come to this country. First, someone had to be a sponsor and pay for the family's transportation: Abraham's older brother was their sponsor. They also had to put up a bond to the government of $500 and prove they had a place to live so that they wouldn't become wards of the state on welfare. It is amazing how things have changed. It's much easier today to become a ward of the state and get government handouts.

They moved in with Abraham's brother Hyman and his wife Sylvia, who Aviva's parents had never met. Sylvia was not that happy at having the family move in, as they were disrupting her life, and, of course, having three more people in a one-bedroom apartment was not easy.

For some reason, though, both Hyman and Sylvia died within a year, which is how the Gotteiners ended up with the apartment. That's also where they made friends with Jack and Clara Weissman, whose daughter was Lilly, the bride at the wedding where I met Aviva, and Esther, Lilly's younger sister.

Lilly's family had left Germany in the early 1930s because they realized the Jews had no future there, and they left for anyplace they could go to. They ended up in Peru, where Lilly was born, and the Weissmans eventually came to this apartment building in the Bronx. Jack was a very strong, outspoken, very smart though uneducated man who was toughened by his life's experiences: you couldn't put anything over on him. So when Abraham's brother and sister-in-law died, Jack went to their apartment and took out anything that the Gotteiners would need to survive or that had any value, since the sister-in-law's family quickly showed up at the apartment to try to strip it of everything. Jack knew the Gotteiners had nothing, so he put as many things as he could in his own apartment. And when the sister-in-law's family complained, he told them, "Well, that's all there is. Nothing else is there. You have to leave." He protected the Gotteiners in his own wonderful way. Aviva's parents were much more educated and sophisticated, yet there was this wonderful relationship based on trust and love between the Gotteiners and the Weissmans. And again, that relationship is what brought Aviva and me together.

The Gotteiners were the most wonderful, loving people. I learned so much from them. They came here with nothing, but they made a new life. Abraham couldn't become a dentist, although eventually, he was accepted to go for the required year of dental college at the University of Alabama. But this was in 1949, and the south was a dangerous place for Jews and blacks. Abraham didn't speak English very well, had no money, and was a very fragile person, so he made the right decision and never went to Alabama.

Abraham was really a broken man; he was a wonderful man, but he was broken because he had lost everything because of the war. But they survived through Lucy's strength. They received a monthly reciprocity check from the German government (which agreed to pay Holocaust survivors these payments for all their loss and suffering for the rest of their lives). He made some additional money by putting a used dental chair in his bedroom, and he did some dental work on a few patients. Interestingly, his patients were mostly policemen and firemen—in fact, they were usually the captains and the officers of those departments. They came to him even though what he was doing was against the law. He was a very good dentist, and his prices were very reasonable. In those days, police and firemen made little money.

He did that because he had no choice. Because of all they had gone through, they knew how to survive. They didn't rob any banks or do anything really criminal. Their lives were only about their child, Aviva, and surviving.

Lucy was a registered nurse, but she couldn't practice nursing in this country, so she went to work in an umbrella factory in the Bronx. In the late 1940s and early 1950s, those factories were still sweatshops. People who worked there were given low pay. Long hours and hard work. But that's what Lucy did: anything, so her family survived.

Almost all their friends were also Holocaust survivors. Most were not held in Soviet work camps but in German concentration camps. They all had numbers imprinted on their arms. Almost every one of them had lost their spouses and most of their families. They came to the United States to find some family member, and then found each other, so that was their new family. Some knew each other from before the war; others had never known each other, but they heard about each other and became very close friends. These immigrants had nothing—zero—and yet they were determined to restart their lives. They remarried mostly to each other. Even though they were in their forties, they had children. They built their own new businesses. They worked their butts off. And they never asked the government of the United States for anything except for the opportunity to be free and live out their lives in peace. I don't know any one of them who became a ward of anybody. They all figured out how to survive. Some made a lot of money, and some just made a living, but they all survived with grace and dignity.

One thing I learned from the Gotteiners is the importance of sharing a family meal. No matter how many times I went to their apartment, they were loving to me and we would always sit around the dinner table together sharing our meals and talk. That made a big impression on me, and I always say to my kids today, "We have to sit around the table and talk." It is the most constructive way of building character and staying close as a family, and I still believe that. They did that at every meal.

When Abraham and Lucy had a guest in their house, Abraham always wore a suit and a tie. If somebody was coming to his house, he would respect them by being what we called in those days, "appropriately dressed." There were social rules: for instance, when someone visits, you must always serve something, even if it's just tea and cookies. Abraham and Lucy always did the right thing, no matter how poor they were. It was a matter of pride to them.

I learned all those things from them. And they respected me but still watched me like hawks. They were protecting their daughter, and until we got engaged, I wasn't allowed to sleep over. After we got engaged, I slept on the living room couch. Aviva was on a cot in the hallway or upstairs at the Weissmans. But we were very happy because we got to spend a little extra time together.

Lucy and Abraham were so proud that Aviva was now engaged to this American boy, Jerry, and they wanted to celebrate, with an engagement party. Engagement parties were important, because people wanted to share their happiness with their friends. They had such a small apartment that they could only have maybe 12 to 15 people at one time. So Lucy and Abraham threw us six or seven engagement parties, with 12 to 15 people at each!

Of course, we got engagement presents. We got many ice buckets. There was one design that was popular at the time, with a penguin on it, and we got six of them. I see them now in the collectible shops today. We got a lot of stuff, but what was most important was meeting all of Aviva's parents' Polish friends. They all were uncomfortable speaking English, so when they saw each other, they spoke Polish. I don't speak Polish, so I just stood in the corner and smiled. Everybody would look over at me and say how good-looking I was, how lovely Aviva was, how wonderful it was that we were getting married, and I was always smiling. I didn't understand a word they said. I found out later they said to each other, "What a wonderful person Jerry is: he gets along with us foreigners. He accepts us!" All I had to do was stand in the corner and smile.

Aviva understood what was being said, though. She can understand Polish, but she has zero desire to speak it. I guess she had a mental block about speaking it. When she came to America, she knew a little bit of German, because they were in Germany briefly. She understands a bit of Russian, from her time in Siberia. She knew some Yiddish words, because her family spoke Yiddish, and of course she knew Polish, that's what her parents spoke at home.

But when she came to America and went to public school in the Bronx, she didn't want to speak Polish. That's also when she changed her name to Vivian, because she thought it was an American name, and she wanted to be accepted. She desperately wanted to be an American, because this was the only country where she was free to be a child. She wanted the kids at school to accept her. And within six months, she spoke English fluently. Aviva always said knowing a second language is good, but when you're an American, you must speak English.

I believe if you want to have a second language because of your family and your tradition, that's great, but there's no reason that young children (or anybody) can't learn to speak English. It is a common thread that unites our country; there is no reason speaking English should become a political issue. It should be a requirement for citizenship.

Interestingly, when Aviva graduated high school, she was not yet a citizen. To become one, she had to take a test, which she found offensive since it asked very simple questions. Needless to say, she passed the test and became a naturalized citizen, and she was now able to vote.

Aviva also had a very difficult time as a child because she never had any toys. While she was growing up, there were no dolls, no new children's clothes or shoes, no toys at all. As a result, all those things she missed are still with her, so she loves to buy toys for kids, to buy dresses for little girls. The big benefactors are her two granddaughters. She will always miss that in her life: the war took that away from her and can't be replaced.

She won't go to a World War II movie; she cannot emotionally handle them, whereas many other Holocaust survivors see these movies to revisit their memories. If I want to see something about World War II, I have to go on my own.

The Marriage Factor

Aviva and I got engaged on January 18, 1957, and we had all these engagement parties, and life was great. I was in college. I was happy. I was getting married. My parents didn't talk much about things like that, but my mother loved Aviva, because she was a sweet, beautiful person.

Then we had to decide about the wedding. There was no doubt that we would get married in the same place that we had met, at the Avalon Ballroom on Burnside Avenue in the Bronx. After all, we met there, so why not get married there? Her parents insisted on paying for the wedding, even though they had little money, and I still don't know how they managed it. But they were not going to let their only daughter miss out on having a special event, for themselves and for Aviva.

The discussion that Aviva and I had was *when* we were going to get married. I wanted to get married a year from the day we got engaged. But Aviva said she couldn't do that, because she was working for the Teachers Insurance and Annuity Association. She worked in the accounting department, compiling the year-end reports necessary to file tax returns. Since that was her busy time of the year, she felt she couldn't disappoint her employer. Unfortunately, I interpreted her response as "them against me." That was the ego of a young man (and maybe older men, too): *Who's more important? Your company or me?* And I made this a big issue, since I was very hurt and insulted that she would rather do her responsibility on the job than agree with me on my requested wedding date. Now, of course, I say God bless that she did the right thing, because I've had people on my payrolls walk off the job at very difficult times. But at that time, my ego and my sensitivity influenced what *I* wanted to do, not the right thing. There, I said it: I was wrong.

JERRY'S LAW #8: "If it's worth doing, do it right."

So we got married on February 15, 1958. Aviva looked absolutely gorgeous in her wedding gown. She wore the same wedding gown that Lilly had worn at her wedding to Paul, where Aviva and I had met. It was a lovely gown, but Aviva wasn't happy that she wore a borrowed wedding dress. But she knew her parents didn't really have the money for an expensive wedding gown, and Lilly's wedding gown fit her perfectly. And it probably still would: Aviva was about 5'4" and weighed 115 pounds when we got married, and 55 years later, she's still 5'4" and she weighs 120 pounds. What's 5 pounds between friends?

The night of the wedding, it started snowing about 6:00. But it was a light snow. We had invited about 150 guests, which was typical in those days, and only two people didn't make it. We had a great wedding and reception, we all danced, ate, and laughed, everything was beautiful—but nobody knew what was going on outside. That was the night of the great blizzard of 1958.

When everybody was ready to leave, it was snowing so heavily that you couldn't see in front of you. Cars were buried. It was an adventure that everybody who attended our wedding still talks about, how they got home. Some people drove, and it took them up to six hours. Those drivers needed to have the person in the front seat continuously cleaning the windshield and then stop the car to clean the other side, since the windshield wipers couldn't work fast enough to clear the snow. Also, many cars didn't have snow tires in those days; some had snow-tire chains. So the guests who drove home that night had all kinds of problems: the roads iced up, and the snow formed barricades. Fortunately, everybody got home eventually. Some got home on the subway. Some stopped at a friend's house in the Bronx.

Aviva and I were also driving, to her parents' house, with my best man Peewee. (Another nickname: the only reason he was called Peewee

Let him eat cake! Fifty-five years and still being fed, 1958.

The Portrait.

was because he was smaller than the rest of us; his real name was Sid Berlof.) Peewee was sitting on the hood of my car, wiping the snow as I was driving three miles an hour. Normally, it would take only 10 or 15 minutes to get there, but in that snow, it took us about an hour. We were going to her parents' house to change our clothes; we were scheduled to go to the Nevele Country Club in the Catskills for our honeymoon.

Another reason we went home was to open the gift envelopes! We wanted to know who was cheap and who was a sport. It was a guessing game. For example, some people gave a $25 savings bond, which you could buy for $17.50 (it would be worth $25 after 10 years). And some surprised us with their generosity. Opening gifts with the bride's parents was a tradition of that time.

Soon enough, though, we realized we weren't going to the Nevele, because we couldn't get out of New York City. So we stayed that night at the Concourse Plaza, which was a very fine hotel on the Grand Concourse in the Bronx. Peewee drove with us to the hotel, although to this day, I don't know where Peewee slept that night: either he slept in the lobby of the hotel, or he found his way home on the subway. We stayed in the hotel for three days—which was how long it took to clear the roads.

And then we went on our honeymoon, and we had a great time. I should only hope so: if not then, when? We met other wonderful honeymooners, and we stayed friendly with many of them for years.

We were supposed to spend seven days in the Catskills, but we left a day early. I had tickets to the New York Rangers hockey game—I loved the Rangers, and I still do—and my wife was such a wonderful partner that she said we should go. So we went to the hockey game on our way home. The Rangers won—a very good sign for our future together.

Playing House Together

After we got married, we moved to Brighton Beach, into the same apartment building on Brighton 6th Street where my father's two sisters lived: as mentioned earlier, my Aunt Pearl and Aunt Hannah had lived there forever (in separate apartments). They knew the landlord and got us a rent-controlled apartment that was $52 a month in 1958. There was a bedroom and a Pullman kitchen, which means the kitchen was in the wall, and it was part of the living room. We had no dining room, so we bought a coffee table that we could open up, spin it around and up, and it became a dining table. It was made by Castro, a company that made convertible furniture.

I was making $85 a week, and Aviva was making $75, so the $52 monthly rent was doable. It was our first apartment, and we were very excited. We furnished it together. We also had my two aunts, who would visit us and also invite us to dinners. It was a special time.

But we also had a tough first year, like most young couples. We disagreed on everything. We had to learn to live together.

My First Full-Time Job: Amalie Oil Company

In the fall of 1956, I decided to transfer from Hofstra University (where I had been taking classes full-time) to night school at New York University, and get a full-time job during the day. I was on the G.I. Bill, and as I learned more about how it worked, I realized I could attend NYU for very little, maybe a few hundred dollars a year.

Once I began looking for a full-time job, I traveled into the city every day for interviews. One morning, on the train, I ran into a man who worked for my father and his neighbor. His neighbor was a man named Al Block, who was the sales manager for the New York region of a company called Amalie Oil, which was a division of L. Sonneborn Sons. Amalie Oil was a premium brand of Pennsylvania motor oil. The finest motor oils came from the Pennsylvania fields, and Amalie sold oil products to first-class repair shops, and new car dealerships. They, Quaker State, and Kendall were the three Pennsylvania premium oil companies. Sonneborn, which owned Amalie, also produced industrial oils, which were used in shipyards, as well as grease and other lubricants for conveyor belts and other heavy machinery. (Amalie was the name of Rudolf's daughter.)

Al Block interviewed me, and he offered me the job of office manager of a little branch office at 1 Park Avenue South, which covered the New York/New Jersey region. It was a great job: I did everything from creating sales aids, to making sales calls, to handling bookkeeping, and making collections, which ended up being my next job.

First corporate job, Amalie Oil. Al Block, Sales Manager; Carmen, my secretary, 1957.

Most salespeople don't like asking their customers to make payments when they fall behind. They don't want to antagonize the customer, fearing they will lose the next order. From my perspective, though, if you don't get paid, there may not be a next order! So it doesn't work well when the sales rep is also the collections agent. So I was given that responsibility, along with everything else, which proved to be another important experience for my future in the corporate world.

Rudolf Sonneborn was a fascinating man. He was a German-American Jew. It was a family business. Rudolf showed up at my office periodically, and although we met, I didn't know much about him. Later, I read that he went to Palestine in 1919 to help start a Jewish state. Many German Jews in America were not very religious. In fact, many of them converted to some form of Protestantism, because they didn't think they could make it here as Jews. Rudolf never converted, and he went to Palestine and fought for a Jewish state. He lived to see that dream come true in 1946. Rudolf was a strong supporter of Jewish causes, and he spent a lot of his time promoting them.

Rudolf was married to a prominent woman, Dorothy Schiff, who was from another very important and wealthy German-Jewish family: she was the editor and publisher of the *New York Post* for many years during which the *Post* was the prominent New York newspaper. She was born in 1903, bought control of the *Post* in 1939, and was a very influential person—a New York powerbroker. She, too, would show up at the office occasionally. When I look back on my career, I realize I was surrounded by extraordinary people, which was a blessing, since almost everybody else I knew was middle class. In those days, the wealthy class was very involved in charitable work. They didn't have to roll up their sleeves and go to work every day. I know they respected me for my hard work and ambition.

JERRY'S LAW #4:
"Start at the top and work your way up."

That was the Sonneborn's lifestyle but GL still had to learn that lesson.

Our Couples Club

In March of 1959, I was 26 years old, and a group of my childhood friends who were now married started a social club. The club included Paul and Lilly, Larry and Carol, Norman and Phyllis, Lenny and Elaine, Smokey and Marilyn, and Marty and Charlotte. This was all about young married kids getting together monthly to talk about our young children and have some laughs. The boys knew each other from the time we were 6 to 8 years old, and the girls met when they were 16 to 21 years old when we started dating, and we all became friends. There was the normal backbiting, but basically, we all got along.

I recently obtained copies of the minutes taken from our get-togethers from Marilyn Smolen. The minutes usually included long discussions about when the next meeting would be, whether we would go out, where we would eat, or at whose house we would meet next. We discussed things like each other's sex lives, circumcisions, who gained weight, who was going to rent a summer place in Rockaway. Then we ate. Those are the kind of silly conversations we had: we were all struggling financially at that time, which was normal for my generation, and the club was a great way for us to get together and have fun without spending money.

As I read over the minutes recently, I found it interesting that our meetings usually started around 8:30, we never ate until 11:30, and we never ended the meetings until around 1:30 AM—yet today, not one of these people has stayed up that late in 20 years!

The members of the couples club took trips together: we went to the Catskills, where we always stayed at the same hotel, the Nevele, because the weekend rate was only $20. We always spent New Year's together, and we probably spent eight months discussing where it was going to be, though it usually took place in somebody's basement.

About a year and a half after we started the club, we had picked up other members, including Rock and Barbara, PeeWee and Irene, and Ted and Ruth. We were growing by leaps and bounds. Our first president was Martin (who we called "Pierre"); probably the only reason we had a president was to have someone to harass. We all took a turn as president, including Vivian (as Aviva was called in those days) and Benny (as I was called back then). Our dues were $5 per couple monthly . . . but I can't remember what we did with the money.

We did go to the occasional Broadway show: one year we got balcony seats for *How to Succeed in Business without Really Trying,* for only $5.75 each. Those were the good old days.

The last recorded official meeting of the couples club was the 71st meeting, held on December 16, 1972. We made a schedule for 1973, but we have no recorded minutes, so I don't know if we continued meeting after 1972. We are still friendly, but Banana Nose, Smokey, and Goofus are gone. The rest of us still keep in touch, without computers or cell phones. Most of our children admire our long-lasting friendship. In our children's generation, it seems most early friendships are long gone, and their closest friends are from college, work, and neighborhood relationships, but those friendships are nothing like my generation's. Our grandchildren's friends come and go with the cell phone and computer listing their hundreds of "best friends." I'm not sure what that term even means anymore. My crowd never let geography or personal success affect our friendships: we are all still Arverne Demons at heart.

Now There Were Three

In 1959, only a little more than a year after we got married, Aviva became pregnant. We had decided to try, and it happened on our first attempt. We were shocked but both very excited. Aviva had told me it could take years to conceive, but not so for our firstborn, Michelle. But with our son Dan, she was right: it actually took two-and-a-half years.

The prospect of our losing almost 50% of our income, and to have a baby to raise, was a bit daunting to me, and I pushed her a bit to keep working. She worked until probably her seventh month (though she claims she worked into her ninth month). But once she became a mother, I always wanted her to stay at home and take care of the children and me, to be my support system for the rest of my life. And she didn't object: she wanted this, too. It was my obligation to support my family—I had to find a way, and I did.

There were a few times over the years when she said to me, "Maybe I should go back to work," and I asked, "What kind of a job do you want?" To me, it didn't make sense to just go to work as a file clerk or some other job that was "just a job": what's the point of that? It was more important to me to make sure our children were well taken care of and loved, and that Aviva was there for all of us. Her support was very important to my success in life—that I had somebody who took care of what we all needed and who made everything better for the family. Success is built on a strong foundation—and Aviva provided that.

I know sometimes it's the woman in a relationship who goes to work and the man who takes care of certain things, and I have no problem with that. I believe that if you have a successful, happy marriage (or relationship), it's not 50-50. Nothing in life is 50-50. I do the things I do best, she does the things she does best, and if that works out to be 50/50, it's perfect. If it's 60/40, that's fine, too. If it's 70/30 and it works, it's good. There's no specific number that makes a relationship right or wrong, and if you're going to fight for that number, then you're going to be fighting all the time, and you're going to be losing a lot in your life. I have no doubt that Aviva's job of 100% caring for our family was the major factor in my success and that of our two wonderful, unique children.

Sometime during Aviva's pregnancy, her cousins Helena and Leon Kleiner, who also lived in Brighton, recommended a gynecologist. The gynecologist was 70 years old, and Helena trusted him because he was older and experienced. (This was a European philosophy.) He also had a son in his practice who was probably 45, so Aviva saw both of them.

In those days, a woman would see the doctor once a month during her pregnancy, the doctor would deliver the baby, and she would see him once or twice after giving birth. That cost $300, which we paid $25 a month.

But Aviva developed some kind of disorder late in her pregnancy, and the doctors told us they weren't sure they would be able to deliver the baby in the normal way, because it might be a danger to my wife's life, so they might have to do a C-section instead. In those days, a C-section was the exception, not the rule: it wasn't anywhere near as common as it is today. So I said, "Okay, do whatever you have to do, Doctor." It was in their experienced hands.

Then about a week or so earlier than she expected to deliver, she developed a complication and the doctor told us, "You've got to take her to the hospital now. Let's immediately try to deliver this baby." I was sitting in the waiting room with Lucy, Abraham, and my mother, Esther, and we waited hours before we heard anything. Then the doctor (the older one, in his seventies) came into the waiting room, and I asked him, "Doctor, what's going on?" And he said, "It's in God's hands. It's in God's hands." Can you imagine what that was like for us, the two mothers and the husband, to be told, "it's in God's hands"? He was a religious man, with a terrible medical protocol.

Fortunately, my daughter was delivered. Aviva was fine, and our baby was healthy. So if it really was in God's hands, thank God, because everything worked out great. Aviva and I went home with our baby, who we named Michelle. And we went on with our lives.

Shortly thereafter, then we got a bill from the doctor for $600, which was double what the bill was supposed to be. We had no insurance, so that was a fortune for us in those days.

So I called the doctor, because I was a young (very young) businessman, and I asked him, "Doctor, why is the bill double?" He said, "Well, we had to do the operation, the C-section." I thought about that for a minute and then I said, "Look, we made a deal. A deal is a deal. You told me $300. I paid you $300. If the baby had fallen out of my wife and been delivered by a nurse, would you give me a refund?" That was my logic. And it wasn't about the money; it was about the agreement we had made about how much it would cost, and in my mind, the doctors weren't living up to that agreement. They never told me that if it something unforeseen happened, it would cost me more.

About two weeks later, the younger doctor called me and said, "Jerry, I'm not going to ask you for any more money. If you want to send me a few dollars, that's fine. If not, there's no problem."

Anybody who hears this story still doesn't believe that I did that, but I didn't see anything wrong with it. It was second nature to me to call the doctor and remind him of our deal. Of course, today, everybody knows that a C-section costs more.

And what does my daughter, Michelle, think of this story? She laughs: she thinks what I did was great.

The same cousin who had recommended that doctor also suggested we hire a nurse for the first week after we brought Michelle home. It's fairly typical for Jewish parents—whether or not they have money—to have a nurse or somebody to help the wife get through the first week or two. This was Aviva's older cousin, who was also a Holocaust survivor: she had done this, so we did it, too. She told us we shouldn't get a young nurse; instead, we should hire somebody with experience. So we found this woman who was in her forties, and we hired her.

We decided to keep her for a few extra hours one night, wanting to go out, just for a pizza and a movie, something in the neighborhood. When we came back to the apartment, the woman was drunk and babbling. We were shocked. And the baby was crying: she hadn't been changed, and she hadn't been fed, the woman had done nothing to take care of Michelle. Of course, we fired the woman immediately.

After that, we looked into her background. I was young and inexperienced, but since this incident, I always look into somebody's background before I hire them. We found out she had lost her own daughter (who was also a redhead, like Michelle), when that child was only a few months old. We later realized that this woman was so lonely and so upset about losing her child that she could very easily have taken our daughter from our apartment, and we might never have seen her again. I cry just thinking about that possibility, about how lucky we were and that we could have lost our Michelle forever. So we learned that lesson about how precious our baby was, and how we needed to be very careful who took care of her.

JERRY'S LAW #14: "Inspect what you expect."

JERRY'S LAW #19: "Verify to clarify."

My Long Day's Journey

So there I was with a baby, a wife, and a new apartment—a lot of responsibility—and without almost half our income. Of course, our whole life changed when our daughter was born. It was planned, but who expected it to happen so fast? We were very excited. It was part of our American Dream. One first parenting experience we both remember is when our baby Michelle slept for many hours, we thought she had stopped breathing. In a panic, we called our pediatrician, who obtained some facts and then advised us that we had two choices: either wake her up, or let her sleep. Oh, to be young and innocent! ·

We had to get a crib and figure out how to fit all this baby stuff in our small apartment. We very rarely went out since we couldn't afford it, and we had a young baby. I was also going to night school at the time: I knew I had to keep my job, but I never stopped attending night classes, because I still wanted to fulfill my dream of a four-year degree.

I attended NYU four nights a week. Many times I went straight from my job to school, returning as late as 10:00 pm. Aviva was always up no matter what time I came home; she always had a hot meal waiting for me. Anyone who knows Aviva knows she loves to go to bed early, so waiting up until I got home was quite a loving sacrifice. I always had a good, warm meal waiting for me and my loving wife to talk to, which meant a lot to me after a long day that started at 7:00 in the morning. But I was young. I was excited. I was ambitious. I wanted to live this American Dream.

Even though I was working full-time and going to school at night, I realized I had to find a way to earn additional income. I decided to sell mutual funds and life insurance in any spare time I had. I mainly sold mutual funds; I didn't like selling life insurance, which was, for me, like death insurance. So I kept my job over at Amalie Oil, but I also took a job selling mutual funds for Dreyfus, which was the first and most important company in the mutual funds industry.

I sold mutual funds to anybody who would listen to me, so my customers were mainly friends and relatives. The idea behind investing in mutual funds was to contribute $20 to $30 a month, which the fund then invested in stocks. I even sold a mutual fund to my mother, who had gone back to work as a skilled seamstress in a very fine shop in Lawrence, Long Island, New York.

My mother chose to invest in a $25-a-month fund. I guess she did it to help me: I got a nice commission for those days. She paid $25 month, $300 a year for 10 years, for a total of $3,000. And the funds proved very successful: in fact, 11 years later, those investments had grown to $11,000. Those investments might not sound like much today, but they worked out well for my parents, who were part of a generation that never imagined investing in the stock market.

My father retired on the day he reached 65—that very day, he closed the doors to his small factory and never went back. In those days, your life expectancy was barely 65, and Social Security allowed those who did retire to relax and enjoy the rest of their lives. This is the way Social Security was supposed to function. This cannot happen in 2012: it's too expensive to retire and live on only your Social Security benefits.

We later discovered that he owed the IRS $6,000; for what reason, we still don't know, since he never made any real money, but probably had the worst accountant in the world. When he retired, my mother told him that she had some money, and he always wanted to move to Florida. She had never told him about the mutual fund, which annoyed my father, but he was happy when he heard she accumulated $11,000. They bought a one-bedroom apartment in Point East, in North Miami Beach, for $9,000. He enjoyed the rest of his life there with a bunch of fun-loving cronies, people like him; they sat around the pool every day, talking politics, and complaining about everything, but they enjoyed themselves. They had this little, modest Shangri-la in South Florida, they kept their lives simple, and they couldn't have been happier. Something we can all learn from.

One of his friends was the founder of Nathan's. He may have been rich, but he was just a regular guy who wanted to be around people he felt comfortable with. That was important in those days. He was smart enough to want to have his cronies around.

My father lived in Point East until the day he died. He was 87 years old. He was hit by a car crossing Biscayne Boulevard. He was holding hands with his girlfriend; my mother had died 10 years earlier. I would never have believed he would have another woman in his life: he was a very demanding husband, to say the least. I think that after my mother died, he finally realized how special a human being she was, and he didn't want to be alone.

Of course, I sold mutual funds to other people as well. In those days, they were a wonderful thing: only wealthy people bought stock, and Dreyfus funds were a way for the average person to buy a group of stocks with only a small amount of money. Many people who didn't have much money benefited from those investments. I never wanted to sell mutual funds full-time, though. I had a dream of doing something bigger. The American Dream.

Benny the Book Graduates

In 1961, I graduated from NYU, with a BS degree in marketing and finance. I was the first person in my family to ever graduate college. My father was smart, but he went to work when he was only 13 years old, so he didn't even graduate from high school. My mother had the same experience. I had that determination to do it. I took a roundabout way, going to night school, but I was very proud that I graduated.

JERRY'S LAW #3:
"Multiple projects lead to multiple successes."

I was so proud of myself. I was married, supported my family with three jobs, and still graduated. Today, people ask how I did it; at the time, I didn't think about it. I just did it. Can't was not an option.

We couldn't afford a graduation ring, which I really wanted: the NYU graduation ring was really beautiful, but it was too expensive for me, with a wife and child to take care of. Twenty years later, on September 18, 1981 (on my birthday), Aviva gave me a small box, and when I opened it, it was an NYU graduation ring from 1961. She had found the company that made these rings, in Wisconsin. The company still had the design mold, and they made me a ring, which I wear all the time. Everybody says it's a beautiful ring. And it was a special gift, from my wonderful wife. She also gave me the "B the B" license plates (for "Benny the Book") for one surprise birthday gift. Aviva knew that thoughtful gifts were more important to me than expensive ones, and she still delivers those, to this day.

My our lifetime friends (l to r,) Paul Rozansky, Marty Holzberg, Lilly Rozansky, and Charlotte Holzberg, 1959.

Our honeymoon table, Nevele, February 1958.

Niagara Falls, second honey - moon, summer 1958.

5

A New Job
at Olivetti-Underwood

I worked for Amalie for about four years, until 1961. I was very happy there, but I wasn't making a lot of money. I had just graduated from NYU, and I wanted to move on. I always had dreams about what my future would be, and that dream did not include oil or mutual funds. So I started interviewing for other jobs.

I was the only one of all my friends who wanted to work in a big corporation. At that time, most Jews coming from a lower-middle-class background were told that it was a tough world (by which they meant Jews weren't wanted in the corporate world) and that we were better off being on our own—as an accountant, a doctor, a lawyer, or in your own business of some sort—or working in the garment industry, which European Jews pretty much controlled in those days. I wanted to be part of the real America, the giant corporate world. I don't know why; I guess I was driven by the challenge.

Anti-Semitism in the Corporate World

My first interview was with TWA, Trans World Airlines, which at that time was one of the biggest airlines in the world. It was an international air carrier (which has since gone bankrupt). My second interview was with IBM, which in 1961 was an up-and- coming computer technology company. Both companies had placed help-wanted ads in *The New York Times*. The warnings about big corporations were pretty accurate: at both interviews, I was asked in slightly different ways what to me, at the time, were very unusual questions: *Was I ever in Israel?* I was only 27 years old, but I knew what that question meant: my name was Leberfeld, a somewhat German-sounding name, so they wanted to know if I was Jewish. Needless to say, neither company hired me. Fortunately, the world has changed: TWA is out of business, and today IBM has many Jewish executives. Today, minorities should not let rejection deter them; they should keep moving forward. If they have what it takes, they will persevere.

Despite these experiences, I didn't give up and look for a job in the garment center or set my sights on another profession. I persevered in my goal of finding a job in the corporate world. I accepted the fact that being Jewish was an obstacle, but, for some reason, that made me want it even more.

JERRY'S LAW #20:
"Winston Churchill said, 'Never give up.':
I say, 'Never give in.'"

The Credit and Collections Game

An ad appeared in the *New York Times* for a job at Olivetti, which was a very large and important Italian corporation. A few years earlier, in 1959, they had bought a controlling interest in the Underwood Corporation, which was the largest typewriter company in the world until the electric typewriter came out. IBM, a small technical company that had done work for the government during the war, developed the electric typewriter. IBM became a giant in that business, and Underwood, because of poor management, closed all its typewriter factories and made rifles and other weapons in their plants. After the war, Underwood went back to manufacturing typewriters using old technology, but companies like IBM and Smith-Corona developed electric typewriters, virtually ending Underwood's empire. The acquisition by Olivetti, who developed their own electric typewriter, gave new life to the Underwood name.

At Olivetti, I interviewed with several executives from Italy, who hardly spoke English. They knew they needed to hire Americans to better understand the American market. I had just received my college degree, and I looked pretty good (in fact, they told me I looked Italian), so they hired me to work in the collections department. Although it had nothing to do with sales, I took the job since it got me in the door. Always get into the door of a good company, and other opportunities will always develop.

I later learned that Olivetti (the founder) was born a Jew, although he converted to Catholicism. In fact, people at the company told me that Olivetti was imprisoned for his antifascist activities during World War II and was liberated by an American Special Service person, who parachuted into the prison with some other Special Service troops and brought him out safely. I worked with the American soldier who saved him. He never did much—he wasn't a businessperson—but after he retired from the military, the Olivetti family gave him a job in appreciation: he was a true American Hero.

Olivetti brought in executives from Italy to work as branch managers in New York City and in other large cities around the country for they trusted them. It was a difficult adjustment for these Italians. Eventually, many went back to Italy and were replaced by Americans; only a few select made it. When I worked in the collections department, I was very focused on detail and always motivated. As a result, I had the best record in the company collecting "past dues"; in fact, I had the lowest percentage of past dues in the country.

So the company kept promoting me in the collections department. I was successful at collecting money because I was persistent. I just kept calling. The world is made up of marginal customers, who pay those who push them. I learned that if I just kept calling, I eventually got paid.

JERRY'S LAW #16:
"Patience is a virtue, but persistence to the point: of success is a blessing."

I tried to convince the salesmen to make collection calls, but they never wanted to: they were afraid they were going to lose their customers, which is a totally wrong concept. As with most people or companies who have a limited amount of liquid capital, somebody is going to be paid first, and somebody is going to be paid slowly. The one who is paid first usually gets the next order: if your account is 60 or 90 days past due, you can't get an order through the credit department, and that company loses business. That is why, in the end, it's better for the salesperson and the company to take on the difficult task of collecting the money.

Customers always say, "I'll pay you next week; come back next week," but the salesmen would not come back next week. They didn't feel comfortable doing that. I tried to convince them to do it by explaining that once they collected that money, the customer would be able to place another order that the credit department would approve, and the salesmen would make their commission on that new sale. That is really the way it works.

When making collections, I used different tactics with different customers: sometimes I was polite, sometimes I used humor, sometimes I was aggressive. It depended on whom I was talking to and what their history was. Every customer has its history. If one always paid in four months, then I knew they were going to pay us in four months, unless I pushed to collect it in three months. That customer is going to pay eventually, but the customer plays the game of stretching out his payments in order to have working capital at our expense. It's not very complicated. I'm sure it's the same today.

Many of our customers were small businesses, not major corporations. In these cases, if a customer who owed us money didn't answer the phone or was no longer at the address, if they owed us a large enough sum to be worth my time, I actually visited the customer's last-known location. The store or business might be closed, but I stood out front, and in 75% of the cases, if I asked enough passers-by, I found somebody who knew where they had gone. I then went to the new address, and I discovered that if I faced the person directly, in most cases, they would pay me something of what I owed. That's something that not everybody did. But it worked for me. Remember, I had the lowest past-due percentage in the company. I must have been doing something right!

One of my favorite collections stories involves the president of Olivetti, Gianluigi Gabetti, a wonderful, very intelligent Italian man, relatively young, probably in his forties. Before he was the president, he was the treasurer, which is how I got to know him. One day, he received a letter from a Jewish orphanage school for young girls in Brooklyn, called Beth Jacobs. The school owed us about $12,000 for typewriters and adding machines it had purchased, and the people who ran the school wanted to meet with us to discuss their bill.

On the day of the meeting, ten bearded men wearing tall black hats and black suits showed up. Every office at Olivetti was glass enclosed so that everybody could see what everybody else was doing. It was company policy, and a good one. Gabetti joined the treasurer and me and these ten mystical-looking men sitting around a large glass table in a conference room in the middle of the collections department. We couldn't imagine what they wanted. They had quite a tale to tell: they said the equipment we had sold them had been stolen, and the kids—these poor orphan kids—didn't have any typewriters or adding machines to work with. I was sitting next to Gianluigi Gabetti when he whispered to me, "Give them anything they want. Just give them anything they want." He was scared: although he was a Roman Catholic and was familiar with the mystique of the Catholic Church, these strange-looking religious people were nothing he had ever seen, and he didn't know what they might do to him, so he was very uncomfortable and obviously superstitious.

I whispered in his ear, "Let me handle it." I ended up collecting 50 cents on the dollar, which was $6,000. I then allowed them to buy additional equipment at a slightly better discount than we normally gave. When they left, Gabetti hugged me. He wouldn't let go. You'd think I had saved his life. From that day on, I could do no wrong with him.

Moving Up the Corporate Ladder

After a few more years, Olivetti promoted me to national credit manager, which is a pretty big job for an international corporation. As credit manager, I developed many new procedures for the credit and collections division under me. My colleagues knew I was always there working with them and not a lame duck or an absentee manager. I worked harder than they did, and I put in longer hours. I led by example. That's how you gain respect and get ahead.

But whenever you work for a big company, there will always be corporate politics. For example, Olivetti had two sales divisions selling its products. One was a branch division, our own self-operating branch offices, located in large American cities, and staffed by people who worked directly for us. The other was an agency division where we were represented by independent business machine companies in smaller cities throughout America.

I was national credit manager when Matt Meek, the vice president in charge of the agency division, called me in his office. Matt had been with the original Underwood Corporation, which in those days was a WASPy company, and he came from a very old line, wealthy family. One day, I asked him why he wore the same suit every day, a dark blue suit, white shirt, and red club tie. His answer surprised me: "Jerry, I have *eight* of these suits. All the clothing I buy is the same. I wear a different one every day." That was the nature of the beast in those days. He would never wear a gray suit today, a black suit tomorrow, or a striped suit; it was always a dark blue suit. He was very conservative and old-fashioned in that way. I eventually worked for him directly, and I did okay: even though we were worlds apart culturally, he respected me because I got the job done and made his life easier.

That day, he asked me if there was anything I wanted him to bring up at the agent sales meetings that Olivetti organized periodically, in various cities around the country. Rather than have him bring up issues for me, I suggested I attend the meeting and make a half-hour presentation, on how the sales agents could handle their finances more efficiently. I convinced him to let me go to one meeting: I wanted to do it myself because, instinctively, I believed that all aspects of the company should be integrated. I thoroughly believed that we were all working together and that the work I did was important to our overall success. The salespeople always thought that what they did, sales, was the only worthwhile function, which isn't true. It's the *combination* of all our efforts that makes a company successful.

As it turned out, the sales agents loved me, since these agents were independent businessmen, not company salesmen (who only want to make the sale, earn their commission, and have nothing to do with collecting money). As independent businessmen, these agents understood that the money they collected from their customers benefitted them in increased profits. When they bought something from Olivetti (or any other major company), they had terms of payment that usually gave them a 2% discount if they paid within a certain amount of time, usually 10 days (and commonly referred to in bookkeeping as "2/10, net 30"). If they collected the money that was owed them, they were able to pay us and take advantage of that 2% discount. Similarly, I explained that if they were not taking their 2% and were paying in 30 days, they were losing 20% interest a year on their money. Even if you have to borrow money from a bank, it's a lot cheaper than what you gain from paying your debt in 10 days. So I taught the agents how to make money without much effort. I also showed them how to best interpret their financial statements and profit by that knowledge.

After the success of that first presentation, Matt Meek quickly invited me to speak at all upcoming meetings, not only about how the agents should collect money and finance their businesses, but also about how to obtain reasonable bank loans and other similar topics. Our sales management couldn't believe how interested its agents were in my presentation. It was obvious that these small business people were trying to find ways to maximize their profits.

How I Negotiated for a Better Salary

As national credit manager, I reported to the assistant treasurer, Burt Haggerty. He was a very cautious man who was reluctant to make decisions. I was doing well, but I was raising a family, and I felt I was underpaid, so I told him, "You've got to pay me a decent wage. You tell me I'm doing a great job, but you gave me only a five-dollar-a-week raise." Even in those days, $5 was not much money, so I kept after him: "Burt, what are you doing about my raise?" He always told me, "Well, the budget, it's very tight. Very few employees are getting any raise at all," and all the usual excuses for why you don't give somebody an appropriate raise.

So one day, I said to him, "Burt, the person you're hurting most is *you*, because if I get a $10 raise, you're going to get a $20 raise, and if I get a $5 raise, you're only going to get a $10 raise. If you want to make more money, and you think I deserve more money, then get me this $10 raise." That worked: he got me the $10 raise, and guess what? He got a $20 raise. It's common sense.

JERRY'S LAW #12:
"You learn more by listening than by talking."

Working for Burt was discouraging. He was very nice, but he was a very conservative man who was scared for his job. That wasn't helpful; more than not helpful, he was a barrier between me and my future success.

At the same time, Matt Meek desperately wanted GL to work for him since he had gotten to know and respect me during those agent meetings we had attended together. The agency division was overwhelmed by the amount of paperwork it had to handle, Matt (who was VP) and Claude Hurley (the general sales manager) went to the president of the company (Gabetti) and told him that to get their work done, they needed *me* to be the administrator to the agency division. That was not exactly what I wanted to do, and although they pushed and pushed for me, and even when they offered me a large raise, I still didn't want the job. I didn't trust them, although I liked them personally. I knew I wouldn't be happy because I knew that if I made a suggestion, they would ignore it. What they wanted was someone to do the detail work they were not willing or capable of doing.

So I pushed the envelope and asked for an even larger amount of money as well as the title "Assistant Director of the Sales Division." I also asked for a television set, because I knew the salesmen in the agency division received these premiums from suppliers. I wanted a color television set, which we couldn't afford, and was certain this would squash the deal. And Matt Meek said, "Okay, you got it."

But I still sensed that something was not exactly right. I didn't trust Matt completely. So I told him I had changed my mind, explaining that I hadn't received the offer in writing, which had been promised.

At my insistence, he scribbled the offer on a tiny piece of notepaper, including the amount that I was to be paid, that I was to receive "one

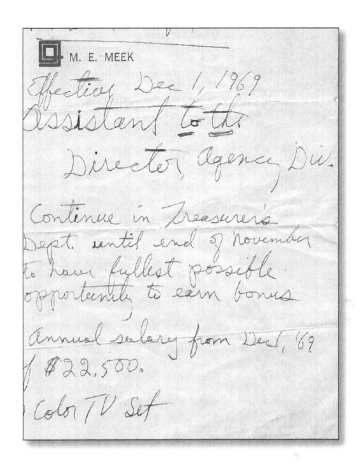

color TV set," and last he wrote my title, "Assistant to the Director of the Sales Division." But that wasn't the title I had asked for and which he had agreed to: he had added the words *"to the"* Director, not *Assistant Director*. I was already the Credit Manager for the entire company, so "Assistant to the Director" made me sound like I was just his administrative assistant, without much authority.

Unfortunately, my job change had already been announced to the entire company: it was too far gone, so I had to move forward.

From Credit to Sales

Once I started working in the agency sales division, I rolled up my sleeves and did the job. The salespeople knew I had a good reputation, and I could help solve their paperwork problem—they were very weak administratively, and their customers were not happy. They didn't even understand what they were doing wrong. They just knew that there were complaints, so they talked to the president, John Gabetti, who had been my direct boss when he was head of the treasury. They told Gabetti, "Jerry can straighten it out." So I was traded to the agency division.

I already knew most of the salesmen, because when I was the credit manager, we attended meetings together, and I issued reports evaluating them based on how many past-due customers they had. It was important since their bonuses were contingent on the results As soon as I became a member of the sales division, they began to think of me as one of them, and our friendships grew.

Working at Olivetti was a wonderful experience. When I joined the company in 1961, I had just graduated from college, and it was my opportunity to move into the corporate world. I was there from my mid-twenties through my mid-thirties. I met great new people from all over the country and the world. I formed many great friendships and shared great new experiences.

For example, Olivetti threw great Christmas parties. Back then, during the week before Christmas, just about every major corporation held a fabulous Christmas party, usually at the Plaza or the Waldorf Astoria. In fact, if a company didn't book well advance, it was impossible to find a ballroom in a decent hotel. Olivetti's parties made us feel good about the company and strengthened ties among employees. I'll never forget them. There was always a big band and the best food. Everyone in the company, from the mailroom to the president, was invited, with their spouses. Everybody attended, and we all dressed to the nines.

Unfortunately, some of the men stopped bringing their wives and a few too many drinks resulted in unpleasant incidents involving married men and single women; eventually, because of incidents like these and because of the expense of such lavish parties, Olivetti stopped holding them. All employees got a Christmas bonus in appreciation for their efforts during the year: mine was in the neighborhood of $250. Bonuses were based on your job, your seniority, and other factors.

In those days, Olivetti had a kind of unwritten policy, especially in Europe, that if you had a job with them, you had a job for life. Yet as I look back on my career, it seems that every nine years, I got the itch to change jobs. Back then, though, you were expected to stay in a job for a long time. If your résumé demonstrated that you stayed at a job for only a short time, there was a good chance you would have a hard time finding the next job. Employers took that as a sign that you couldn't keep a job. Today, it's perfectly acceptable to stay for only a year or less and then move onto a better job. In fact, today it's a plus; then, it was a minus. I think it was better then—by this I mean you can't learn and grow in your job—in such a short period of time. As I see it, it takes six months before a person feels comfortable in a new corporate environment. In the beginning, most of us keep our mouths shut while we're learning. It's totally impossible to become an expert at your job in only a year. Today is different: your resume is more important than your experiences or accomplishments. If you have the right names on your record—such as Harvard, Yale, Wharton, Goldman Sachs, Morgan Stanley, etc.—that trumps any other factors such as success at prior jobs. Today, if you're over 50 years old, you're on the down side of success. That makes no sense to me. No wonder the business world is hurting. In my time, businesses thrived on middle management pushing to get ahead over many years. There should be no shortcut to success.

The first thing I discovered after joining the agency sales division was that the salesmen didn't answer their mail; they didn't follow up on customer complaints; they accumulated paperwork; and simply hoped somebody else would take care of it. Their rationale was that because they were salespeople and generated the profits, they were the most important people in the company. To me, that is the most ridiculous idea in the world. In my business experience, I've found that a company's success is based on the complete package, which means that a company not only has to *sell* to its customers, but it also has to *accommodate* its customers, which includes taking care of everything from writing letters to handling telephone calls to making collections, and so on. Whatever your job is, you can't do only one thing, drop the ball, and then expect that there won't be a penalty, down the road. Today, we call it kicking the can down the road—a road, for me, to failure.

In my experience, salesmen are generally shortsighted. The salesmen who go into business and succeed are the ones who understand this concept and probably the ones who will start their own businesses. Most small businesspeople understand this. The sales division staff spent their days having fun, going out to lunch on the company's dime, and playing liar's poker, which is a game based on bluffing (similar to Texas hold 'em), except that you use the serial numbers on dollar bills instead of cards. Claude Hurley, the director of sales and a wonderful man, called a meeting every day, at which five to seven of us played liar's poker for about two hours. Among the players were managers from other sales divisions. It may sound cynical, but it's true.

Matt Meek was the vice president of this division. Once in a while, Matt would knock on the door, see all of us, assume we were in a meeting, and then say, "You're busy. I'll come back later." Whenever anyone knocked, of course, we put the dollar bills in our pockets until the secretary signaled that it was OK to continue. Hurley was a good sales director, but his attitude toward work was much different than mine. Mine was work first and play later; with him play usually came first.

JERRY'S LAW #18:
"You cannot do the minimum and reach the maximum."

Eventually, I realized that working in the sales division was not really for me. I tried very hard to organize the sales personnel administratively, and I managed to make some improvements, but it was not what I wanted to do for the rest of my life. I also felt the time had come for me to make a change. I worked in that job for slightly over a year. It was fun, but I wasn't happy, because I wanted to get ahead in the corporate world, and I believed this job distracted me from that goal. It was a dead end as far as I was concerned, and I had young children, a stay-at-home wife, and bills to pay, so it wasn't easy to walk away from a secure job.

Then something happened that made the decision to leave easier. In the fall of 1970, Olivetti sent over an executive from its personnel department in Italy to look into the U.S. operation, with the goal of cutting expenses. Like most companies, periodically Olivetti's profits were not up to expectations, and the senior executives wanted to cut costs. The manager interviewed many people and influenced some to leave, with a reasonable severance package. When he called me in, he didn't have my file in front of him, just a piece of paper with my name on it. He had no idea of my corporate accomplishments and that I had started at Olivetti as a young man and was now a rising star in the corporation. He asked me what I considered silly questions, like, "Are you happy here? Do you like your job?" He told me the company was terminating some of the staff, and for that reason, he was interviewing everyone, and he asked me how I would feel about leaving. He explained that there would be a benefits package.

I was very annoyed—not reading my file was the ultimate insult. So at that moment, I made up my mind to leave. I asked him what was in the benefit package. He said they were giving two months' pay, although he pointed out they only had to give one. I was angry, so I said, "Do you understand that I'm part of the top management of this company, that I was formerly national credit manager, and I know a lot of things going on in this company, that you have my trust in keeping corporate secrets. I expect to be treated like a member of management if we're going to terminate this relationship." I went on: "I understand that in Europe, employees get a month's severance pay for every year they were with the company. I've been here nine years, so I expect nine months' severance." "Well, that's in Italy; not here," he said.

But I didn't back down, "I'm part of Olivetti Corporation world-wide, and I'm part of its management team. I expect the same rules and regulations to apply to me." I was probably the only one who spoke like this to him. He held fast to his position, "We're not going to do that; we can't do that." Nevertheless, I pushed a bit further and told him I also wanted to be paid for unused sick days and my vacation days.

I didn't hear from him for a few days. Then he called me down and agreed to my terms. When I left, I received almost 10 months' pay, which was $11,200. I told Aviva, who was upset initially—she was always concerned about the future and our security—but she totally supported this decision, as she always supported me. Each time I left a job, we bought a bottle of champagne, and toasted the future; this time, we also drank to the $11,200 check. The way I figured it, that money staked me for six months. It meant that, for the first time in my life, I didn't have to worry about where the money for tomorrow or next month would come from. I had six months in which to make a decision about what I was going to do. It felt great.

When I left Olivetti, Aviva had some medical problems. At Olivetti, I had a Blue Cross/Blue Shield medical plan. When I left the company, I wasn't able to remain on the company's plan, and COBRA (which is a good thing) didn't exist back then. So I immediately called Blue Cross/Blue Shield and transferred to a personal plan with the same coverage I had at Olivetti. As soon as I went off Olivetti's plan, my new plan was supposed to kick in.

Not long after, Aviva went to the hospital. The bill was for $6,000, but Blue Cross/Blue Shield refused to pay, because they claimed the hospitalization resulted from a pre-existing condition. She was ill when I had to change from the company plan to the private policy; therefore, they said it was a pre-existing condition. It didn't matter that I was insured by the same insurer for nine years. If COBRA (which requires an insurance company to carry your policy for 18 months from termination) existed then, I wouldn't have had a problem. What they did was despicable.

I could have sued and probably won. In 1970, $6,000 was a fortune to me, but I didn't sue. Maybe it was because when you ask an attorney about suing an insurance company, even today they say, "Well, by the time we get our fee, is it going to be worthwhile? Do you want to spend the next six years pursuing this?" because insurance companies always drag it out. It's their modus operandi. The companies are able, just as the government is, to make these things go on for as long as possible, since they have lawyers on staff who they have to pay regardless. I had just gotten that $11,000 severance package; and, as it happened, I soon became very busy and was making good money, so I was able to pay the bill, although it still annoys me: principle was always very important to me.

This is an instance where the government should be involved, not in running insurance companies, but in protecting the public. The way it works now, each state licenses only a couple of insurance companies. People should be able to do business with any insurance company that meets certain criteria; it would increase competition, which would benefit the consumer, both medically and financially.

My Own "9-9-9" Plan

There is one strange coincidence about my working life: I worked for Olivetti-Underwood for nine years, from 1961 to 1970. I worked at my next company, Prentice Hall, for nine years (from 1970 to 1979). I sold the first trade show I organized, Art Expo, after nine years (in 1987). I was way ahead of Herman Cain (the 2012 Republican candidate for president) who ran on his own financial plan called 9-9-9. I lived "9-9-9" long before he even thought up the idea. Obviously 9 was my magic number. And although I did well at Olivetti, after nine years, it was time to move on.

6

Our Growing Family

While I was changing jobs, we were also moving up in terms of where we lived. Aviva and I had moved to Brighton after we got married (in 1958), and we lived there for about two-and-a-half years, when we realized we needed more space. After all, by that time, we had a young child, Michelle. My parents lived in Far Rockaway, so I thought maybe we'd move there so we would live close to them, and Aviva could have help from my mother when she needed it. We didn't want to move to the Bronx, where her parents lived, since the neighborhood was changing.

That's Right—a Housing Project

Then my mother told me that she read about a housing project that was being built in Arverne, not far from where I grew up. There was a federal law that if the city built low-income housing projects, it would get federal funds that it could use for other things. So New York City built a lot of housing projects, and almost all were built in places like Rockaway, which had many people in the summertime but didn't have enough full-time residents year-round that would have provided the voting power to prevent these projects from being built. I didn't really want my family to move into a project, but when I told my mother that, she said, "No, no, this isn't a low-income housing project; it's what they call a low- and middle-class project. The city is trying to get low-income people and middle-class people living together in harmony." In other words, *Kumbaya.*

So what did we do? We moved to a housing project, which today, I can say I'm very proud we did. We met some very nice people: real diversity, with Hispanics, Blacks, Christians, although very few Jews. We made friends there and developed an interesting social life. It was a place we financially needed at that time in our lives, but didn't expect to live there forever.

And after about two years or so, the government, in its inimitable style, started dumping drug addicts and welfare creeps who just didn't want to work. Welfare, in general, is not bad—except if you take it and don't put any effort to doing more with your life. It was a bunch of bad characters who moved in. The politicians in those days were the same as today's—promises made but never kept.

The first people to move out were the middle-class blacks. They knew, from their life experiences, what was going to happen to our housing, how it was going to deteriorate. The rest of us were more naïve, since we had never lived in a place like this before. Then eventually, everybody we knew moved out, and it became a haven for drug addicts and criminals. The government gives, and the government takes away.

We lived there for about three years, which was a long time. I think about that place when people say to me today, "Oh, you live on Sutton Place?" When I hear that, I always say, "You don't understand. You know something? I *do* live on Sutton Place, but I also lived in a housing project." I'm not a snob. I'm a guy who appreciates everything I have, everything I've worked for and earned. But when I lived that life, I learned great life lessons on how people of all backgrounds shared our dreams of improving our lives. It was a character builder. Aviva and I are proud we did it, so we moved on from there, to a new, upscale apartment building. We were moving closer to fulfilling my and Aviva's American Dream.

Moving On Up—to a High-Rise Apartment Building

I was making more money, I was succeeding in my work, so my pay scale was up to a point that we could move to our own apartment in a new building in Far Rockaway called the Georgetown, which, my God, was so much different from where we had been living. It had its own outdoor swimming pool, and it was a lovely new place. It was a 20-story building, which was something people had never seen in Far Rockaway apartment houses. In 1963, we rented an apartment there, and during the time we lived in that building, we met our friends Bernie and Lorraine Shakter, whom we're still very close to today; we spend many holidays together. We became close because our children were similar ages: my son Dan was born in 1964, while we were living in that building, and he's about the same age as their son, Richard. We spent a lot of time with them, since we had so much in common: Bernie also grew up in Rockaway. It's great to have friends and stay close for all these years: there's no way to replace them.

Also, my mother and father lived very close to that building, right up the street, which was great. I guess we're old-fashioned: we liked being close to our parents. Some of today's generation can't move far enough away from their parents. I still had to commute to my job in Manhattan, and Aviva was still my support system. I often said to her, *you're my world*. Aviva is a beautiful, amazing person: she put up with me all these years. I'm really a type-A personality, but we were the right combination. That was important, because I had a personality such that, after a certain amount of years, I left my job; I wasn't necessarily fired, I just reached a point where I had to go, I had to move on.

Today, I tell everybody that after leaving a job, we always celebrated with champagne, but my wife was always crying because there was little money to fall back on. Still, she was my support system, and I tried to reassure her by saying, "We'll make it. We'll get along," probably using this language to reassure myself as well as her. I left a number of jobs without having a new job. Fortunately, every single time, I found work quickly, a better job. I would never recommend to other people to do that: people always say, *get a job before you leave a job*. But that wasn't what I did. There was just something in me that said, *I've had it*. Either I had outgrown a job, or I couldn't stand what was going on around me, or sometimes the company changed, or the person I was working for changed. Still, it worked for us, always drinking champagne and celebrating our next adventure toward living the American Dream.

Married two years, with Aviva's parents in Rockaway, 1960.

Aviva pregnant
with Michelle,
1960.

Our First House

We lived in the Georgetown apartment building in Far Rockaway for five years, from 1963 until 1968, when we bought a house in East Rockaway, which was about 10 miles east of Rockaway, so they called it East Rockaway. It was further out on the south shore of Long Island. We moved to a very nice diversified, balanced neighborhood. We didn't have many black people living there, but we had a lot of Irish, Italians, and Jews. That diversity was a very good thing for our kids, since they got to know people of different backgrounds.

We bought our first house for $36,500. The address was 17 Sachem Street, in East Rockaway, on a beautiful block lined with 100-year-old trees, a lovely 80-year-old Dutch colonial house. It was perfect for us: it had a bedroom for everyone, a family playroom, and a real fireplace. It was the American Dream for a girl from the Holocaust and a boy from Arverne by the Sea.

We moved there in 1968: me, Aviva, our 8-year-old daughter, Michelle, and our 4-year-old son, Daniel. We stayed there for 18 years until 1986, when Aviva and I became empty nesters and moved to Manhattan. The house was only two blocks from the Marion Street School, so they could walk to and from a very fine public school. All our public schools were within walking distance.

Through my whole life, even when I made money, I never spent more than I thought I could afford. In fact, a lot of people said I was *too* conservative, because real estate was the best investment, and if you buy a little bit more than you can afford, then you have a better house and a better location, and obviously the value would go up. That was quite true, but still our conservative approach worked out fine for us.

It didn't start off fine, though: we had some difficulty with the sellers at the closing. We bought that house from a couple who had lived there for many years and raised their family there. They said we reminded them of themselves when they first bought the house, and they said they *loved* us, and they wanted to do anything and everything for us. They said they would leave us anything we wanted—the chandeliers, accessories, almost anything, because they "loved us so much." Everything sounded great—until the closing date approached.

First of all, they postponed the closing several times. Their attorney said they needed more time. But with every postponement, we got increasingly anxious: after all, this was our first house, so we weren't familiar with the process; we hadn't expected that there would be delays; and we were worried that the deal wasn't going to go through.

Then when we finally got to the closing, the situation changed from wonderful to Hell. The sellers told us they wanted to stay in the house for at least another month, since their new house wasn't ready. We had already pre-paid many of the bills associated with the house—including the heating oil that was left in the tank, the electric bills, the taxes, and other expenses. So the sellers would be living in the house at our expense. More important than the expense, we had no place to live. We were living with my parents, and we had two kids, and it was very uncomfortable. We had already lived with them for well over a month; we were excited to move into our first house!

Then I found out from our attorney that the contract stated that the sellers had the option to stay in the house for three more weeks, but it also stipulated that they had to pay $21 a day. Even in those days, that wasn't much money—but the sellers refused to pay the $21 a day. So then, the lawyers, of course, tried to resolve the situation by saying to us, "Oh, Jerry, and Aviva, why don't you compromise after all?" But the sellers had already delayed the closing several times, so I said, "No. If I have to let them stay three more weeks, at least let me have my $21 a day." At that, the sellers stormed out of the room.

So the lawyers got together, and they realized that, on principle, I wasn't going to give in. And the sellers were obstinate and didn't want to give in either. So the two lawyers agreed to pay, out of their fees, the $21 a day for the sellers to continue living in the house.

Then when we finally moved, everything had been stripped out of the house. This was the couple who had promised to leave us everything—but everything was gone: every light fixture, including bulbs, switch plates, curtains and shades, etc. was gone. Even in the back yard, there had been a concrete bench that must have weighed 200 pounds, yet somehow, the sellers had found somebody to move it.

So this was a life experience. And over the years, I've heard from many people who have bought and sold real estate that most closings are more difficult than not. But once we moved in, we loved that house.

Meeting Neighbors and Making Friends

After we moved in, we started to get to know our neighbors. In those days, everyone joined the Parent/Teachers Association, the local synagogue, and other organizations, so it was easy to make friends. Our new home was in one of those communities where mostly small stores—the bakeries, the diners, even the clothing stores—were small and privately owned, so you knew everybody. It was lovely.

The trouble for me was that everybody in the suburbs seemed to hang out in their backyards. If you didn't see your neighbor in an organized community function, you didn't see them. So what did I do? I decided to sit on my front steps on weekends and sometimes after work. Then something wonderful happened: my neighbors started joining us. All ages enjoyed this experience of becoming a family of neighbors. It can't happen in the backyards of today because everyone is using electronics. This idea probably came from my youth in Rockaway, were my front porch with a television and my basketball court in the back became the focal point for my friends and my parents' neighbors—the local candy store was also our social meeting place. This is why Starbuck's crazy idea of expensive coffee became so successful: human beings need human connections.

Our next-door neighbor on one side was one of my former high-school teachers. On the other side were Mike and Mary Candel and their kids. Aviva and I became best friends with them, and we're still close after all these years. They still live on Sachem Street. They had two boys, and we had a boy and a girl, and our kids were friendly, too. I remember Mike and Mary used to kid me that every time they looked out their window, Aviva was cutting the hedges. They kept accusing me of sitting and watching television while she was outside working in the yard. I worked tons of hours, and there were certain things this Jewish guy couldn't do—or didn't get himself to do, that Aviva did instead. To this day they still kid me about that. Marriage is a balancing act; over the years neither of us complained about who was doing more.

I'll never forget one conversation Aviva and I had with the Candels as our children were growing up: we talked about what we would do if our children got into a great college, how much could we afford to pay? In those days, our children could have gone to New York's city or state schools for virtually nothing, but we wondered what we could afford if our children were accepted to a top private university. I said that if my daughter or son could get into an Ivy League school, I would find some way to pay for it. But if not, why not go to a city or state school, which in those days had very high academic standards. Nothing else made any practical sense.

Then lo and behold, my Michelle got into Yale! Both instant excitement and shock. Did I put my foot in my big mouth! A few years later, Dan went to the University of Massachusetts, a school with a major sports program, in which Dan could and did secure his successful career in the sports world. And one of the Candels' children went to the University of Pennsylvania and one went to Yale. I was happy that the Candels followed my advice, and they thanked me for that wisdom. All our children and their children are doing great, which meant that instead of us having to support our children during their lifetimes, they could support us if needed. What a great investment that was. I firmly believe that if your children want to go to some party school and you don't have the money, don't do it. But if they get into a great school that will establish them for the rest of their lives, the answer is very clear: find a way to do it.

JERRY'S LAW #4: "Start at the top and work your way up."

Aviva got very involved with a group called the National Council of Jewish Women, which is a world-renowned charitable organization. Aviva eventually became vice president of the Peninsula chapter. One year, they held their national convention in Washington, D.C., and the attendees were invited to the White House for lunch. The President at the time was Jimmy Carter, and the luncheon was hosted by his wife, Roslyn. But what Aviva will never forget about this luncheon was that when she walked in, the first thing she saw was lox and bagels with butter, and right next to that was an enormous ham! We laughed about that for years, but we realized that her organization had been invited primarily for the Jewish vote. The shame of it is that so many important people know so little about different cultures and religions. They served ham at a National Council of Jewish Women luncheon!

I spent much of my leisure time playing tennis. I was very busy at work, and doing well, but working very long hours. I was a singles player, and that was intentional. In fact, Aviva and I encouraged our children to learn a sport or an activity that they could continue to do as they got older. Team sports are wonderful for kids, but when they grow up, they probably won't find enough people to play with, on a team. So we taught our kids to play tennis, to ice skate, and other more independent sports and activities, which Michelle and Dan still do, to this day. I think that's good advice to anybody: to learn something you can take with you, that you don't have to depend on somebody else to do.

Michelle and Dan: Proud to Be Their Parent

Michelle decided at 10 years old that she wanted to play the cello, so she borrowed one from the high school and started taking lessons. Of course, the cello is a large instrument. And we had a very small car—an Austin America. It was red, it was adorable, and it could barely fit the four of us. Also, there was no trunk. Aviva drove Michelle to her lessons, and the cello took up the entire back seat.

Once Michelle progressed on the cello, we wanted to buy her a better instrument. Cellos are very expensive, so we put an ad in the local *Pennysaver* that read, "Young student needs old cello."

We got a call from a woman who told us, "My deceased husband was a professional cello player. I have two cellos, and he always wanted some young music student to have one of his cellos." So we got this fabulous instrument for a price we could afford. I don't remember exactly what we paid for it, I think $800 or $900, and that was a lot of money for us. But we believed that if something is important, you can always find a way.

Michelle became very skilled on the cello: she made New York's all-state orchestra, and the cello was one of the reasons she got into Yale. My daughter was also editor of the high school newspaper and did other extracurricular activities at school and in the synagogue. My advice: get your children away from today's electronics and into things that separate them from the masses: they will never regret it!

JERRY'S LAW #11: "Perfection is not optional."

In addition to being accepted to Yale, Michelle was also accepted by many other fine schools, including West Point. In fact, she was one of the first women to get a scholarship to West Point—and she didn't even apply! West Point went after her, because newly enacted laws required that the military academies begin to accept women cadets. Today, of course, there are many women in the military academies. Going to West Point was the furthest thing from my daughter's mind, although she was flattered that they pursued her.

At Yale, Michelle continued to play the cello for a few months, but there were so many *other* fabulous cello players (and even the professors were part of their great orchestra) that she felt overwhelmed, so she dropped out. Instead, she did something that I wouldn't have believed if I hadn't seen it with my own eyes: she took up crew! Aviva and I went to watch her once, and we were amazed at how physically fit the women were! Of course they needed to be strong: they carried their boats into the water and rowed for hours. I couldn't believe my daughter did this.

I believe my daughter's Yale experience did much to encourage me to push harder and to believe that in America, anything is possible if you want it badly enough.

After graduation, Michelle took a year off to decide what she wanted to do. She spent six months in Europe, and she worked for me for a year at Art Expo (in 1982), then she went to Hofstra Law School, where she made Law Review. After graduating from law school, she was offered a job with a midsize firm that was competing for talented graduates; she was offered $95,000 a year to start, which was an enormous starting salary in 1987. After six years, she quit that job: she hated lawyering.

Michelle is a creative type. I believe she really only went to law school because there weren't as many opportunities for bright women as there are today. She could have gone to medical school, but medical school was a hard road for many women who deep down wanted to get married and raise a family. Like many young women of that generation, she opted for three years of law school instead of committing to seven years in medical school. Today, probably more than 50% of the students in law school are women, but in those days, that wasn't the case.

Michelle worked in the real estate department of her law firm. The firm wasn't making much money in that department, and although she was offered a job in corporate law, which was the firm's main focus, she decided she didn't want to do that type of work. She had soured on her law career, even though she was making well over $100,000 (today, those jobs are probably worth $250,000), and just like her father, she moved on. Aviva and I didn't understand, but it was Michelle's decision, and we accepted it.

I had just started Art Expo-New York and was doing seminars, and I had a budget of $10,000 for someone to create the programs. It was only a three-month job, and Michelle said she wanted to try it. She did a wonderful job. After three months at Art Expo, Michelle went on to work with several big companies running conference programs.

I'm happy that Michelle is now almost a full-time mom. Today, in my opinion (an opinion not necessarily shared by Michelle), she has her best job taking care of her family: her husband, Scott, and their two fabulous daughters, who are now 12 and 16 years old. After some years of struggling, her husband is doing well financially, so Michelle doesn't have to work, but she still accepts consulting jobs and regularly assists her husband at his work. That's the way Aviva and I lived our lives: I was the primary breadwinner, and Aviva looked after our children.

When Michelle had her first child, she chose the name Maxine, which was unbelievable to Aviva and me. My eldest sister Maxine was someone we didn't discuss much, although we'd visit her tombstone periodically. My daughter also loved Maxine Andrews, the most famous of the Andrews Sisters singing group. The combo closed the deal. You never know what special things you can expect from your children: remember that the next time they annoy you!

My biggest regret is that I didn't have enough time to spend with the children since I worked so many hours. I don't know how my children feel about that, but Aviva was always there for them. Honestly, I always believed that Aviva had a harder and more respectful and important job than I. We were a team, and together, we were very successful. There's no questions that without her doing her great job, taking care of the children and the husband and all the other things that matter, I would have never reached the level of success we both strived for living our American Dream.

My son, Dan, was somewhat like his father as he was growing up, a bit of an underachiever. It was quite normal for boys to mature slower than girls, and they preferred to play sports and hang out with their friends. But everything changed when Dan got into college. Dan was pretty much a self-taught man in a field where most young men would work for nothing and then go on with their lives; it's a dream for every young man to be involved with a sports team. But Dan never lost his desire and kept pushing his own envelope, continually improving his writing and broadcasting skills. Today, he is well known in the sports world and well respected by his peers.

Dan always wanted to be in sports, and he wrote about sports for his high school and college newspapers. In fact, one of the reasons he went to the University of Massachusetts was because it had a very large athletic program. He had only been at college for a short time when he started doing his own sports program on the University of Massachusetts radio station.

He was the second person ever to get an internship with the New York Jets football team (the first was Roger Goodell, who later became the Commissioner for the NFL). Although everyone hires interns today, at the time, they didn't readily hire them. But Dan was persistent and continued to press the team's management, and he finally got the job. Dan knew what he wanted to do, and he kept pushing, and that paved the way for other college students to become interns and have successful sports careers.

Dan went on to start a sports newsletter about the New York Jets football team, even though everybody said he wouldn't make any money doing that. It's called *NY Jets Confidential,* and he built it into a monthly magazine. He also has a website, jetsconfidential.com, and he has a radio program every Saturday morning on Sirius NFL radio covering the entire football league with his broadcast partner Vic Carruci. Dan does other radio and TV programs, too, and he travels across America as a recognized and well-respected sports writer. Dan always knew what he wanted to do, and today he is doing what he loves. He may never make a fortune, but he's a success in his dream job.

JERRY'S LAW #3: "Multiple projects lead to multiple successes."

7

An Amazing Consulting Career
at Prentice Hall

Three days after I left Olivetti in August 1971, I received a call from Dan Rosenberg, a former director of the branch division at Olivetti. He had recently left Olivetti for another job. At the time, I didn't know where he went; our relationship hadn't been personal, but strictly business. I didn't know him well; we had met occasionally at business meetings.

He said he heard I had left Olivetti, and told me he was now with Prentice Hall publishing company, as the vice president of PH's Mergers & Acquisitions Division. He explained that they had just bought a company and were having problems collecting their accounts receivables. He asked if I could consult for a few days to help him out. Prentice Hall was in Englewood Cliffs, New Jersey, and I was living in East Rockaway on Long Island, which I knew would be a bit of a commute, so I asked, "Okay, but how much do you want to pay?" He offered $75 a day, which wasn't enough for a short-term consulting job, so I said, "I think it's worth a little bit more." I thought this was just a few days' gig: in other words, no big deal, and nothing ventured, nothing gained. He asked what I wanted, and I responded with $150 a day. I thought that if they paid enough, they might even listen to my advice. We settled on $125 a day, which included my expenses, like gas and tolls.

The commute actually wasn't bad, not more than 40 minutes, since I was against rush hour traffic, and I didn't have be there at 9:00. We agreed that I would come in for three days a week, and that I could arrive at 9:30, which let me avoid rush hour traffic.

A funny thing happened to me one day, when I was driving home from Prentice Hall, during a snowstorm. I was on the Grand Central Parkway, and the road iced up, and it took me six-and-a-half hours to get home. That meant traffic was moving inches at a time. Eventually, I had to go to the bathroom. I was really suffering.

At the time, I played tennis: it was a big part of my life, so I always had tennis balls in the car, so if somebody asked me to play, I was always ready. I noticed there was a new can of tennis balls in the back seat. This vision came to me: perfect! There were people in cars all around me, but I opened up the can, flipped off the top, took the balls out, and relieved myself. I looked forward and kept smiling. Of course, I didn't want anybody to take too close a look at me. To this day—I'm much older now, and, of course, I have to go to the bathroom more often—I never leave home without a tennis ball can in my car. Necessity really is the mother of invention.

Turning Paper into Money

Dan Rosenberg had hired several other men I knew from Olivetti, so working at Prentice Hall was very comfortable for me. The company Prentice Hall had acquired was a book distributor that distributed books under a 1970s federal government program to make library books available in schools all across the country. The idea was that every school in America, including religious schools and American-Indian school districts should have a library. The program paid the school districts, and the school districts were then to pay the distributors for the books received. It was a great idea, but it wasn't properly administered, and from that point of view, it was a disaster.

The distributor Prentice Hall had acquired was at the forefront of the government program to sell the books to the school districts. Unfortunately, because the distributor could purchase any books it chose, it often purchased those that were very inexpensive and weren't selling well. In addition, instead of distributing one or two copies of a book to a district, the distributor gave them as many as 20. There was no government control over the quality or the quantity of the books distributed.

JERRY'S LAW #19: "Verify to clarify."

The distributor's attitude was that because the government was giving away this money, there is only so much time to take advantage of it so they pressured the school districts, who of course wanted to take advantage of the free library books the program offered. After all, who can say no to a something-for-nothing program? And the school superintendents, who never had enough time to look into what books were available, said to themselves, "I can get 500 books for free, so let's do it." But there are no free lunches in this world.

The superintendents gave the distributors carte blanche. "Whatever you think is good, send it," was their attitude. But you usually get what you pay for in this world. As Abraham Lincoln allegedly said, "You can fool some of the people all of the time, and all of the people some of the time," and that's enough to make a good living if you were one of these book distributors. In the end, the scheme backfired because many school superintendents refused to pay the distributor, even though they received the money from the government. The books were so bad and there were too many copies of some of the books. As a result, the schools were stuck with the books, and the distributor (now acquired by Prentice Hall), was left with $6 million in past-due accounts receivable.

When Prentice Hall bought this company, it assumed it would collect that $6 million, which they thought was government-guaranteed and would reduce the cost of the acquisition, which was in the neighborhood of $15 million. That was big money in those days. Also, Prentice Hall's management was embarrassed, because its due diligence had clearly been less than thorough. They bought the company because it seemed a good fit with Prentice Hall, which published high-quality educational texts, which they could sell to these school districts under the Title V program, something companies like Prentice Hall should have done to begin with, adding to their revenue. There was virtually no federal government control over what books were sent to the school districts. Again, the federal government had a great idea that turned into a disaster and was shoved under a rug. After all, it's not the politicians' money; it's the taxpayers' money. After this acquisition, the Title V program was halted leaving Prentice with nothing but a bad investment.

I was hired to recommend steps to minimize the damage and to help save face of the corporate managers who were involved in the acquisition. In those days, stockholders actually went to meetings.

Prentice Hall had a very good reputation in the educational world. The PH managers knew this was a bad situation. They had tried unsuccessfully to collect, but all they got in response to collection letters were complaints.

I had to come up with a formula to collect this money. They had already written off $5 million of the $6 million accounts receivable. They wanted to get it off their books as quickly as possible. Perhaps, they had a good year that year, and could afford to take the write-down. I did find a way to collect $4 million of the $6 million. The management of Prentice Hall held me in very high esteem—to them, I was a hero—not only because I actually collected the $4 million, which was important, but also because they landed on their feet, and there was no management embarrassment.

When I came aboard as a consultant, I told them that when I left Olivetti I was in the sales division, and hadn't actually done collection for many years. If you have good work experience and results, you should never say, "I don't do that anymore." If you really commit to something, I guarantee it won't take long before that knowledge comes back to you in spades.

Indeed, it came back to me. The first thing I did was write a series of letters designed to get input from the school districts. The thrust of the letters was that Prentice Hall, a large Fortune 500 company, had just bought the distributor, and wanted their school district or library to be satisfied, but we see you have an outstanding bill from this company; is there a problem? Of course, the answers we received expressed their dissatisfaction.

We followed saying how sorry we were; we had just acquired this company and that we would do better in the future. As a result of the series of letters, some school districts paid in full—all because we showed an interest in dealing directly with them, communicating with them. They respected Prentice Hall, and wanted to do business with them in the future. Some of them essentially said, "We got paid by the federal government. Let's just settle this, even though we are annoyed." They were rightfully disgusted with what they got for their money.

I got some to pay 50%, which to me, was better than nothing, especially in this situation. After all, the debt was a few years old. With my success, they asked me to put in more time. I was working five days a week for the same $125 a day. That was the equivalent of an annual salary of almost $35,000, which was very good in the 1970s. In addition, I had $5,000 left from my severance pay, after paying Aviva's hospital bill. I was living on top of the world. I went in every day for many months. Collections kept coming in and I was their one-man collection department. A win-win for all.

After about nine months, the president of Prentice Hall, E.J. Donnegan, called to say he and some other top executives wanted to meet me. Donnegan had just taken over the year the acquisition occurred, but he probably had nothing to do with it; these acquisitions usually take a few years. He was a real gentleman, and very appreciative of the work I had done; in fact, he liked me so much that I consulted full-time at Prentice Hall, reporting to him for nine years.

To collect the $5 million, it took me about four years, during which time I had no other work assignment for Prentice Hall. When there was approximately $1.5 million still uncollected, I suggested that I hit the road and visit some of the remaining school districts in person. I explained that after so much time had elapsed, the chance of collecting was low, but they okayed it. So that summer and the next summer (when my kids were 7 and 11 years old), my family flew to Portland, Oregon, and we drove across the country together visiting school districts. I drove 11,000 miles the first summer in a rented station wagon.

JERRY'S LAW #13:
"'No' simply means begin again at a level higher.:
Deal direct and always qualify."

Driving Across America on Prentice Hall's Payroll

The United States is about 3,000 miles long, but we didn't travel in a straight line. We began heading east, but we zigzagged, sometimes heading north and other times going south. Eventually, we worked our way east. Along the way, we got to see all the great national parks, including the obvious ones—Yellowstone, Grand Teton, the Grand Canyon—as well as some many people have probably never heard of, including Crater Lake, which is this giant lake in the middle of a volcano in Oregon, and Mesa Verde National Park in Arizona, where you can see the Native American cliffs dwellings. We saw virtually every national park in America on those two trips.

Some of the school districts I visited were on Native-American reservations, which were located in the middle of nowhere. Often, Native Americans were given land that nobody else wanted. As it happens, many were located close to national monuments and national parks. It all worked out beautifully for us.

As we drove, my daughter read; she seemed to have no interest in the terrain, which changes considerably as you go across the country. In states like Montana, Wyoming, and Idaho, you could not go more than a few miles without seeing something special. Aviva and I got excited about everything we saw. Each time I spotted something, our kids were unimpressed; the conversation would go something like this: "Michelle, take a look at that." "I'm busy reading, Dad." "But look at this." "If you've seen one tree, you've seen them all." That was her attitude, but today both kids remember those trips as great experiences. Today, children traveling would be playing games on their tablets or on their cell phones. So many people travel internationally but never see America's national parks, which are so special: there's nothing else like them in the world.

Success in Rural Kentucky

Two experiences stand out. In Lexington, Kentucky, I met with a local attorney to get some advice, since I was attempting to collect a pretty big amount, about $8,000. I told him I was going to Carter High School in Carter County, which was a very rural area about an hour and a half from Lexington. The attorney said, "Don't go. Carter County is the most corrupt county in Kentucky. It's owned by the Carter family. If you go, you'll be lucky not to get thrown in jail." He told me I'd be better off just going home. I hadn't come all this way not to go. Of course, I went, though I left Aviva and the kids at the hotel.

As I was driving through Carter County, I noticed Carter County Hospital, Carter Library, Carter Courthouse, and Carter Police Station: everything was named "Carter." I didn't know much about the Carters, except that they were politically connected. In 1974, the American south was pretty rural, and there were certain counties that were outside the jurisdiction of anybody but locals, which I didn't know coming from New York. I arrived at Carter High School and met the superintendent, who said, "My name is Carter."

I introduced myself and told him that I represented Prentice Hall, and this company, which was now owned by Prentice Hall, had sold his school district a great many books: "Our records show you owe $8,000." He smiled and said, "Son, what are you doing here? Nobody comes here asking for money." I persisted, "We sold you these books trying to help the kids of Carter County." He said, as others had, "Well, the books weren't any good, and we don't think we should pay for them." He was adamant. Nevertheless, I continued with the usual arguments: that they had an obligation; the books were sold to them in good faith; we can work out an arrangement that will satisfy both of us, etc.

I didn't expect his response: "All you Catholics are alike." You can be sure that in Carter County, there weren't any Jews, so, although there weren't many Catholics in Carter County either, I guess some of the local businessmen were Catholic, and that's why he assumed I was Catholic. My being there had pushed some button.

When he still refused to pay, I said, "Okay, here's what I'm going to do. I've got my station wagon outside. Let's pack up the books, and I'll take them all back." That must have surprised him, and he asked what we would do with them. I told him we were going to sell them to Catholic schools because they welcomed used books, since they had limited funds and could use them.

Of course, I was bluffing; I made up the idea of selling them to the Catholic schools on the spot, although I had used the technique of suggesting we take back the books before. Nobody ever wanted to take the books off their bookshelves and pack them up, even though the books weren't very good.

But Mr. Carter could see that this was an unusual circumstance with an unusual person, and he responded with, "You know something? I respect you. What deal can we make?" I told him 50 cents on the dollar, and he cut a check and handed it to me. I think he enjoyed the negotiation, because, in his mind, I was this Catholic young man, who came to the middle of nowhere to collect a debt. It was a great experience: probably one of my best collection efforts.

I had to travel a bit farther than I did when I made collections for Amalie Oil, but I always believed that personal, face-to-face, contact often worked. If people don't make that extra effort, it's unlikely they are going to collect the difficult debts; in fact, they are probably not going to succeed at anything. My visit to Carter County was a great experience. When I got back to Lexington, I went to see the lawyer, because I was so proud of what I'd done, and he was the only person I knew in Kentucky to whom I could tell what happened. He was amazed.

JERRY'S LAW #6:
"When forced to compromise, ask for more."

Seeing Native-American Poverty First-Hand

The other experience I still remember was my first visit to an American Indian school. I almost had tears to my eyes seeing how impoverished the people were. You don't realize it unless you've been there. Some of it results from the fact that this country has never done the right thing when it comes to Native Americans. Then, and still today in some places, many are dependent on subsidies, and they don't know how to do what I did, which is to take advantage of the opportunity America offers. Some Native Americans have escaped poverty, but there are still too many living in impoverished neighborhoods, where they get a poor education. They live so far away from cities, which offer greater opportunity, and are isolated from the real America. We should be doing something about this situation. Until I visited these schools, I never realized this. Today, I'm politically conservative, but that doesn't matter. What matters are the facts, not the politics.

My Proposal to Collect Student Loans

Those trips were a fabulous experience. After that, there was almost nothing left to collect, but Prentice Hall management still wanted me around.

So during those last few years at Prentice Hall, I had time to work on a number of my own projects (which had nothing to do with Prentice Hall). Among them was a proposal I made to the federal government having to do with collecting past-due student loans. I had read articles that aroused my interest: On November 21, 1976, the *New York Times* ran a lead article that said, "Many students avoiding payment of loans by filing bankruptcy," and, at the same time, the *New York Post* also carried an article about students defaulting on their loans. I actually knew people—lawyers, doctors, and businessmen—who weren't paying. Once again, the government had a great idea, but it couldn't administer it properly. Honest people like my daughter and others I knew paid back their student loans, even though the government wasn't pressing them for the money. But others thought, *why should I repay my loans when no one is coming after me for the money?* It bothered me that people weren't living up to their obligations. Today, we again see the same problem, where so many Americans believe they are entitled to government funding, even if they don't need it.

So I decided to write what turned out to be a 30-page proposal to the Department of Health, Education, and Welfare, which, at that time, was in charge of the student loan program. I submitted it and made an appointment to go to Washington to meet with them. HEW was located in a very large building, and I was struck by the fact that every inch of it was filled with government employees, each of whom had a typewriter, an adding machine, and a copier. I immediately thought to myself, *can't they share them?* I was there on other business, but I couldn't believe how wasteful it seemed.

My proposal was short and simple. It explained how they should collect this money; my role would be to administer the program for them. I proposed that they hire privately owned collection agencies around the country—professionals—who knew what they were doing and worked on commission, so it wouldn't cost the government anything out of pocket. There was much money owed, so the commission could be substantial. This would not be a small account: these agencies would have to hire additional staff, but they had the expertise and incentive to succeed.

HEW said I had submitted the best proposal, but they couldn't hire me because I ran a small consulting business, and I lacked a big business résumé. When government bureaucrats make a decision, they don't want it to come back and bite them if anything goes wrong. It's much safer to hire the best-known and biggest company, which, in those days in the area of consumer collections, was Household Finance Company. HFC had thousands of retail locations around the country to lend money to poor people who had trouble borrowing money from a bank. It lent them money at very high interest rates, and the borrower had to put up substantial collateral. It's now part of HSBC.

HEW hired HFC since it was a New York Stock Exchange company and I was Jerry Leberfeld, consultant. It was a safe decision; it was also a dismal failure. HFC didn't have the staff or the ability to do this job. In contrast, an independent small businessman (like me), who is working to survive and raise a family, has the major incentive to collect the money. A person working for a giant corporation and being paid a minimal salary and who doesn't earn commissions, doesn't have the experience or motivation. Small, privately owned business has always been the backbone of our country.

Several years later, HEW announced it was going to give the job to collection agencies around the country, and the program was a tremendous success. HEW collected hundreds of millions of dollars; these private collection agencies were motivated. In a way, I'm proud of the fact that I had the idea first.

Fast forward: today, the student-loan past-due debt is even worse than it was then. Every lesson the government learned about lending and collecting money has been lost. In my day, the most a person could borrow for one year of college was $2,500, and the most a student could borrow over four years was $7,500, which meant students had to spend some of their own money to pay for their education. Even in those days, $7,500 was a manageable amount to repay. Today, a student can graduate owing $100,000 to $200,000 worth of loans—a sum most college graduates can't afford to repay. I don't know what they are thinking. In my opinion, if they lend less, and the kids couldn't pay $40,000 or

$50,000 a year, the colleges would reduce their tuition. In that sense, a college is like an airplane or a hotel room—an empty seat is worthless. The price of a college education will go down significantly if the government, through student loans, stops tampering with the process of competition then supply and demand would positively affect prices. They don't realize that they're hurting themselves in the long run, but who cares? It's the citizens' money, not theirs.

With loans this large, many college graduates spend a large percentage of their salaries repaying the government, for the first 10 or 15 years after graduating. That's an *incentive* for people to try to cheat the government. It's going to come back to bite us, and we should really deal with it. Raising the interest rates on student loans from 3.5% to 7% is not a terrible thing. If I were a parent of someone attending college now, paying 3.5% interest, I would tell my child to take the loan. After all, if I had to go to a bank and borrow the money, I'd have to pay around 8% for a personal loan. I could use the money for something else. When money is cheap, it's abused because people borrow more money than they need. It's called kicking the can down the road. Much too common in today's society.

In addition, many of these student loans will never be collected since there is no collection vehicle. We're back to the way things were—with politicians making nice by giving away taxpayer money. When a professional did the collections job, students knew they'd better pay, because someone was coming after them and charging them interest and penalties. When you send out the right message, which is that if you do something wrong, you'll eventually get caught and there will be consequences, fewer people do something wrong. Now, students are rewarded for bad behavior, which down the road only makes the problem bigger.

It Ain't Over till It's Over

Other than my proposal to the government, I'm hard-pressed to describe exactly what I did during the last four years at Prentice Hall. I reported directly to Donnegan, and I was still friendly with Dan Rosenberg and the men who had come over from Olivetti, but I was not working with them anymore. Periodically, Donnegan would call me for some special project, mostly a small job here, and a small job there. Occasionally, I came up with a suggestion: I had to, since I wanted to keep getting paid. I no longer went into the office every day since they didn't need me. I thought they would terminate my contract, but they didn't: they liked the idea that I was there for them, if they needed me. On the plus side, the extra time allowed me to start working on other projects.

The contract I had with Prentice Hall had an automatic renewal clause, with a built-in increase every year. I didn't want to renegotiate each time I did work for one person or another in the company. Prentice Hall had additional office space on Sylvan Avenue (also known as Route 9W), right across from its primary location, where I was given my own private office space. I went across the street periodically to help with their accounts receivable system. At the time, they had computer punch cards all over the place. It took a tremendous amount of time to match them up. I helped them automate the system.

I lost favor at the end—although they still didn't terminate my contract—I stepped on too many people's toes when I told them that some of their major divisions needed improvement. The fact is, someone in my position could criticize the acquisitions managers and make changes in administrative and collection procedures, but I couldn't really go to the president, who then went to the manager of the particular division, and say that what they put into effect was wrong. In all likelihood, the way the department was doing things was the present manager's idea. Of course, the managers said no to my ideas and were annoyed with me, because I was criticizing what they were doing, which may have damaged their egos or made them feel threatened. From my point of view, I was simply looking for new projects so they wouldn't terminate the agreement. Again, after nine years, it was time to move on.

Finally, my consulting arrangement with Prentice Hall was terminated in 1979, since there was no longer anyone who wanted to protect me. They let me use their office for a period of time to look for something else, and they gave me a beautiful letter of recommendation. In truth, I knew it had to end eventually, and I was already involved in producing and selling art as a tax shelter and was just at the beginning of creating my new nine-year adventure of Art Expo-New York.

8

Discovering the Magnificent World of Being an Entrepreneur

The next stage of my life and career had actually already begun, almost 10 years earlier. As early as 1969, while I was still at Olivetti, I began to get involved in other side businesses, in addition to my full-time work. This was the beginning of what would become my most successful and interesting work—my new career in the art world.

After I transferred from the credit department to the sales department at Olivetti-Underwood in October 1969, I met a great many of the sales managers, and they were always coming up with ideas to make money. One of the sales managers—Jerry Cammina—left Olivetti to open a big warehouse on Long Island from which he sold picture frames that he imported, mainly from Mexico, as well as lithographs and prints by artists and what he called "original art." None of it was very expensive.

At that time, the art world was booming. Middle-class people were becoming interested in art. Jerry Cammina invited me and Paul Matick, another Olivetti sales manager who was a very close friend of mine, out to see his operation. At lunch, Jerry suggested that Paul and I get involved in the business of art, specifically auctions to raise money for charitable organizations. He explained that you make an agreement with a charity, acquire the artwork, create the catalog, and schedule and run the auction. In return, you receive 80% of the sale, and the charity gets the balance.

Although we didn't know how the auction business worked or much about art, Paul and I decided to try it. The first charity I booked was my local Marion Street (East Rockaway) PTA, and Paul the New City ORT, both scheduled in the fall of 1970. We went back to Jerry Camina and asked what the next steps were. To our surprise, he replied, "Well, to tell you the truth, I never ran an auction in my life. We'll have to learn together." So Paul and I decided to go to Sotheby's to see how an auction was run.

To say the least, we were confused, but we were resourceful. We created invitations and decided on how to promote and advertise the auctions. We bought some framed art from Jerry. The first auction to be held was the PTA event, in September 1970. Paul was the auctioneer, and I did the administrative work and set up the room.

We had a wonderful turnout. We brought in about 200 pieces of artwork, a combination of oil paintings and prints, mostly landscapes that were hand painted in Asia, probably in China. They were not really original pieces, as I later learned: each artist was expert in painting a particular thing like a tree or a bird or a river and together, several artists created these paintings. The framed landscapes were very attractive and didn't sell for a lot of money—maybe $25 to $150 at the most—so no one was taken advantage of. The pictures were comparable to the kind of art you find in malls today: the prints were mainly framed copies of famous artists' work, which primarily have decorative value only.

In those days, middle-class people weren't art collectors. Most people believed collecting art was done only by the very wealthy, elite, and sophisticated few. Still, the middle class was growing and had more disposable income and wanted to learn more about art, but mainly were just interested in hanging something attractive on their walls. It was a way of accessorizing and distinguishing your home from others. After all, every couch, chair, table, and lamp looks pretty much the same, but artwork can change the personality of your home.

The PTA auction was a big success. People bought just about everything—198 pieces out of 200—and there was great enthusiasm in the building. Almost everybody took something home; it was a happy, fun-filled event.

Since we did so well at the PTA auction, we brought 300 pieces to Paul's ORT sale, and we sold virtually all of them. One moment stands out—a Picasso print of two hands clutching a bouquet of flowers. The print was a copy of a famous Picasso painting. We paid something like $5 for it and framed it for a total cost of $25. The people went crazy: at least six people were bidding on it, and when the bidding went to $185, I grabbed Paul's arm and told him to stop the bidding. I was embarrassed, but the people were happy. In fact, the under-bidder asked us if we could find another one for him.

That was how I started my art career with success, and, of course, we learned some lessons. For example, within the first year, we learned that Jerry Cammina wasn't the only person from whom we could buy art. As a result, the quality of what we sold improved. As with all businesses, we learned as we went, improving at each and every auction.

At the same time, we made good money. Usually the charity got 20%, the merchandise cost us about 50%, so we grossed 30%, but, of course, we had other expenses. We had to rent a truck and pay for promotional materials, which included invitations and advertising in local papers, but still made a nice profit from a part-time weekend job. The auctions were held on Friday or Saturday nights, and Paul and I continued to work at our regular jobs at Olivetti for several more years. I was always really motivated, and we were both young and raising families. This was my first step up the ladder of becoming a major player in the art world.

It was a wonderful experience, but very difficult, since we were doing it in our so-called "spare time." People don't realize what's involved. We had to find the artwork, frame them, and number and catalog each piece. On the day of the auction, we had to carefully load each piece on and off a rented panel truck, and then display them—usually on tables or against the walls. It involved a lot of manual labor, and usually it was just the two of us. Occasionally, we hired some local kids who would work as movers, picking up each art piece in numerical order, bringing it to the front of the room and placing it on the easel, and then removing it so we would go on to the next item. They had to move quickly, because in an auction, the audience quickly gets tired and begins to lose interest.

Even after I left Olivetti for Prentice Hall, we still did auctions together and stayed close friends.

JERRY'S LAW #18:
"You cannot do the minimum and reach the maximum."

Flying Solo at Lambert Hill Galleries

Then in 1973, about four years after we started the art auction business, Paul told me he no longer wanted to be involved in all aspects of the business. "The only thing I want to do," he said, "is show up and be the auctioneer." By that time, we had built the business up to 12 or 15 auctions a year. Paul was a salesman, and as mentioned earlier, my experience with salesmen is that they always think they're the most important part of any business. But my view has always been that to be successful, all the parts of a business have to work together.

I didn't think it was much of a partnership if Paul wasn't going to help with the physical work, so I decided I didn't want to continue on that basis, and Paul agreed to end the partnership. We signed an agreement dissolving our partnership, and I paid him for his half of the inventory.

I decided not to ask Paul to work for me as the auctioneer, because I believe that when a relationship becomes strained and your partner doesn't want to do his share, there's no place for things between you to go but down. Still, I was very nervous, since I had never worked as an auctioneer.

Although my auctioneering style was very different from Paul's, I did very well. As with anything else in life, I had to try it and commit myself to it. This led to many new opportunities in my life. I had always been administratively strong, but as an auctioneer, I was *selling*. Once I realized I could be a successful auctioneer, it gave me confidence in my overall ability.

When we started the business, Paul and I spent many days trying to come up with a company name. Paul had just moved to Steep Hill Road in Weston, Connecticut, and for lack of another idea, and because he thought it sounded impressive, we called ourselves Steep Hill Galleries. When Paul and I split up in 1973, I changed the name from Steep Hill Galleries to Lambert Hill Galleries. I sometimes used the name "Jerry Lambert" to avoid being stereotyped because of my religion. In those days, in the art world, it was best to have some kind of generic—unidentifiable—name. (Lots of Jewish people used to change their names: for example, most people now know that the actor Tony Curtis was born Bernard Schwartz.) I decided to change the company name because I wanted to change the corporate setup, and it was much simpler to dissolve the old corporation and start a new one. I used the Lambert Hill name for many of my new ventures until I started Art Expo.

After Paul left, I started to expand. I did my first two-day auction in Atlanta, Georgia. Norman Zipkin (alias *Pussyfoot*), one of my Arverne friends, had moved to Atlanta, and he lined up a couple of charities for me. A member of one charity owned a gorgeous Mercedes-Benz showroom located in a circular glass building situated in the center of Buckhead, one of the most prominent sections of Atlanta. The auction was very well-promoted, including to the dealership's customers. I had to ship a lot of art for a two-day auction, so I hired somebody to drive a rental truck from Long Island to Atlanta, and I flew down on Friday. By this time, I was working as a consultant for Prentice Hall so I had flexibility, and the charity auction business was making good money, so I could afford the airfare.

Even so, it was very demanding physically, but Norman got his son and his son's friends to help me by bringing the art up to the front, removing it once it had sold, and helping the buyers pack up their purchases to take them home. I did other auctions in Atlanta over the next two years, and they were the best auctions I ever ran.

During all this time, I was fortunate that Aviva was very supportive of my working weekends and traveling out of town. She knew the art business was beginning to make money, and she understood that, since we had started with nothing, everything I did was a step toward building a better life together. I'm sure she was unhappy that she was alone with the children. Without her, I don't know if I would have been able to push myself as far as I did.

On the other hand, I always push myself. It's part of reaching my

American Dream. You reach one goal, and there's always another step upward. It's not that there weren't problems along the way, but every time I took a step, I did better and better.

JERRY'S LAW #3:
"Multiple projects lead to multiple successes."

My Bermuda Art Adventures

My next art venture began in 1972, about two years into my job with Prentice Hall. Another Olivetti sales manager approached me with another new business idea. His name was Claude Stone, and we had stayed friendly after I left Olivetti, and we're still great friends. He had befriended a business-machine dealer from Bermuda, who told him they didn't have any art galleries there. Claude suggested that we might open an art gallery there, since he knew I had connections to that world from the charity art auctions. Although Claude hadn't been involved with those auctions, he knew I had done well.

We decided to pursue the idea and discovered that a non-citizen could not own a business in Bermuda. A Bermudian had to own at least 51% of the business. Also, non-citizens are not allowed to work in Bermuda unless the job is advertised in the newspaper for two 30-day periods, then if no qualified Bermudian applies, a non-citizen can get a work permit. No locals applied, so I was able to get a six-month work permit. As a result of this government policy, there is virtually no unemployment in Bermuda. (Congress, take note!)

Claude Stone and I went to Bermuda and met with two locals, Joan Aspinall and Wally Pitman, who was an Olivetti typewriter distributor. Joan and Wally became our local business partners, and they suggested we set up our gallery in the brand-new, beautiful Holiday Inn that had just opened in St. George in April 1972. Most people go to Hamilton, but St. George is the other major city in Bermuda, and it is really an interesting place. It's closer to the airport, and it's a very historic city, built on top of an old fort. The hotel was willing to give us free space for a gallery, to draw tourists to this less-famous area of the island. We made an arrangement to open a gallery and also to run weekly art auctions at this Holiday Inn and at the world-renowned Princess Hotel in Hamilton.

My job was to teach Joan and Wally how to run an art gallery and art auction. Since my work permit was for six months, it was imperative that I complete this training within that timeframe. I was still working for Prentice Hall, so I did this mainly on long weekends. There was no limit to the amount of work I was willing to do. I didn't think about it in that way. I saw it as an opportunity to get into my own business, and it was very exciting.

We had the galleries for about a year and a half. The problem was there were four partners in this business—Joan, Wally, Claude, and me—so we really made no money at it. Another problem was that Joan and Wally had full-time jobs in addition to running the gallery, and they weren't as interested as I was in working hard to build something that might have value in the future. They complained they weren't making enough money. Most people want instant gratification, whereas my business plan dictates if you are not willing to give a new project three years, don't do it.

You learn in business (at least in a small business) that if you don't invest the time and energy and if you don't make adjustments along the way, you won't succeed. In the end, we dropped the project, but it was a great experience. I went to Bermuda at least six times over a year and a half, and it was another building block in my road to the top of the art world.

There's one other incident that stands out in my mind from that time. As mentioned, during the time I worked at Prentice Hall, I began working as a consultant on other projects. I did well enough that I even hired people to work for me part-time. One of them was also a hairdresser, who put my hair in pin curls to create a white "Afro" look. It was very attractive, and it became a weekly exercise. I kept that hairstyle for over 2 years, then she began to experiment with me on other hairstyles. Once she wanted to cut it very short, not a military crew cut, but almost, and I let her do that. It was comfortable and easy to maintain.

What I didn't know was that in those days, having short hair was sometimes code for being gay, like a man wearing an earring in his left ear later was. But I didn't know, and so one night, in Bermuda, I was at the bar by myself. A man sat down next to me, and we started to talk.

He got chattier and chattier, and finally, he said he knew a better bar that we should go to. I became uncomfortable. Up until that point, I hadn't thought about the possibility that he was gay; I just thought he was too pushy. I decided I had to get away from him, so I went to the bathroom. Less than five minutes later, I heard pounding on the door, and he started screaming, "Let me in! Where are you?" I didn't realize he thought that my going to the bathroom was an invitation. I was 39 years old, but I was naïve. I climbed through the bathroom window and started running. And he ran after me, screaming.

I guess I was attractive to a gay man; maybe it was my hairdresser's fault. I never told that story before to anybody, not even Aviva.

Selling Art as an Investment for Tax Credits

My next venture into the art world occurred in 1977, while I was still consulting for Prentice Hall, when my friend Ted Nussbaum approached me with an idea. Ted and I were childhood friends: his nickname was *Moon* because he had a moon-shaped face. Ted was a partner in a law firm that worked almost exclusively for Atlantic Records, an important music label at the time.

His idea involved tax shelters. He explained that if you bought commodities—such as oil, gas, minerals, real estate in certain rural areas, or art—the government let you write off the investment over 25 years and gave you a special tax credit. It sounded crazy, but I am not a tax attorney or an accountant, and Ted assured me it was legal. He said, "We've got to do it, and I want to be your partner." Many attorneys have wanted to be my partner. The idea was to invest in art for ourselves and also to sell art as a tax shelter investment to others.

At the time (and this is the shame of it), the major investment banks, law firms, and accounting firms were recommending these investments to their clients. I figured if they could recommend it for their important clients, I could do it, too. I knew where to get the appropriate art product; I knew I could sell it (which I did), and I thought that if all these established companies like Price Waterhouse, Goldman Sachs, and Lehman Brothers were doing it, it had to be legal. All the accountants and lawyers working at these big firms wrote opinions saying that it was legal—a loophole in the tax law.

I set up two new businesses, Arverne Art and Arverne Art Distributing Company: one to acquire art and the other to distribute it. I chose the name *Arverne* since that's where Ted and I grew up in Rockaway. Ted received a percentage, because in addition to finding customers among his clients, he handled all the legal work. I did this for about four years, and I made some real money.

Here's how the business worked: I commissioned important artists to create a series of limited-edition lithographs. There's nobody—including artists—who doesn't want to make money (at least, I don't know anybody who doesn't). The artists produced and signed their work, and we sold the editions to various people as a tax-sheltered investment. I sold many of these tax shelters, mostly by word of mouth, and Ted had a large base of clients who were interested in legal tax deductions. We didn't even have a shop or a gallery; I worked out of my Prentice Hall office. We kept our overhead low—a business principle I followed in later successes.

Most of the buyers didn't care about the art itself; they were buying the tax deduction. They were told that if you invested in art, you could take a legal tax deduction, because you were supporting the arts—something the government wished to encourage. It was another government idea that sounded good in theory but had unintended consequences. In this case, the government presumably wanted to encourage art and help struggling artists, but, in practice, the only artists who were helped were the rich artists. I couldn't choose an artist that nobody knew; I had to choose recognizable names, or buyers wouldn't be interested and the deal would lose credibility.

The idea caught on like wildfire, but as it turned out, it wasn't legal after all: 10 years later, after I had sold about 100 of these tax shelters, and after the investors (including me) had taken their deductions, the government said it was illegal, and we had to pay back the entire tax deduction—plus penalties and interest! It came to about double our initial investment.

Meanwhile, the giant firms barely got a slap on the wrist. Just like today, they collected gigantic commissions. Although I'm a pro-business conservative, I think that's just wrong. The government should have been involved from the beginning. This type of investment should have been approved in writing before anyone sold a single one; it shouldn't have taken the IRS 10 years to say the deduction wasn't legal. I was annoyed, because the big firms that recommended these investments were rewarded for it, and those relying on their professional advice were punished.

The upside for me from this venture was that I got involved with some great artists, including the sculptor Marisol, Richard Anuszkiewicz, Salvador Dali, James Rosenquist, Mark King (who painted sports subjects), and Irving Amen, who was well-known especially to Jewish people, because he did woodcuts and other art related to Jewish themes. Others were less well known but important, including Herbert Schneider, an artist from Austria whose work I produced with partners. Later, we brought his work to an art fair in Washington, which turned out to be the beginning of my next career in the art world. (Everything has a connection.) Someone I knew said he was a very good artist, very well-known in Europe, whose work was a little different, so I said, *let's do it.*

The Idea for an Art Expo in New York City

As a result of my earlier part-time job of running art auctions for charities, I met many people in the art world, people who sold, distributed, or framed art. Phil was a framer on Long Island who I met when I was doing the art auctions. He seemed to be a very nice guy, and we became friends. By the late 1970s, the auctions were of higher quality: I was no longer dealing in $25 paintings and prints; now they were original lithographs and paintings that sold for hundreds of dollars. In 1978, Phil told me about a very fine art show in Washington, D.C. called Wash Art. It was similar to European-style shows: the venues were large, the exhibits lavish, and very fine galleries exhibited at them. Phil invited me to join him and his three partners, Irwin, John, and Bridget, to exhibit together at Wash Art. Irwin was Phil's cousin through marriage. He was a self-proclaimed accountant, but I never saw him work a day in his life. John was a French poster publisher and dealer. Bridget was a French art dealer.

Phil convinced me to join the four of them and exhibit at this show, which was held in 1978 at the Armory in Washington, D.C., not far from RFK Stadium. The four of us each put up $3,000, and we didn't do very well: we sold only a few pieces. The Armory had no air-conditioning, the exhibit was held in May, and the temperature was 90 degrees outside. The neighborhood was bad: taxis didn't cruise the area because few people would walk in this area, so people had to call for cabs to get in and out of the area. There also were no hotels nearby. All in all, it was a difficult place for the exhibitors to attract the fine-art buyers to this show.

Despite these drawbacks, it was an esthetically beautiful show, with very good exhibits; Europeans always want to expand their market and attract American clientele, who are still the best art customers in the world. Still, there wasn't an exhibitor I spoke with at the show who wasn't bitching about the management—the attendance was low, the exhibit hall was too hot, the show hadn't been sufficiently advertised, and on and on. All the complaints from all the exhibitors made us realize one thing—that for an exhibit like this, New York was the place to hold it; forget about Washington. So Phil suggested, "Why don't we do it in New York?" And I reacted that if we did it, we had to do it *before* the Washington show, which was scheduled again for the following May. You always want to be first.

It was a big undertaking to start a new show in a different city. It's always hard to lure exhibitors away from an existing show, even when they are not happy with that show. They're afraid to give up what they have for something they don't know. Some exhibitors do well at any show, but those are few and far between.

When Phil suggested New York, I jumped on the idea, saying, "I have an office in New Jersey. I'll hire somebody to help send out mailings. I'll see if we can get space at the New York Coliseum," which was the major exhibit center in New York City at that time. As soon as we left the Wash Art Show and got back home, I sent letters to everyone who had exhibited at Wash Art (their names were listed in the exhibit's catalog) to see if they had any interest in exhibiting in New York City. Very quickly, we got enough answers to know we should go ahead. Many of them said, "New York is the best place; we're interested." That didn't mean they were ready to send us a deposit check, but they were definitely interested.

At first, we called the fair the International Art Expositions, but almost immediately, we changed the name to Art Expo-New York. The key ingredient for our success was emphasizing *art* and *New York* in the name. Every art gallery and artist in the world wants to show their wares in New York: it's the center of the art world. When I started Art Expo in New York, some galleries had doubts about us. They were concerned about the level of customer we aimed to attract. My biggest concern was whether art that sold in Europe would translate to American tastes. At the same time, I didn't want everything to look alike. The art had to be important, but also had to conform to American tastes.

From the start, I understood the market, and most of the art dealers who participated in Art Expo were successful, and their success attracted others. My instincts proved to be right, because most of the exhibitors kept coming back and brought their European and Asian colleagues.

I knew little about trade shows, or the buildings where they were held, or even about art at that level. But I was a good businessman. Since we had received a positive response to the letters, I suggested we move forward. Despite my lack of knowledge, I wasn't intimidated. I always wanted to learn, and I learned so much as I went along, but, when I started, I only knew what I liked. Over time, I learned more about art and what my customers wanted to buy. For example, when I traveled to Europe later, some of the art I saw was very avant-garde, and I didn't try to sign those artists as exhibitors because I knew Americans wouldn't buy that type of art.

The experience I gained from doing all the things I had done made me feel that I could compete in the art world. When I began in the charity auction business, if ordinary middle-class people went to an art gallery, the staffs at those galleries wouldn't even look at them because they thought they weren't potential customers. At the time, there were only a few thousand art buyers in the entire high-end art world. And that was really the only art world there was at that time.

I was successful because I understood where the people I sold to were coming from and what their level of understanding was. I had always been more of a businessman than an art connoisseur, but, from the beginning, I had a very good sense of what middle-class people—not people who collect Picassos and Rembrandts—would want to buy. I was always instinctively good at selecting art, even though I grew up without art. The only art work I can remember from when I was a child was a framed photograph of my oldest sister, at about two years old, nude on a bearskin rug, which hung over the living room couch. That I came from that background makes it amazing that at my peak, I was one of the leading personalities and experts in the art world. Still, I have to give Phil credit since he was the one who suggested we exhibit at Wash Art, and that show sparked the whole concept of Art Expo-New York, which became a huge success.

Planning Our First Art Expo

So the five of us put up $8,000 apiece, and we found a small office on Madison Avenue. My French partners said that to be in the art business, you had to have a Madison Avenue address, which in those days, was probably true. It's a matter of perception, and the art world has always been elitist, so we had to at least play the game. So just before the first show, we moved from New Jersey into an office on Madison and 53rd Street.

By this time, I was no longer working for Prentice Hall, and I needed an income. I told my partners that until we made money, I would work for a $30,000 salary, which wasn't much money even then. At first, they objected, because I was an equal partner in the business, but I explained that since I was doing the day-to-day work and they weren't, I deserved to also be paid a salary.

They continued to object, and they actually interviewed people to replace me. They chose a retired assistant principal of a public school, who agreed to do the job for $18,000. It was obvious to me that she lacked the business experience and know-how to run a brand-new venture for an international art fair. After a while, my partners realized that although she was a nice person, she didn't have a clue about art or business. It was ridiculous, but I was dealing with men who thought small when it came to business. Nevertheless, I went ahead with what had to be done, because that's my nature, probably my Achilles' heel. (Later on, when we were in a dispute, although things were really going well, a couple of my partners said that my "weakness" was that I "back off.")

When you think about the Rockefellers, Carnegies, or the Vanderbilts, you realize that they all got rid of their partners before their great successes. They knew that a business can't be run by four or five partners; *one* person has to run it and make the day-to-day decisions. Of course, the Rockefellers, Carnegies, and Vanderbilts were also sued, but, in the end, they all won or settled in a way that left them in charge. I didn't have the courage to do that. The company was growing and had great potential. I figured it would work itself out in the long run, which it did, in a way, because two of the partners left before the second show opened (in 1980).

Back then, the New York Coliseum was the only major convention site in New York large enough to handle a big art fair, and it had only one date available in 1979: March 6, which was perfect because it was two months before the Washington show. We wanted the fair to run for five days and we wanted to be open Thursday through Monday. The building had four floors, but only the mezzanine level was available, and I didn't think we needed a bigger floor at the time.

What I didn't know was that the mezzanine level didn't go full circle: it was shaped like a horseshoe, which is a no-no in the exhibition business, but it worked very well, because the visitors had to circle back to look at all the art a second time. In that first year, we had 150 exhibitors and 275 ten-by-ten spaces—which was less than two booths for each exhibit. Usually, art dealers average between two and six spaces. But the dealers who participated that first year were just testing the waters, and they didn't want to go overboard in the beginning.

We were trying to emulate all the wonderful art fairs around the world: all the important fairs were in Europe. They all had exhibitor catalogs, which are important since they allow each exhibitor to illustrate in a page or two what they're bringing to the show, and to list the artists they represent, the people who will be working the booths, and other vital information. So my first adventure in producing a major art fair was to offer our exhibitors space in our fine-art catalog.

A friend of mine gave me the name of a printer, an immigrant from Yugoslavia (as it was called in those days). He gave us a good price, about $20,000 for 3,000 catalogs of about 250 pages each. We were able to get advertisements from art magazines, *The New York Times,* and other publications, which helped cover the expense of producing the catalog (which was printed in black and white). We gave the catalogs to all the exhibitors and attendees. The catalog included a floor plan and a list of exhibitors and artists. These catalogs have become collectors' items because they documented the changes in art during this period.

There is a lot involved in putting together a catalog. All the exhibitors had to provide photographs of the art they were exhibiting, so we could reproduce them in the catalog by a certain deadline. Sometimes exhibitors forgot (or ignored) the deadline, and we'd have to call them and push them for the material we needed. This was especially difficult when an international exhibitor was late. We wanted the catalog to be complete, since it was our first year, and an impressive-looking catalog was very important to our future success.

Then a week before the show, close to the time the catalogs were supposed to be delivered, the printer told us he needed twice the amount of money he had contractually agreed to, and he threatened not to deliver the catalogs unless he got what he wanted. I called my attorney friend, Ted, who had worked with me on the tax shelters, but because the printer was in New Jersey, we needed a lawyer who was licensed in that state. Ted recommended an associate of his who was excellent. He got a restraining order from a judge, the printer was ordered to deliver the catalogs immediately, and I agreed to put a certain amount of money in escrow with the court, in case the court ruled we owed additional money. The courts later ruled in our favor since we had a contract, so we had to pay only the original amount.

But it wasn't over. I got an outrageously large bill from the New Jersey attorney. I told him, "I think you did a wonderful job, but you didn't spend that many hours." He had sent me the telephone bills and other paperwork detailing how many hours he had worked, which still didn't add up. His answer was, "Well, to tell you the truth, your friend Ted wanted a very big commission for recommending me." I was furious, because this wasn't how I thought a friend should behave. Ted and I had also done business together. I had asked Ted to recommend an attorney, and now he wanted to make a lot of money on that simple referral.

The New Jersey attorney, who I used again later, was also upset at Ted's request, but he couldn't do anything about it. So I contacted Ted, who said he "thought it would be okay, but if you're upset, I'll drop it." The final bill was more in line with the work performed.

JERRY'S LAW #14: "Inspect what you expect."

Is the New York Coliseum Ready for an Important Art Fair?

Putting together a show not only takes tremendous effort, it is also very expensive. In addition to the rent for the space, the cost of printing the catalog, and paying my administrative staff, I had to hire a general contractor. We needed a union contractor to carpet the whole floor, not just the aisles. Visitors to a show do a lot of walking, so the space must be comfortable and plush. After all, we were selling expensive art. Normally, a show's producer provides what is called *pipe and drape* as well as tables and chairs, but we also needed hard walls to hang the art, and we also needed fancy furniture to give more of a living-room effect.

The New York Coliseum recommended three union contracting companies that had agreements with the building: Freeman, United, and Atlantic Coast Contracting. I chose Atlantic because it was the smallest and the only local company. The man who ran it was named Tex Perrino. I never knew why they called him Tex, since he was from New Jersey, but we became very close. What I didn't know at the time was that Tex was also the president of Union 32B, which even today is a service employees union with tremendous power. But Tex and I worked well together. He quoted a reasonable price. His was not a national company; he worked only New York and New Jersey. That was his union contracting domain.

As it happened, Tex didn't have any carpet that I wanted, so we worked out an arrangement using some of my own materials. In those days, most shows used multicolored tweedy carpets because they don't show dirt. They were reds and pinks, which typical trade-show organizers liked because it was perky, but it wasn't right for our show. I knew from visiting European art fairs that gray was the color to have, because it's neutral. Tex didn't have gray and he couldn't even get it from another contractor, since nobody in the business used such a bland color. So I called my friend, Marty Holzberg (aka *Pierre*), a lifetime friend then and now, who owned a carpet store in Paramus, New Jersey, and I said, "Marty, I need 4,000 square feet of gray carpet." It sounds like a ridiculous amount, but I needed to carpet the whole coliseum floor. Marty wasn't sure if he could get it from the carpet mill he bought from in Griffin, Georgia (which was where most of the carpet in the U.S. came from). Luckily, they had some gray carpet, and they sent us samples. For $2 a square yard, we got the carpet. It was a bit thin and it needed padding, but it looked great on the Coliseum floor, and it lasted a few years. It cost us more money to have the union guys install it than it did to buy it.

Next, I had to get walls on which the exhibitors could hang their paintings and framed lithographs. In New York, you must hire union contractors, and they have strict rules. For example, they must plug in any electrical equipment used in a booth, and they must hammer in every nail. I could not imagine having to pay them to hammer a nail to hang a fine-art painting, especially since paintings are always being readjusted. Also, artists and art dealers don't like outsiders touching their expensive artwork. So I came up with a plan: we covered pegboard with beautiful off-white burlap material. The paintings would hang from hooks that went through the burlap and into the pegboard, so no nails were needed. We didn't want to get into a dispute with the unions, and this system prevented that. If I must say so myself, this was an ingenious idea.

Some of the burlap walls got dirty during the show, so our guys would recover those pegboards with new burlap, to keep it fresh for the next few years. Once our fair was successful and the contractors knew they'd get paid, they all wanted to make the walls and supply gray carpet for us, but, in those early years, there wasn't a person in the trade-show business who thought we would succeed.

I hired off-duty policemen and firemen to work for us during the show, doing security and floor management. They were street-smart, strong, and hard-working, and they loved the excitement of this new life experience.

We also hired a public relations firm and an advertising agency. I was convinced that choosing the proper promotional people was essential to the fair's success. I found both firms by interviewing every major art gallery owner who would speak to me and asking them, "In your opinion, what's the best advertising agency/public relations agency in the art world?" Based on their recommendations, I hired two small art-oriented firms.

Madeline DeVries was my PR specialist; she was a beautiful, sophisticated woman. She was so well respected that when she visited an art gallery, everyone would stop what they were doing and talk to her. So of course I hired her. These visits helped open doors not so much to exhibitors but to the right contacts for our seminar program. I also hired Gerngross & Co., the husband-and-wife partnership of Hans and Frances Gerngross, who were well respected in the art world and whose advertising agency represented most of the important New York art galleries. These two connections helped encourage the participation of the major artists and dealers in our seminar programs, and this made an impression on people during the early days of Art Expo. It gave us instant credibility in the highly insulated fine-art world.

Another great thing that DeVries and Gerngross did was get Governor Hugh Carey and Mayor Ed Koch to declare the week of our show to be "Art Week" in New York, which generated great publicity. However, neither firm was able to do much bringing in customers or to get publicity for Art Expo in the mainstream media; it was very difficult to get a story in the *New York Times* (which was the main media organ for the art world) even though the *Times* was supportive of the show. The *Times* policy was that it couldn't run any general entertainment stories (which included the arts) anywhere but in the Arts section, which is controlled by the art critics. I always believed that through Art Expo I was bringing art to more people than they could ever imagine, but *The New York Times* Arts section and its art critics apparently did not see it that way. They were always elitist and not really interested in popularizing fine art; they were more interested in maintaining their own importance.

Based on my positive experience with DeVries and Gerngross, throughout my career, I hired ad agencies and PR firms that were run by successful entrepreneurs; that way, I was always able to speak to the boss, who was the decision-maker. This is not the case when dealing with large agencies, which make elaborate presentations, but when it comes to the day-to-day work, they assign the account to someone else, who may or may not be very good. The ability to talk to the owner gave me much more bang for the buck than I ever imagined I would be able to get, and I never forgot that lesson.

JERRY'S LAW #13:
"'No' simply means begin again at a level higher.:
Deal direct and always qualify."

Although it sounds as if we needed a lot of money to produce Art Expo, that was not necessarily so. To operate in the trade show business with limited capital, you have to be savvy. We needed initial startup capital to see if the idea was workable, to reserve exhibit space, to invest in advertising and promotion, and to pay the staff and the rent on the office. Each exhibitor had to pay 50% upfront as a deposit and the other 50% 60 days before the show began, which meant we were paid in full well before the show even opened.

The Europeans' attitude toward this method of payment for trade show space was much different from the American exhibitors. The Europeans were unaccustomed to doing business this way. They made deals on the basis of just a handshake: they told me, "Oh, I'll come to the show, but I won't pay until I show up at the door." Of course, half of them wouldn't show up. I told them I would not do business that way. I wanted this to be an international show, because it's more interesting if you have people from all over the world exhibiting, but I stuck to my policy. In the beginning, I lost exhibitors, but eventually, as we became successful, they all agreed to do it *my way*.

I tried to set our exhibitor fees so they would cover all of our expenses. Our profit came mainly from the gate—the admission fee paid by attendees. I always did it that way, and it worked very well for me. I spent every penny I took in from exhibit fees on promoting the show. After all, if the show isn't promoted well, there's a good chance that attendance and sales will be poor.

Many people thought I wouldn't succeed. For example, Howard Sloan, the president of the Coliseum Corporation who had a contract to manage the building, said he loved art and what I was doing. He also told me there had been six other art shows in the building, and none of them had ever gotten past the first show. "It's nice knowing you," was how he put it.

Obviously, I got way past the first show.

Before Art Expo, prior art shows never drew enough people to support the event. But that didn't daunt me, since I was always optimistic. (Remember, *can't* is not an option.) In 1979 when I began Art Expo, there was a recession in America. Interest rates under Jimmy Carter were 15 to 20%. Nevertheless, I pushed ahead. I knew that if we attracted enough exhibitors, we wouldn't have to dig deeper into our own pockets.

The dealers we attracted sold limited-edition lithographs, original photographs, and paintings. I decided to also let artists—good artists—exhibit. I had to fill up the booths. Usually, dealers, galleries, and artists don't mix: they don't want to be in the same room together. Some of the artists from around the world who exhibited were fabulous. Letting artists participate in this way is a concept I don't think occurred to others. The reason I probably got away with it was because I didn't mention this fact in advance to exhibitors.

Most artists don't want to exhibit their own work, but after coming once or twice, either an attendee from some gallery or an exhibitor would often ask if the artist would like to be represented by their gallery. In this way, I put many marriages together, and I'm proud of it. In the art world, when a gallery represents an artist, it sticks with that artist, even if there's a better artist around, since the gallery has committed its time and money to that artist. It takes years for art dealers to build a new artist's reputation.

Letting artists in was a wonderful thing, since everybody benefited: the public, the artists, the dealers, even the art magazines, because the more people who get interested in art, the more subscribers they can attract. The '80s were a great time, and I'm proud of the fact that we made art an important part of more people's lives. At Art Expo, everyone could comfortably buy something. It allowed for the Nouveau Riche and growing middle class to bring art into their lives, without being intimated by the elite art galleries.

The first year was a success. The art world is very small, and word travels. Every dealer in the world either came to the show or knew somebody at the show. Even the high-end, elite galleries that would never exhibit at my shows came to look, and when they were in the building, the other dealers saw them, which was important since it demonstrated that we were being noticed. I bumped into many people famous in the art world, including Leo Castelli, Holly Solomon, and Ivan Karp, three of the most innovative, creative, top-of-the-line art dealers in the world. When they returned home from the show, they must have said, "The quality wasn't great, but so many people attended, and business got done."

I called on these high-end gallery owners many times, but I could never get them to exhibit, even when we were at our most successful period. With hindsight, I see that having them wasn't necessary, but, at the time, I wanted everybody to be part of my shows. I realize now that an art show can't grow to 1400 booths (which Art Expo did by the time we sold it in 1986) and get the elitist galleries in the mix. No matter how successful the show, the elite galleries wanted to remain in a smaller, limited circle.

Still, during those first years, every one of them, to a person, told me, "Jerry, I don't know if I like the show or not, but I can't believe that you can get this many people to pay to look at art." They had no idea that so many American people could enjoy art, even fine art. I believe we opened their minds to the full potential of even their art world.

I succeeded where others hadn't because I was inventive in the way I promoted the show—not using the old, established rules for selling fine art. I expanded the art-buying base twenty-fold, bringing many more interested people under my Art Expo umbrella. In addition to getting the governor and mayor to declare the week of Art Expo to be "Art Week" in New York, every year we held our show, I created a free Cultural Events Program of important seminars and special exhibits, thus creating an important comfort zone for attendees and exhibitors while boosting our credibility in the art world, which is standoffish and elitist.

One of the best ways to promote the show was to be covered by every art magazine—such as *Art News, Art in America, Connoisseur, The New York Times Arts* section. They might not have known much about the show we were planning, but they were excited about the idea of a new art fair in New York. I bartered with every one of them for full-page color ads, in exchange for giving them a table and chairs in the entry of the New York Coliseum, where they would hand out free magazines to promote their magazines and brands. We got almost every magazine in America and Europe to give us advertising space, which was probably worth more than $100,000. Everybody wanted to be involved. If you associate with the best, everybody else wants to come to the party. My job was to make perception reality.

Our seminar program included people like the senior vice president of Sotheby's Park Benet (as it was called then) and representatives of the Museum of Modern Art. The VP from Sotheby's spoke about art as an investment. Mark Hampton, one of the most famous interior designers in the world at the time, spoke about art as it relates to interior design. Patterson Sims, then-curator of the Whitney Museum of American Art, talked about the permanent collection of the Whitney Museum of American Art. Wow: all of these people spoke for free, no expenses paid, which was well within our budget.

JERRY'S LAW #4:
"Start at the top and work your way up."

Opening Day of the First Art Expo: March 6, 1979

As mentioned, my formula for success was to open in New York City before Wash Art: that's one of my rules of business—*always be first*. We did, and our success caused Wash Art to close the following year. But before that happened, we didn't know if anybody would even walk through the door of the New York Coliseum, let alone if we'd make any money at it. We projected that about 10,000 people would attend. We thought we'd get good publicity, which would draw in the crowds. The daily pass cost $4, $2.50 for students, and a five-day pass was $10. The prices were reasonable, even in those days.

At last, March 6 arrived, and we were all excited. One hour before opening, there was a line around the block. I didn't know what to do.

I was sweating. My heart was pounding. I was in a panic. I had put so much effort into this: we had found a way to break through, to a certain extent, by developing our relationships with the art and design magazines and *The New York Times* and having important and well-known art experts and artists speaking at our seminars. I obviously developed a winning image and formula that was accepted by the elite fine-art world.

Finally, it was time to open the door. People rushed in to buy their tickets. Within 10 minutes of the opening, someone from the fire department served me a summons since not all the doors were open, which was a fire hazard. I asked him why he was giving *me* the ticket when I was only renting the building: I explained I didn't even have a key, and I didn't know the rules and regulations. His response: "It doesn't make any difference." So I called over the manager of the Coliseum, who just shrugged his shoulders, and I was stuck with a $400 ticket.

The show went on, and it was a big success. I even forgot about the ticket and the fact that I had to go to court—although I did try to fight it later on, just on principle: I shouldn't have gotten the ticket, so why should I pay it?

I don't know how many people came to our first Art Expo that morning, but there was a line around the block. The show went on for five days, and we recorded a paid attendance of around 12,000 people. Not bad for a first-time venture!

I think part of the reason for our success was because of how we scheduled the five days of the show. The truth about American trade shows is that most of the trade doesn't want to see members of the public. They wanted Art Expo to be open only to the trade, but the professional art world is too small to support a trade-only show. I also knew that in Europe, the public was encouraged to attend. So I suggested a compromise: the show would be open only to the trade on the first two days. That gave the professionals the first shot at everything, and they were able to talk business in a quieter atmosphere.

The public came on Saturday and Sunday; then on Monday (which was the final day), the dealers and the public came back to make deals at the end of the show. I also made Monday students' day, something I am very proud of. The exhibitors didn't like the idea of kids coming to the show: they were afraid young people would touch the artwork and drop food everywhere. But I thought it was good for young people to come and learn about art. For the most part, the only kids who came were high school art students on class trips with their art teachers. In all, in the first year, maybe a few hundred art students attended, but as the years went on, that grew to a few thousand, and almost all of them were from private schools. I'm not sure why no-one came from the public school system—maybe because they were inflexible and couldn't adjust their schedules because of bureaucracy, or maybe because the teachers weren't interested in taking the extra time for the students to see fine art.

Art Expo is still around today, and students who attended that first show became aware of certain artists who were represented at that time, and, since then, no doubt many of them bought art. Not everything provides instant gratification. People grow into their art collections; many of the public that attended over the years have become major art collectors. The same is true of those students. Art Expo was a growing experience. What these dealers didn't understand was that, as with any business, they had to build their clientele. Today, everyone has to have everything immediately. People don't hang in long enough. A business doesn't always make money in its first year. In the first year of Art Expo, we did okay. We broke even, and we took a giant step toward our future success.

I tell people, if you see your business slowly growing but you're unwilling to put in at least three years without making real money, you are not putting in the right effort. Sometimes it doesn't take three years to make money, but a person has to be willing give it that much time. This philosophy enabled me to build my other shows.

JERRY'S LAW #8: "If it's worth doing, do it right."

After our first Art Expo ended, I lost two of my four partners when I told them, "We might have to invest another $5,000 on top of the original $8,000, but we've got good potential." We needed additional working capital to be able to run the office for another year, which meant paying the staff's salaries and the rent. When I informed them we would need to invest more money, Bridget and John (my French partners) panicked and ran. What a blessing in disguise. (*Viva la France!*)

As I see it, the French are like no other people in the world. They think differently. They don't understand business, they don't like to work very hard, but they like to play, and they don't like investing their own money. As a result, what did they get? Bridget felt she'd already invested too much and didn't want to put in any additional money. She asked for her money back, and we gave it to her.

We didn't give John his money back because we found out he had kept three-quarters of the advertising posters (designed by the Belgian artist Jean-Michel Folon) that we had paid him $20,000 to create and distribute. John kept them so he could sell them privately. When we discovered that, John resigned from the partnership, and we made a deal that he would lose his investment, but he could keep the posters.

We also gave both of them two free booths at two future Expos, just to get rid of them, but I had no further contact with either of them. They exhibited at the show for a few years, but they didn't know what they were missing. I'm sure they will never forget their unbelievable mistake. *In God we trust, but not your partners.*

The lesson I learned from my experience with partners is that if you don't have at least a 51% interest, or an agreement making you the general partner with control over the day-by-day operations, it's almost impossible to run a successful business. Somebody has to be in control, and somebody has to be able to make the quick decisions. You can't have five people making decisions, especially when four of them are not involved on a day-by-day basis.

Today, those two must go to sleep each night thinking about Art Expo: it must haunt them to know that from their initial $8,000 investment, they could have ended up millionaires. And when we sold the business nine years later, I had only two other problem partners with whom I had to share the profits, instead of four.

JERRY'S LAW #1:
"If anything goes wrong, fix it. (To hell with Murphy!)"

9

The Excitement of Building My Own Business

Our first year of Art Expo was more a psychological success than a financial one. We emerged with a good reputation among dealers in the world of fine art: they began to believe that Art Expo might become the major fine-art showcase in New York, something they had always longed for. Even at our first show, we had some of the most important people in the art world participating in our lecture/seminar program.

In 1980, for our second art fair, we had two floors at the New York Coliseum, which was tremendous growth from the previous year. We now had about 250 exhibitors—but they took more spaces than the exhibitors at the first show: 550, which was more than two spaces per exhibitor, a sure sign they had confidence in the show.

I also discovered, to my amazement, that the participants in our seminar program for the 1980 show were even more important in the art world than the 1979 fair participants. Clearly, in our first year, there had been good buzz in the art world about the seminars, which in 1980 included participants like Brendan Gill, the drama, film, and art critic for *New York* magazine (which was an extremely influential magazine at the time). Henry Geldzahler was New York City's Commissioner of the Department of Cultural Affairs and very prominent in the art world. And we had famous gallery owners, including Mary Boone, Ivan Karp, Max Protetch, and Holly and Horace Solomon, who were the most prestigious art dealers in the world: they participated in a seminar on "the role of galleries in the 1970s and '80s." In the second year, we offered a seminar called "The World of Prints," led by Marian Goodman (who still has a gallery in New York), Kenneth Tyler, and Manson and Wood International. We featured famous artists, including Christo, the installation artist who created the gates in Central Park in 2005, James Rosenquist, William Wegman, and Laurie Anderson. All participated, gratis. If I were to get that group to exhibit together today, I would become world-famous, but in 1980, we were able to get them to participate. What you don't know can't scare you.

JERRY'S LAW #4:
"Start at the top and work your way up."

In the end, we had a wonderful cultural events program. The exhibitor list grew, and attendance grew. We raised the price of admission from $4 to $5.

JERRY'S LAW #8: "If it's worth doing, do it right."

Dealing with the Unions

By the second year, I also learned more about the business side and how to deal with the unions. They didn't understand the art world, but they really wanted to work with us since ours was the kind of show where they could make good money. Our exhibits required a lot of electrical work (lighting in the booths) and a large amount of freight handling, because art isn't tightly packed, and therefore there are more pieces to load and unload.

But it wasn't all easygoing with the unions. One incident that stopped work on the show had to do with a special sculpture exhibition. It was called Sculpture at the Coliseum and was curated by Alanna Heiss. She was the head of the Institute for Art and Urban Resources, which was devoted to creating installations in otherwise unused or overlooked spaces (and eventually became P.S. 1 Contemporary Art Center, which she also directed). Alanna Heiss was very well connected with galleries, museums, and artists. Some of the most important sculptors in the art world today presented their work at that exhibit, including Louise Bourgeois, Mark di Suvero, Jackie Ferrara, Tony Rosenthal, Alann Sarat, and Robert Yasuda.

All these sculptors were there—in person—setting up their work in the New York Coliseum. Since it was not a normal venue, they were very nervous about setting up in a building where work was controlled by union workers, and we did run into some problems. The artists insisted on handling their own artwork, which meant bringing the sculptures in piecemeal and setting them up piece by piece. To get the unions to allow them to set up their own work, I went to my friend Tex Perrino (the general contractor), and I told him I would pay six union guys not to touch the work, just to stand there and do nothing. And they agreed. So the artists started bringing everything in themselves.

But in the 1980s, modern sculptures were made of unusual materials, such as rusted metal, pieces of wood, sand, concrete, anything and everything under the sun. So when the sculptors started bringing in these materials, the construction workers simply stopped putting up the entire show, and everyone in the entire Coliseum went on strike. I went straight to Tex to find out what was going on, and he told me, "The union guys say you're breaking our union rules. They say they know construction material when they see it." They assumed the wood, the concrete, the metal were all construction material, which they were supposed to handle, exclusively. They didn't understand that those materials were parts of the sculptures themselves.

The only way I could see to solve the problem was to add another six-man crew to do nothing but watch the artists build their own exhibits. And everybody was happy. If you can make it here you can make it anywhere. Frank Sinatra was probably singing about New York unions.

Also during the setup of the second show, one exhibitor walked through the front door of the Coliseum carrying a giant box on his shoulder, and he banged right into a union official. It was clearly against union rules to carry anything but a small package into a union building; all freight was supposed to be delivered through the freight entrances by the Teamsters. So the official said, "You can't bring that in here." And the exhibitor, who happened to be very hotheaded, started screaming and cursing at him. It got extremely dangerous.

I was in the lobby and ran over to calm down the exhibitor and to try to settle things with the union official. But before I could, the official lifted his right arm toward his head, which is a signal to all union workers that someone was breaking the rules and that all work in the building should stop, which it did. I didn't realize this union official was the head of the joint New York City Council of Unions. In other words, he was Numero Uno, and in New York, egos run rampant.

Now I *had* to calm things down so work could resume. After a while, the exhibitor realized the union official probably could have killed him had he wanted to—because in those days, the Teamsters were very connected to the Mafia. The exhibitor was a hotheaded Austrian, but he wasn't stupid, and he got his temper under control. And I got the two men to shake hands: I told them, "You have to go along to get along." We fought the unions many times, but overall, we really got along very well. There was a feeling of mutual respect between myself and the working men.

Everything did not go back to normal right away, however. Once the official raised his hand, he had to show the men that he was fighting for them; he couldn't just tell them to go right back to work. It's psychological. So the workers sat around smoking and chatting for an hour and a half while the other exhibitors went crazy since nothing was done during that time. And there was nothing I could do. Eventually, the workers went back to work, and fortunately, the show was assembled on time.

Getting Cheated by the Ticket Takers

Another essential part of my job was to deal with the union ticket takers and ticket sellers we had to hire. They always wanted more men, but more important, I discovered how to control the box office. It took me time to figure it out, but in the second year, I realized that the ticket sellers and takers were working together to steal some of the box office receipts.

The scheme worked like this: The ticket seller sold a ticket, the attendee gave the ticket to the ticket taker, who pretended to tear it up but who actually palmed it. The ticket takers did this with somewhere around 5% of all the tickets sold. The palmed tickets were then given to one of the supervisors, who returned them to the ticket sellers, who then resold the ticket. Since they had to account only for the number of tickets sold, they could pocket the excess cash.

I never suspected anything was wrong; I caught them only because I was frequently in the lobby, observing what was going on around me. I guess I was in the right place at the right time, because I just happened to notice that the son of the head of the ticket takers union hadn't torn up a ticket. I continued watching him, and I saw him palm a few more. He was new on the job and still in training; perhaps that's why I noticed him. He probably hadn't perfected the technique. (The experienced ticket takers were like magicians; they were experts in sleight of hand.)

Once I was certain that's what he was doing, I called over one of my security guards, who were off-duty police officers, before I confronted his father. I wanted a policeman around just in case he reacted violently.

His father was in charge of all the men, so I knew that if one ticket taker was doing it, they all were, and I told him his son was fired. The father, who had to be in on the scheme, would have to tell the rest of the men that I was onto them. He tried to defend his son by saying his son was new on the job and had simply made a mistake in not tearing up the tickets, which was a total fabrication. I wouldn't accept his excuses and told him that this type of behavior couldn't continue. I explained that we spent a lot of money to promote the show, which, in turn, provided jobs for him and his crew. I added I would prosecute the next person I caught palming a ticket. He apologized, and as far as I know, they were on their best behavior for the next number of years.

After that incident, I always placed an off-duty policeman or fireman behind the ticket takers to watch them. And I did something else that still stands to this day: I made the ticket boxes Lucite, so you could see through them: that way, if nothing dropped through that box, it was obvious. Using Lucite has become a standard in the industry, and we eliminated most of the sleight-of-hand experts.

JERRY'S LAW #14: "Inspect what you expect."

In general, the union men respected me: they knew I was there with my sleeves rolled up, so to speak, even though I always wore a suit and tie. In contrast, many show managers leave the building, especially during set-up. They go to a bar, because they don't want to be involved in handling exhibitors' complaints or other problems that always arise. But I was always there, on site. That was my style.

In fact, one of my trademarks, especially in the early days, was that I visited every exhibitor's booth *twice* during setup, with Tex Perrino, our general contractor. I was a very hands-on guy, and the exhibitors were glad to see us so they could vent their frustrations: "Where are the lights?" "Where's my freight?" "A box is missing." "Where are my table and chairs?" Everybody had some sort of complaint, but as long there was somebody with authority to vent to—and Tex and I were the two most important people in the building—we got through it, and they got over it. The exhibitors as well as the union men knew I was always there. I was never hiding. I was the true hands-on entrepreneur.

This approach is very important in the tradeshow business, and I am certain it helped us get through the first few years, when we were still proving ourselves. When the show grew to 1500 booths, I really struggled to get around, but I still tried to see them all. It was important to prove I was interested by asking, "How's it going?" And they told me. Whether they were happy or unhappy, they told me, and in either case, they always remembered that there was somebody to vent to. A very important key to my success.

JERRY'S LAW #1:
"If anything goes wrong, fix it. (To hell with Murphy!)"

Choosing My Own Vendors

Just as my exhibitors liked having a personal connection to me, I wanted to have control over the vendors we used at the shows. Each venue had a preferred list of contracts with service providers, such as shuttle bus companies and caterers. To get on the preferred list, a company had to make an arrangement with the building's manager, who received some kind of favor in return. I don't believe it was legal to rebuff competition, so this preferred list was questionable, but most people went along with it.

I wanted to use a different shuttle bus company. At the time, the Coliseum used the Gray Line Bus Company, which was (and still is) a big New York guided-tour bus company. Judy Brightwater (who had worked for me since near the end of my days at Prentice Hall) had a cousin whose husband's father owned Academy Bus, which at the time was a tiny bus company in New Jersey that mainly transported students. The cousin also helped out during the show—everybody loved to work at Art Expo, because it was special.

I asked Judy if she thought this cousin's dad's company could replace Gray Line and provide the shuttle buses. The job involved running shuttle buses for the exhibitors and customers in a circle from the hotels, which were located in the areas between West 50th Street and Central Park South, to and from the Coliseum. It wasn't a huge job. We didn't need hundreds of buses, since everything was fairly close. The cousin's husband, Francis (the owner's son), loved the idea, and Academy gave us a lower quote than Gray Lines, a big corporation, whereas Francis and his father were entrepreneurs and therefore had more flexibility. Remember my motto, *deal with successful small businesses:* it enables you to deal direct.

I fought like hell with the building's management to let me do it, which they finally agreed. Today, Academy is the biggest private bus line in the New York area. I am very proud of the fact that I opened that door to a small father-and-son business. We both benefitted: they were flexible and did a great job.

I also wanted to change caterers. At the Coliseum, the preferred institutional caterer's food was awful, but it took me until 1984 to get the management to agree to let me bring in my own caterer, Zaro's Bread Company, which was run by entrepreneurs that owned a number of bakery restaurants.

JERRY'S LAW #6: "When forced to compromise, ask for more."

Having the right caterer is very important since good food keeps the customers in the building. If visitors leave the building to eat, they may not come back. This was especially true in the neighborhood around the Coliseum (on Columbus Circle), where visitors could easily walk to any number of good restaurants. It's less true at the Javits Center, which is not located in a prime restaurant area. On the other hand, if attendees leave the Javits Center and take a cab somewhere to eat, it's almost certain they won't be coming back. One of the most important jobs of a tradeshow manager is to make sure people stay at the show for as long as possible.

Working with My Partners Wasn't Easy: The Great Understatement

We were on our way, but my two remaining partners were making my life hell. The problems between us were growing. As the director of Art Expo-NY, I signed all the letters, so mine was the only name anyone knew in association with Art Expo. My partners continually threatened to sue me because they wanted their names to appear on the letters, too. I explained to them that in the art world their names lacked credibility. If potential clients investigated their credentials, the show could be harmed since neither one had *any* art-world credentials!

I suggested that we instead put together a group of museum curators and major art dealers to serve on our board of directors, list all their names on our letterhead, and then throw my partners' names in as well.

My point was that we shouldn't put ourselves in jeopardy. What people don't know can't hurt you, and when you're in the elitist, snobbish art world where everybody puts everybody else down, you don't want people to find out that you have no fine-art background at all. (Years later, after I sold Art Expo, I learned that one of my partners, Phil, had gone to jail for three years for art fraud, so I was right to be cautious!)

My argument did not persuade Phil and Irwin, whose lawyers continued to send letters threatening to sue me. I ignored them. It was the smartest thing I ever did.

The early days were filled with conflict between me and my two partners. After the second show opened, Judy Licht, the entertainment reporter for New York's *Channel 5 News*, showed up with a camera crew.

I was thrilled: she was very well known in New York, and she wanted to talk to me, the show's director, about our show on that night's 6 o'clock news. Without a doubt, having a major New York news affiliate covering your show at 6:00 and 11:00 is the coverage every show manager dreams of but very rarely accomplishes.

This interview created a difficult situation with my partners, because *they* wanted to talk to her, too; they wanted to be on the 6 o'clock news, even though they were unfamiliar with the exhibitors, artists, and the seminar people. A situation like that could have destroyed everything we had worked for. Besides, Judy had made it clear that she only wanted to talk to the person in charge of the show. While my partners and I argued about it, Judy and her crew walked out with their cameras without covering our show, and she never came back.

This wasn't an isolated incident, either. My partners caused many other problems because of their egos. Finally, I told them, "You're my partners, and you're equal financial partners. But you've got to stay out of the day-to-day management of the business." I recognized that there was a mystique that we had to maintain: this was a fine-art show, and we had to maintain that image. Perception is reality, and my partners' egos were messing up the show's image.

For example, I always wore interesting clothing at the show. I had a talent for dressing well, if I do say so myself. Business executives dressed well back then: it was a status symbol. One of the exhibitors at the European Basel Art Fair told me later that he felt good about doing business with me since I dressed well and my shoes were always shined. I tried to emulate a cultured, European effect by wearing velvet suits, white linen suits, whatever stood out—I really dressed up. I also did it so people would recognize me. "Where's the director—the guy in the blue suede suit, or the white linen suit (or whatever I happened to be wearing that day)?"

What kept me going during all the strife with my partners was that instinctively I knew I was onto something great, something that would not only make me money, but would make me a unique person, someone people would know for this special thing I had done. You can invest in the stock market and make money, but unless you are Warren Buffett, nobody will know who you are. Every time I was tempted to say to my partners, "Either you get out, or I get out," I backed down. Aviva said I was a softie, but I knew how stubborn my partners were, and I didn't want to jeopardize what I knew we had going. It wasn't worth ruining the opportunity of a lifetime. In hindsight, I wish I had pushed the edge of that envelope.

JERRY'S LAW #9: "If you can't win, change the rules."

JERRY'S LAW #10: "If you can't change the rules, ignore them."

Managing All the Logistics

A great deal is involved in putting together a show like Art Expo. For example, we had to reserve hotel rooms for our exhibitors and attendees. I did everything myself, including choosing the hotels and negotiating with them for favorable rates.

The hotels had to be as close as possible to the exhibit site; in this case, Central Park South was where the closest hotels were located. That's an expensive area, but I was able to keep these costs down. For the first few years, our headquarters hotel was the St. Moritz, and our secondary hotel was The Essex House. The ace up my sleeve was that I was bringing wealthy art dealers and collectors to their hotels, and even for these fine hotels, these were special clients. I got good rates. We virtually filled these hotels. We also negotiated lower rates with the Hilton and Sheraton, which were not on Central Park South, but were also close to the Coliseum.

The St. Moritz gave me a suite gratis for the duration of the show, which I very rarely used except to sleep, since I put in a great many hours working. I was still living in East Rockaway, and I couldn't go home every night. I'll never forget the terrace at the St. Moritz: it must have been 2,000 square feet, overlooking Central Park. I would go out onto it and just gaze at Central Park and the city, and say to myself, *Oh, my God*. I was living the American Dream.

Two nights before each fair opened, I hosted a cocktail party for my staff on the terrace overlooking Central Park, and then we went out to dinner. I know they are still talking about those evenings.

Aviva didn't come until the day of the show, because there was nothing for her to do during set-up (except get upset); I was so busy working and dealing with all the yelling and screaming behind the scenes, but never in front of my exhibitors. People have always commented on the fact that I have an enormous ability to keep a calm demeanor when everything around me is chaotic, which made people feel that I had everything under control. Of course, Aviva always knew what was going on inside of me, but nobody else ever saw that, which helped, particularly at Art Expo shows, where every exhibitor is an owner and/or an artist.

In addition to the occasional strike, the police ticketed exhibitors who tried to move their artwork in through the front door. These were usually small exhibitors, often individual artists exhibiting their own work, who brought their art in panel trucks. They didn't want to wait in line behind the huge freight trucks that were lined up around the building, waiting to unload through the freight entrance in the back. Coming through the front door was a way to get their freight into the building, and the unions looked the other way, because the union workers had sympathy for the struggling artists who were trying to make a living. You would think that the City of New York would let them park for 20 minutes, but for some reason, in the early days, they gave us a hard time.

So much was going on around me, and many people disappointed us. For example, the New York Coliseum management that was assigned to assist us usually disappeared during set-up, leaving us on our own. I believe they didn't want to mediate between us and the union. So they were always at a so-called meeting. But we learned to cope.

JERRY'S LAW #15:
"Bureaucracy is a challenge to be conquered with righteous attitude, a tolerance for stupidity, and a bulldozer when necessary."

To the Trade Only or Open to the Public?

In the exhibit business, there are two types of shows: trade shows and public shows. I wanted Art Expo to be both. Beginning with the first Art Expo, we offered two days during which we were open only to the trade and three days when we were open to the public (and the trade could come on public days, but not vice versa).

Public shows receive bottom-of-the-barrel treatment on everything and, most important, when booking dates with an exhibit site for the following years. Public shows were always the last in line, since hotels believed that the people who attend public shows usually live some-where within a 50-mile radius, so for a New York show, people would be coming from New Jersey, Long Island, Westchester, and New York City, so they would usually come only for the day, rather than staying at a hotel. The New York Convention and Visitors Bureau made these rules to protect the hotel industry, but in our case, they were wrong. Art Expo filled up thousands of hotel rooms, not only because our exhibitors came from all over, but also because art dealers who weren't exhibiting also came from around the world. We filled more rooms than many other so-called trade shows, yet some hotels still treated us as second-class citizens because we were still considered a public show. I argued with the New York Convention and Visitor's Bureau every year: I asked them to ignore their antiquated rules and instead look at how many hotel rooms my shows filled.

JERRY'S LAW #9: "If you can't win, change the rules."

JERRY'S LAW #10: "If you can't change the rules, ignore them."

It was a continuous battle to get my yearly show dates, again because we were considered a public show—a bureaucratic rule that made no sense. It was imperative that the art fair be held at around the same time every year. In the trade-show business, dates are paramount:

both exhibitors and attendees usually plan ahead. I wanted the art world to mark their calendars for each Art Expo.

Also, it's difficult to compete with any other major event. It is imperative to be the main event. For example, I wanted to do an art show in Atlanta during the Olympics. While exploring the idea, the reactions to it were all negative, and I realized that anything I did would be so insignificant compared with the Olympics that nobody would be interested in it. People go to the main event, period, and nothing else.

JERRY'S LAW #5: "Do it by the book, but be the author."

Looking Successful Is Important, Too

For our second Art Expo, one of the best things I did to make exhibitors and art dealers happy was to bring in a limousine company, which I made the official limo company of Art Expo. By the early '80s, a great many fine-art dealers from around the world came to the show. They arrived at Kennedy Airport, and it made them feel great to get into a stretch limo. It was prestigious and fun. In those days, stretch limos were hugely popular and seen all over the streets of Manhattan. Today you see fewer stretch limos because people are cautious about flaunting their wealth, so most car service companies provide Town Cars instead, which are comfortable and private but not as flashy or prestigious.

The limo company did very well, and in return for the business, they gave me 80 hours of free limo service. It was so much time, I didn't know what to do with it. One day, I had the driver pick me up in East Rockaway. He arrived in a black stretch limo and parked it in front of my house. My next-door neighbor's kids, who were around 10 and twelve, came out. Their eyes were wide open. I wasn't ready to leave, so I said to the younger one, "Matthew, would you like a ride?" (His older brother had left for a sports commitment.) Matthew was thrilled, so the limo drove him around for 10 or 15 minutes. When they returned, the driver opened the door for him, and Matthew got out and said, "This is for me. This is what I want when I grow up." Today, Matthew is a multimillionaire. He earned his money working on Wall Street, though he has since left that to do many other interesting things. I'm not saying I had anything to do with his success, but it's interesting that he knew what he wanted and had that in his DNA, even at only 10 years old.

JERRY'S LAW #4:
"Start at the top and work your way up."

Again, 80 hours is a lot of limo time, so I also invited my staff to use it. When I used the limo to leave the show, I always asked the driver to pick me up behind the building, next to the loading platform, because I didn't want the exhibitors to see me in the limo; I thought it would create the wrong impression. One day, the driver and I couldn't find one another; there were no cell phones then, so I couldn't call him to tell him where I was. So I decided to go to the front of the building to look for him, and eventually he found me. Just as I was getting into the limo, many of the exhibitors were leaving the building, and they saw me getting into the car. That had been my worst nightmare.

But I was wrong! What I discovered was that my customers *wanted* me to be successful, and when I showed them I was, they were more supportive of me than ever. It made them believe in me. From then on, I openly used the limo. It's about your peers rooting for one of them to make it big, leaving hope that they will fulfill their own aspirations. Today, some people want to take from the so-called rich even though many took the risk and worked very hard to earn their money. It's important to note that success breeds more success.

Success Invites Competition

When the second Art Expo show ended, more people had attended, more art dealers exhibited, and things were looking great. We were on our way. We celebrated our success, and we began thinking about the next year and how many floors and how much additional space we would need. Then I received an announcement for a new art fair in Los Angeles called Art Expo-West.

We had registered our name and done all the things necessary to protect our brand, yet one of our exhibitors, Ed Weston, had seen our success and decided he could do on the west coast what we were doing in New York. So I called my attorney, who wrote to Weston, but the wheels of justice grind slowly, Weston ignored our efforts, and the show opened in the fall of 1980 at the Los Angeles Convention Center.

He had 400 booths, which by that measurement was a success, but the show was a dismal failure in terms of attendance and sales. He had attracted exhibitors, since they were excited about the success of the New York show, but that alone won't bring in the buyers. The organizer still has to do all the basic things to promote and advertise the show. The biggest mistake he made was to hold the show a few days after Labor Day. A cardinal rule of this business is never stage an event close to a major holiday. Around Labor Day, not only are some people still away, but many of the attendees had children, summer vacation was over, and they had to get their children ready for school. Those factors hurt attendance, and without customers, they had limited sales.

His show lasted only one year, but it tarnished our name because many people didn't know it wasn't our event (guilt by association.) It also hurt our future plans, which included starting a second yearly show in California once we were firmly established in New York. Our goal was to have another show six months after the New York show, which would help keep our staff busy, full-time, and increase our profits.

We dropped our suit against Weston, because his show had been a failure, and we didn't want to spend all the time and money the lawsuit would cost. In the end, he wrote a letter agreeing that he wouldn't use the name again, but, of course, the name was of no value to him since he had failed.

10

On the Road with Art Expo

Our third show in New York in 1981 was only slightly bigger than the second, only because more exhibit space was unavailable. Also, in the exhibit business, it's better to have a waiting list than to fill up only half a floor, which makes the space seem empty. The point is to fill up an entire floor, so that the show looks busy and crowded. That is also why the aisles should be as narrow as possible—a 10-foot-wide aisle may look good, but from a sales perspective, a six-foot aisle (which was the legal minimum), may not look as nice, but it's better since our goal was for the booths and show floor to look crowded.

It's part of the psychology. It is very important that the potential customers *think* the show is busy because it reassures them that other people want what they want. Exhibitors and customers feel the energy of a successful show, and they feed off that energy, which is very important. Crowds bring energy, energy equals sales.

In 1981, we created a special exhibit, which was called "Transformations: Women in Art, '70s–'80s." It was an exhibition of the work of women artists. At the time, there were only a few famous women artists. That's the way the world was: in those days, most of the well-known artists were men. Among the artists whose work was exhibited at Transformations were Jennifer Bartlett, Nancy Azara, Louise Bourgeois, Judy Chicago, Janet Fish, Lois Lane, Alice Neel, Joan Semmel, and Miriam Shapiro, among many others. At the time, I didn't know all of them, yet today, every one of them is important. I don't believe that there has ever been a more important women's art exhibit with all of these famous women artists' work under one roof, together with most in attendance.

Many people came to Art Expo just to see what was going on. In my own weird way, I transformed the art world, since before then, most dealers in the art world thought it was impossible to get that many people to look at art, no less buy it. They believed there were a handful of sophisticated collectors who could be reached only by the fine-art galleries. A broad-based populist Art Fair was unthinkable.

Although we still operated on a low budget, I began to advertise more and more on the radio to attract the general public. I asked two exhibitors—one French exhibitor, the other English—to read the script for the commercial, since I believed that English and French accents (as long as they could be understood) would add credibility and attract radio listeners—especially when the product being advertised was fine art. When I first approached these two exhibitors, they were nervous about doing the ads, but once they did it, they wanted to do it again the next year, which they did.

The commercials themselves weren't stodgy; they had some humor. They were written by our ad agency and me. I always had my own concepts about how the show should be promoted. We created 30- and 60-second spots, and they were a big success. My concept was that I was the average Joe, and if I understand it and enjoyed its humor, most others would, too.

JERRY'S LAW #5:
"Do it by the book, but be the author."

Competing with Street Vendors

Also, in 1981, something upsetting happened. I was heading toward the New York Coliseum from the St. Moritz, which is on Central Park South, when I noticed there were hundreds of art exhibits in the park. I soon found out that New York City bureaucrats had decided it was a good idea for unknown artists to have an exhibit in Central Park, which is just a block or so away from the Coliseum. For a $25 licensing fee, any "artist" could exhibit in the park and along 59th Street and capitalize on our efforts to draw people to the area. As I saw it, it could only make our show appear less important. We were only in our third year, so it was important that I protect my exhibitors and myself. Of course, there was a difference in the quality of what was being sold; nevertheless, the fact that they were there at all sent the wrong message about our art fair. Madeleine DeVries, my PR person, called the Parks Department and the Mayor's office, but we got no direct response. However, the city never did it again. Bureaucracy at work.

I never knew if it affected my show, but it made the area look like a circus. We had worked for three years to present an upscale image, and right next door, people were selling inexpensive paintings and hawking our hard-won clientele as they headed toward the New York Coliseum. What made it worse in my mind was that some people were attending for the first time. The path to success in business never runs smoothly. As some of today's politicians claim, we could not succeed without their help . . . I didn't think so; we succeeded in spite of them.

JERRY'S LAW #20:
"Winston Churchill said, 'Never give up.'
I say, 'Never, never give in.'"

Getting the Unions to Work All Night

It was in that same year, 1981, that another unbelievable disaster occurred. The show was bigger than ever: we kept adding new walls and carpet to our inventory, to accommodate more exhibitors. The day before the opening at about noon, a group of exhibitors approached me looking for their booths. They weren't there; in fact, all of Aisle 1 and part of Aisle 2 had not been built.

I immediately went to Tex to find out what was going on. He told me not to worry: they were going to take care of it. In the meantime, I tried to reassure the exhibitors. A few more hours went by; still, nothing had happened. Again, I asked Tex what was going on. Finally, he admitted that they had run out of walls. I tried to understand how something like that could have happened: they were supposed to have ordered a sufficient number of walls based on the number of booths that were taken. We always submitted a floor plan to the contractor, so he would know exactly the material requirements. Obviously, this was a big screw-up.

The exhibitors in Aisle 1 were mainly Israeli and French, because as we added exhibitors, I began to develop sections—an Israeli section, a French section, etc.—so that if attendees were looking for a particular type of art, they would be able to go to a specific area where they'd find most of it. I put the Israelis and the French near each other, because they were the most difficult people to do business with: they were always complaining. But in this case, they were absolutely right to complain! Exhibitors have a lot to do to get ready for a show like this, and without walls, there's not much they could do.

I immediately told Tex to go to every lumberyard in the city of New York and buy every pegboard wall he could find, even if it was unpainted, even if we wouldn't be able to cover it in burlap, and once they found them, they were going to build those walls in time for the exhibitors to set up before the show opened. We had trucks going to every lumberyard in the five boroughs. By 5:00 PM, they found enough walls.

Of course, union carpenters don't work after 5:00 unless you pay them overtime, so I had to tell Tex, "You're going to hire as many men as you need to work all night if they have to, to build these goddamn walls. You're going to install the walls, and you're going to complete those aisles," which they did. They began at about 5:30 that evening— Tex added 70 union carpenters—and they worked all night. I didn't know if we would have to pay double- or triple-time, but I knew it would be expensive. But it didn't matter: we had to get it done, even if we lost money. They completed installing the walls at about 8:00 AM, the morning of the show.

Then the exhibitors arrived; the show was scheduled to open at 10:00. We had little time, so we made union laborers available as needed to aid the exhibitors. By some miracle, we made it. Someone said, *work expands to fill the time allotted*, and it is absolutely true, and so is the reverse. The less time you have, the less time it takes. They got it done, although the dealers were still complaining, and I couldn't blame them.

JERRY'S LAW #16:
"Patience is a virtue, but persistence to the point
of success is a blessing."

The show opened, and it was the most successful show of any to date. The Coliseum was packed with collectors, gallery owners, art dealers—and just good old-fashioned consumers. Everybody did business that year. The recession of early1980 was ending, the Reagan era was beginning, and the economy was beginning to boom. People wanted to spend money, just as they will now, once they sensed that things were getting better.

By evening, the exhibitors were happy (including our Israeli and French exhibitors). The only thing that makes exhibitors happy is doing business, so they forgave me. On principle, some of them wanted to get a little credit for their trouble, but that was nothing that couldn't be handled.

When the show ended, I got a bill from Atlantic Coast for an additional $70,000, which, in those days, was a fortune. Union construction workers get an unbelievable amount of money for working all night; they couldn't care less that we didn't have the walls. It was my problem and the contractors' problem, which meant that it was my problem.

The way contractors bill is the men get a fixed union wage, on top of which is an additional 20% or so for the contractor. As far as I was concerned, that 20% was obviously going to come off this bill, because I wasn't going to pay Tex for his mistake. Actually, I assumed that a little extra had already been built in for him. I ended up paying an additional $20,000, so Tex's profit was less. Tex was probably also out of pocket for $20,000. We shared the headache equally. My profit was less, but I knew that if I didn't pay him anything, it would be the end of our relationship. If he had to absorb the entire bill, it might have put him out of business. Even though we both knew he was wrong, I had to do something to make it right. He accepted the $20,000, and we went on to the next year.

JERRY'S LAW #7:
"If you can't beat them, join them, then beat them."

Through the entire episode, we remained relatively calm. There obviously was an argument, but anger would have accomplished very little. Tex was also in charge of 32B, which was an important and powerful union that represented the people who cleaned the building; it was essential that we come to an amicable agreement because the last thing I needed was a filthy exhibit hall, including maybe some dead rats on the floor.

Very shortly after this incident, we mutually agreed that he would no longer be our contractor. Art Expo had grown so big that it was too much for him to handle. Our new contracts were national, with companies that dealt with buildings across America. They had inventory in warehouses around the country, so if we needed carpeting or walls, they would have had them. After Tex and I parted ways, these national companies all agreed to build my walls and provide gray carpet (by then, the rest of the trade show world had caught up with us and were beginning to ask for gray carpet, too). In fact, all the national contractors bid for this job, since by then, we were a large successful show, and, unlike in 1979, they knew they would get paid.

Go West, Young Man

In 1982, we decided we would try to expand to the west coast. After the failure of Art Expo-West in 1980, we decide to go to go to San Francisco rather than Los Angeles, thinking we might have a better chance there overcoming the bad memories of the Los Angeles art community.

We rented a very large old railroad station terminal that a man named Adams had developed into a tradeshow center. It was perfect for displaying art. It was unique. It was in the center of San Francisco, and, as it happened, the San Francisco Convention Center didn't have the dates we wanted. Aesthetically, it was probably the nicest show I ever did in all the years of Art Expo. Not only was the venue beautiful, but the dealers brought a great many original works of art and other wonderful pieces, and the whole effect was special. The show, however, was a dismal failure. People in San Francisco just didn't come out for the show.

I always hired local people to handle advertising and publicity, and this time, I hired two wonderful young men. What I looked for were people with experience, but I didn't want to hire a big company. These two men worked their tails off to get me publicity. They did get some, but the art critic at the *San Francisco Chronicle* wrote an article that was published the day before the show opened, saying it was the worst art show he had ever seen. He even mentioned me by name, calling me the art version of P.T. Barnum, which I took as a compliment. After all, Barnum was hugely successful and one of the greatest promoters in the history of the world.

Just as the art critics at the *New York Times* controlled New York's art world, the critic at the *San Francisco Chronicle* controlled that city's art world. From my perspective, he wasn't reviewing the show, he was protecting the San Francisco art galleries. I don't know why he felt that way because, if our show created an interest in art, the interest would remain, and people would visit local galleries.

The show was a failure, and these two men were so upset. They had kept a log of all of the press that came to the show—all PR people do that— and they said the critic had never even been in the building. He made up the review while just sitting in his office, out of a desire to destroy the show. The free press sometimes abuses the truth and can destroy good people and ideas. Sadly, it may be worse today since there are fewer newspapers, almost no investigative reporting with little fact-checking, and no-one can disagree with them. With less competition, power corrupts.

After the show, I received a thank-you note from the two PR men, who had enclosed a voodoo doll with pins and notes with the names of all kinds of punishments. They put the art critic's name on the doll, and I was supposed to stick a pin with a different punishment into it every day. I still have it. When this art critic died a number of years later (I don't know if it had to do with the voodoo doll), they wrote to tell me about it.

Although we didn't lose any money as the show's promoters

(because by this time, we had a following), what made me feel worse was that the *exhibitors* lost money. I also felt terrible for the two young PR men, who got paid but didn't get the satisfaction of making the show a success.

Evolving into More Commercial Art

We held our fifth show in 1983. By that time, we were moving away from the fine-art world, and they were moving away from us. The reason was obvious: we were growing by leaps and bounds, which meant, in their view, that we were becoming too commercial. In my view, that meant we were successful, but they didn't want to be associated with something that drew the masses. They wanted to remain elite. Art Expo proved that more and more people appreciated art, but the fine-arts dealers couldn't handle the idea that we were commercial, meaning more buyers and dollars. In their view, oil and water don't mix. In other words, their importance was clearer in their elite world than being part of mine. We were attracting new collectors, the nouveau-riche corporate presidents and their wives and others who were becoming comfortable selecting their own high-quality, expensive art. The elitists didn't understand, but they benefitted because so many of our collectors began feeling comfortable visiting their art galleries during the year. It was a win-win for both, and perhaps the separation was a good thing for all.

By 1983, we were also attracting attendees who were less interested in the traditional art of famous art dealers or in talking about museums and such; they were more interested in new, avant-garde things like wearable-art fashion shows, which we began to bring in as special events. We also began to include things like functional art, electronic art, art made of glass—all of which are accepted as fine art today. Back then, fine-art dealers wouldn't accept that: they were into antique and traditional art forms, and they were afraid to move away from that. Today, the galleries are much different: they accept all the new contemporary art forms that Art Expo introduced.

JERRY'S LAW #9 "If you can't win, change the rules."

JERRY'S LAW #10:
"If you can't change the rules, ignore them."

Today, museums also bring in exhibits that are geared to the general public; they, too, need to bring people through the door. They have also made their gift shops more interesting and more consumer friendly, which is something that one of my exhibitors started. They didn't understand that everyone who goes to a museum wants to bring home some memento, but they want something they can relate to, that they will enjoy owning. It could be a T-shirt, a tie, jewelry, or even a reasonably priced exhibition poster.

From the time Art Expo started in 1979 to today, much has evolved: back then, most of the dealers weren't ready to accept it. So Art Expo evolved naturally. There was no angry parting of the ways; it just happened.

In our seminar program, we began to cover new topics such as how to start a collection, how to protect yourself from art fraud, and how to do things that new collectors were interested in, such as how to decorate with art. That was another topic that fine-art dealers never liked to discuss, but interior designers were major buyers at Art Expo over the years, and, as a result, we became increasingly involved with decorating and design magazines. As I see it, Art Expo evolved in a good, healthy way.

Working with Andy Warhol

We also did something different with the posters for Art Expo in 1983. For the first few years, we had an official Art Expo poster, which I selected (except for the first year's poster, which my former partner John had chosen). Beginning in 1980, many exhibitors wanted to produce the posters, and they did so at their own expense. They wanted to produce the official poster because Art Expo was something special, and it gave them cachet. Plus, the poster featured the work of one of their artists and denoted the exhibitor as its representative. About 100 exhibitors or more every year would produce their own Art Expo posters for their own use, and they became collectibles. Customers enjoyed collecting posters with the exhibition's name, the date, the place, and the artist, and the posters were affordable: something to take home as a memento of this Art Fair. But the official poster was something special, and we began holding a competition to determine who would produce it.

The competition committee was a committee of one—me. Had it been a group of dealers, it would have taken two years for them to make a decision; still, everyone who entered felt they had a chance, and those who didn't win would use the poster they submitted in their own booth and they would sell it all year.

1983 was the 100-year anniversary of the Brooklyn Bridge, so one exhibitor said he would like to produce a Brooklyn Bridge poster, and he thought he could get Andy Warhol to do it. That was an offer I couldn't refuse: a Warhol Art Expo poster would be a great promotion. We had to get the city's permission, since we wanted to make the poster part of the official celebration of this anniversary.

We also had to get permission from the Brooklyn Cultural Commissioner (who knew Brooklyn had one?) who had the last word. The poster was typical Andy Warhol of the period—a double image of the bridge. The most important thing for any artist is that his work be recognizable—so people will be able to say immediately, *that's a Picasso, that's a Miro, that's a Dali, and, of course, that's an Andy Warhol.* You might be a great artist, but if your work is not immediately identifiable, your chances of success are limited.

Fortunately, the Brooklyn Cultural Commissioner agreed to the poster. Then I told her that Andy was going to sign the edition in the stone, which meant his name would be visible on every print; it would not be an original signature, only the stone produced from his conceptual piece would be signed and that image would be reproduced on each print. Warhol was willing to sign it, because when a piece is signed, the dealer doesn't have to tell a potential buyer that it's an Andy Warhol, and they'll happily pay $30 for it. And the Borough of Brooklyn was going to make 20% on each poster sold.

But the Brooklyn Commissioner said, "I refuse to let Andy Warhol sign it. It's not an original." The dealer who made the agreement with Andy Warhol was a poster dealer, who knew that almost every poster was signed in the plate. But the Commissioner was unconvinced: she insisted that she had learned in art school that this was inappropriate, and she stood her ground. So we created the poster without the signature and, as a result, they sold only a few hundred pieces in all.

Not everyone is knowledgeable, and even for a relatively small amount of money, many people won't buy something that isn't signed. Had it been signed in the stone, we would have sold tens of thousands of posters. Even the dealer wasn't willing to push it. Instead, he made his money by producing a limited-edition lithograph, which he sold for $1,000. Andy Warhol not only signed it, but he was at Art Expo signing them for anyone who bought one. It was unbelievable: people were lined up in the aisle to buy one. At age 53, Warhol was already very famous; he died unexpectedly in 1987, so this was toward the end of his career. He signed one of his original lithographs—an artist's proof—and he gifted it to me. There were 300 pieces in the limited edition and only 5 artist proofs. I didn't take care of it, and it's a little ripped on the corner; in fact, I only recently framed it. I've been told it's now worth about $30,000—but sadly, less because it's damaged. Easy come, easy go.

Warhol was, by far, the greatest self-promoter in the twentieth-century art world. He knew he was disdained by the fine-art community because he was considered commercial. He went everywhere every day: he would walk in the front door of Studio 54, stay five minutes, and leave by the back door. He would go to every party and every event. He *was* Page 6 (the celebrity gossip page of *The New York Post*). The aficionados may have hated him, but I knew it would be wonderful to have him associated with Art Expo. I spoke to him only briefly, and we took some photographs together and also with Mayor Koch. Andy even offered to do my portrait for $25,000. He was doing double-image portraits then, like he had done of the bridge. Perhaps I could have been another Marilyn Monroe, hanging in MOMA. But I didn't believe at that time that any painting of GL could be worth that kind of money.

Fast-forward to 2012. Today, you'll find that works by Warhol are in great demand at Sotheby's, Christie's, or any of the major auction houses, and he's one of the best-selling artists in the world. He was commercial, but he's very collectible: elite art dealers don't call him *commercial* anymore!

Andy was a very hardworking, driven man. He was also an antique collector who bought the entire inventory of antiques stores: he would enter a store and ask, "how much?" The owner would ask him, "for what?" and he'd say, "for the whole store." Then he would buy the whole store. When he died, there were warehouses full of the antiques and other items he had acquired.

Art Expo gave me the opportunity to meet some amazing people, if only for just a few short moments. When you get to know people who are special or famous, you discover that most of them are not only interesting but they also have a certain characteristic that makes them successful. You may not like everything they do, but they have something unique. I enjoyed that. (More about these famous celebrities later.)

Expanding to Texas: The Dallas Show

In 1983, we also decided to do an art fair in Texas. Because of the failures of Art Expo-West in L.A. and our show in San Francisco, we were spooked by California. Still, we wanted to find a second home, so we decided on the Dallas Market Center. The largest interior design centers in the world are in Dallas. There are also a great many entrepreneurs, lots of culture, and galleries featuring western and southwestern Indian art—all of which made it a likely candidate for an Art Expo. So we decided to give it a try.

I went to Dallas and as before, I hired a very prominent public relations person, someone who knew everybody. She immediately told me that Dallas is a very insular town where everybody knows everybody else: every entrepreneur, every millionaire, and everybody who bought art knew everybody else. "It's a big small town," she said, which I found to be true. Her advice was to get important local people on our Advisory Board. Since I didn't know anybody in Dallas, she volunteered to assist me.

She succeeded in getting some big names: Annette Strauss, who was a former mayor of Dallas and the sister of Robert Strauss, who was a long-time supporter of LBJ (and later, Chairman of the Democratic National Committee). He was one of the most powerful men in America. She also got Stanley Marcus, the founder of Neiman-Marcus, and Trammell Crow, the big property developer, who happened to own the

Market Center, which was the gigantic complex in which we were exhibiting. Trammell Crow was one of the wealthiest men in the world and quite a nice person. We met his family, too, because in Dallas, you meet not only the person you are working with but their wives and children, too. Business is done differently there. Those three people were the beginning of a very important Board of Directors, which would prove very helpful.

We also got the support of Ann Richardson, who was the editor of *Texas Homes. Texas* magazine was also on our team. Another advantage was that 1983 was the year the new Dallas Museum of Art opened, which was a major event in Dallas, and we were able to tie ourselves in with the opening.

Art Expo-Texas opened on September 30, 1983, and we sold out the space, with a little less than 500 booths. Not only did some of our regular exhibitors attend, but we also attracted western and southwestern art galleries and dealers, since many people in this part of our country collect Remingtons and other cowboy-related art, as well as Native American artists like R. C. Gorman.

The Dallas Market Center was a very professional venue, which made it an easy place to put on the show; there weren't any union problems, since Texas is a right-to-work state. The attendance was fair; it's very hard to build a large attendance in one year, but it was enough to keep exhibitors interested. They wanted to do it again: they knew we could build a show. That was the start of Art Expo-Texas, and in 1984, we held our second Texas show there.

That second year, we had about 50 more dealers participating, and we wanted to make sure we had buyers and not just lookers. In the trade show business, you have to be able to match the exhibitors with the customers so they do business. If a lot of visitors attend, the promoter will be successful, but if those visitors aren't buyers, the exhibitors won't make money, which means they won't exhibit again.

We did two special exhibitions. One was the wearable-art fashion show, where we had professional models periodically appear in the trade center lobby, wearing artist-created fashions. It was very cool. The other was an electronic art show, which I'm very proud of. We found a group of computer artists working in their basements in the East Village, who were creating computer-generated art using unusual shapes, colors, and forms. At the time, people thought they were a bunch of weirdoes, that it wasn't art. In those days, most people thought of computers as tools for accounting and other business purposes.

These were people who were working with Apple, Hewlett-Packard, and IBM computers, exploring the creative side of what a computer could do. This group of 50 people worked together to produce the most amazing creations. In those days, few people could imagine what the computer was capable of doing. Today, of course, every TV commercial is created using computer-generated art. We now know people can do all sorts of creative work using the computer's unlimited capacity; then, it was people like these young artists who taught the world (even the manufacturers) the potential of computers. We're still learning; they were in the forefront, and some of them moved on to Silicon Valley and became wealthy. I am very proud that Art Expo was in the forefront of these world-changing innovations

Working with Peter Max and Loving It

At that time, I began trying to find an artist I could connect with the show, someone whose work might help us break through to the New York and Dallas news media. It was hard to get publicity because the art desks at major newspapers were not interested in reporting on or reviewing what they deemed commercial art events. Nevertheless, shows like ours needed publicity to get people through the door. No amount of advertising has the impact that being featured on the evening news does; it draws people who are looking for weekend entertainment.

Finally, I hit on the idea of doing something with Peter Max, who was a well-known artist. Many of the nightly news anchors had grown up with his work—psychedelic art—that appeared on posters advertising rock concerts, album covers, and commercial products. He did very well for a while, and then his work fell out of favor. The newscasters of the early 1980s were not interested in the details of what was going on in the art world, but for my purposes, the important fact was that they knew of Peter Max. He was living in a lovely apartment on Riverside Drive in Manhattan (where he still lives today). At the time, he lived with a supermodel, and they were into mind-altering substances, and he had stopped working as a productive artist.

We met in his apartment: he was very friendly, and he showed me the work he had done over the years. I told him, "Peter, you're famous! You've got to straighten up." I don't know if I had anything to do with it, but the supermodel left soon after. They were enabling one another, so the split was a good thing.

Peter got clean and started working again. I introduced him to electronic art. The work excited him, and he immediately wanted to learn more. He had been in the avant-garde with psychedelic art, but this came from a different time and place. It was right up his alley.

He joined us in Dallas, and the PR agency was able to book him for some interviews on the nightly news. Finally, I had broken the barrier! The interviews ran before the show, and Peter was very happy with the outcome. I am convinced those interviews boosted attendance at that year's show.

Peter Max was back in the spotlight. In fact, his artwork is still selling well some 30 years later. From that show on, while I was associated with Art Expo, Peter Max was an important part of the art fairs—especially in New York, where he did interviews on the nightly news and other features to promote himself and, of course, Art Expo.

After I sold Art Expo, Peter asked me if I would be his manager, but I could never do that because his ego is ten times bigger than mine, and mine is pretty big. He still hugs me every time I see him: he believes I helped him, but you can only help yourself. What I gave him was a route back, a way for him to do what he loves to do and does so well.

Great People and Good Times

I had some wonderful experiences at Art Expo-Texas. One of my exhibitors told me he was creating a sculpture of Nolan Ryan, the former New York Mets player who pitched the most no-hitters in the history of baseball and who threw the ball 100 miles an hour (the first person ever to do that). He played for a long time; in 1984, he was playing for the Houston Astros—he was originally from Texas. He later became president and part owner of the Texas Rangers. The artist wanted me to see the sculpture and to introduce me to Nolan Ryan. We had lunch together. Ryan is a very low-key, wonderful man, and it was my pleasure to meet one of the greatest players in the history of baseball.

Later, at a pre-show meeting, another artist told me he was doing a sculpture honoring John Wayne, whose son Patrick had sponsored the sculpture. The artist introduced me to Wayne's sons, who were also actors, but of little note. I was eager to meet the family and learn more about the personal side of John Wayne. Things like these meetings were very special to me. Remember, John Wayne was perhaps the greatest icon of my lifetime.

As mentioned, I always had a staff party two nights before the show opened. I chose that time because no matter how the show ended, at that point, we all knew we had done our best and had worked our tails off. If I had waited until the last night to have a party, and the show hadn't gone well, no one would be happy and everyone would be tired. Whereas, at the beginning, everyone is upbeat. We went everywhere, including Studio 54 in its heyday and the Copacabana, but our best parties were during those two years in Dallas.

The first year we went to Southfork, to the ranch where the TV show *Dallas* was filmed. (The show recently came back to TV, with many of the original cast members.) I took Judy Brightwater to Dallas: she had been my #1 girl since the end of the Prentice Hall days. Judy's real last name was DeBlasio, but when she started working with me in the art world, we gave her a name that everybody would remember, something easy and generic. For some ridiculous reason, we came up with Brightwater, which sounded like an American-Indian name. And people still call her Judy Brightwater: I know since we still talk and laugh about it.

I also brought Judy's father to the Dallas show: he was in his sixties and retired. After all, we had only five people on permanent staff. He was the most wonderful man: he would do anything we needed done, unlike some of the kids who worked for me, who would say, "I don't do coffee." "I don't pick up trash." "I won't go out and get an exhibitor," and who I would ultimately fire. Judy's father was just great to have around. I also traveled with a regular core staff of security men—off-duty police and firemen—who were also our floor managers.

When we went to Southfork, I decided to make the event really special. Southfork is about 50 minutes outside of Dallas, so I hired a white limousine, which could fit a dozen people and which had big steer horns on the roof. We were supposed to be there for lunch on the verandah, but I suggested we leave early, drive around, and find a country restaurant or a diner for breakfast. I told the driver to look for a place for breakfast on the way. We drove for nearly a half hour, but we found nothing except McDonald's. By this time, everyone was hungry, so our big white stretch limousine with steer horns on the hood pulled into the McDonald's parking lot. I bet the people in that town are still talking about the day the white stretch limo pulled in for breakfast. Then we went on to Southfork, visited the set of *Dallas* (which was then the most-watched weekly show on TV), and had lunch and were entertained on the veranda.

The second year, we found a Greek restaurant in Dallas proper, which had a great food reputation. We wanted something a little different—not just a steakhouse. When we arrived, there was a little Greek music playing in the background, but while we were eating, the restaurant was very quiet. We all drank a lot (at least, it was a lot for me), and finally, we called the owner over and asked, "Where's the real Greek music? Where's the breaking of dishes?" We had heard about this tradition, called *opa*, which means celebration. It's a Greek custom. Anthony Quinn did it in the film *Zorba the Greek*. They break dishes on the ground, and the men celebrate by dancing together. The owner told us, "We don't do that here in Dallas—it's so boring here—but you are so much fun and so nice, I want you to break dishes. So I'm going to turn the music up, and I want you to get up and dance."

The owner brought out at least 30 dishes from the kitchen. The police and firemen had no trouble breaking them, but it was hard for me: it seemed a shame to break perfectly good dishes! Still, we had a great time. And the local Dallas people who were dining in the restaurant couldn't believe this was going on, because it was a very quiet, serene place. Everybody had a great time, we laughed so much that evening that we still talk about it. It's times like these that made the Art Expo shows and the staff something special.

Bad Publicity Can Spoil Everything—
Even When It's Not True

The second Dallas show was better than the first, but it still wasn't where I wanted it to be. There's no place like New York: that's a fact. It's the center of the world.

At the end of the show, I stood by the door as I usually did to say goodbye to the exhibitors. My modus operandi was to be there, not to hide in my office. As I walked to the front of the hall and the exhibitors were leaving, TV cameras rolled through the door, and I thought to myself, "The show's over, so what the hell are cameras doing here? Well, maybe it'll be good publicity for next year." It was *ABC News,* Dallas. A reporter pushed a microphone in my face and asked why I had ripped off my exhibitors. I didn't know what the hell he was talking about.

On the next-to-last day of the show, an Italian dealer in paintings had told me his paintings had been stolen. He showed me the frames: paintings are stretched on wood, and these paintings had been cut out of the stretchers. I immediately thought his story was bogus and that he had done it to collect the insurance, because it made no sense: an art thief would steal the whole painting, not cut it out of its stretcher, which removes an important part of the painting and greatly decreases its value. I found out later that this dealer had gone to the media, I assume to put pressure on me.

But I stood my ground, and I said to the reporter, "What are you talking about? We had a wonderful show. It was a beautiful show. Were you here to see it?" The exhibitors were still leaving the building, and I told the reporters to ask them if I had ripped them off. They said, "No, no, no, Jerry's terrific." Some added, "We did well." Others said, "We didn't do so well, but we have no complaints."

Finally, the reporter left, and I got a phone call from one of my best exhibitors, Edward Newman, a Parisian dealer, who had attended the Dallas show. "Jerry, I'm in a cab, and the radio is on, and the promo for the evening news is that you ripped off the exhibitors." The fact that they were running a promo meant they were going to feature this story. Yet they had come to me only an hour earlier, which meant they hadn't investigated or verified anything; they hadn't spoken to any other exhibitors or attendees: in other words, they were ruining my business on the basis of one person's story.

My PR person was as upset as I was. She had worked her tail off, like everybody does at a tradeshow. It's not a piece of machinery; it's real people, real art, real energy. It's exciting. She knew the president of *ABC News* in Dallas, so she immediately called him. That's the advantage of a city like Dallas: everybody knows one another. Unfortunately, he told her he couldn't interfere with the newscast, but he agreed to look at the tapes before they went on the air, and he assured her he would make certain the newscast was fair.

We watched the broadcast. The report took a few minutes, which is long in television-news time, but it was generally positive. They had a clip of the Italian dealer claiming his paintings were stolen. It was a nothing story, but nothing could erase the fact that the dumb, negative, and untrue promo had run.

I had a reputation to maintain in Dallas and beyond; I was associated with many wonderful and prominent people. In addition to Annette Strauss, Stanley Marcus, and Trammell Crow, one of the people I met at the show was a married couple who owned several retail stores, loved art, and took me in as their friend. On several occasions, they invited me to the Dallas Entrepreneurial Club, where owners of the largest companies in the world still got together with other entrepreneurs, so you might meet someone who runs three women's clothing stores alongside the owner of Neiman-Marcus. At the club, I met 75 to 100 of the most important people in Dallas. I was very impressed with the entrepreneurial nature of Dallas. This was the small big city of Texas at its finest. Respecting people for what they accomplished, not for their net worth.

The episode with the reporter had left a bitter taste in my mouth, so I decided to investigate a little. I discovered that some local gallery and frame-shop owners had bitterly complained to their friends at the local TV station that I was ruining their businesses, which was ridiculous. We sold thousands of lithographs and posters at that show, which had to be framed at local frame shops. The show also created interest in certain artists and artwork among people who otherwise would not have visited galleries. No doubt, they would now visit Dallas frame shops and galleries, because they felt more comfortable with art.

When I left Dallas to return to the New York office, Art Expo-Texas was naturally on my mind. I had very mixed emotions, since I loved Dallas and I loved the special people I met there, but I was very upset about how the media had treated us. Also, although the Dallas show had been a financial success, it would always have rather limited potential: it would never be New York. So I had to decide whether I would go back to Dallas for a third show, or move on. The outrageous "news" story on Dallas TV's Channel 7, asking me if Art Expo had ripped off our exhibitors, had damaged our reputation irrevocably—even though the accusation was totally unsubstantiated, with not one bit of fact to support it, just the fact that there had been a story on the news would make people wonder if "where there's smoke, there's fire."

So I decided to move on to Los Angeles and the west coast market, which was much larger and more important in the art world than Dallas. Even before the Dallas news debacle had happened, I had considered moving. The sad part is that Dallas lost a lot more than I did when I decided not to take Art Expo back to Dallas: all those wonderful local galleries that participated no longer had a place to exhibit. In addition, the Convention Center, the hotels, and the restaurants lost so much revenue that we had brought in during that time period, and the people who had attended and really enjoyed the show no longer had this major event in their city.

Art Expo never went back to Dallas. We did only those two shows. I would have had to push very hard to change perceptions. I decided it wasn't worth it. It was time to move on.

Art Expo-LA Rises from the Ashes

Two weeks after the Dallas show ended in 1984, I flew to Los Angeles to secure the convention dates there for the fall of 1985. I wanted a show on each coast, approximately six months apart. I also wanted to make a connection in terms of local PR representation, so we could start promoting the show and talking it up almost immediately.

By 1985, the stigma of Art Expo West was gone. It took time for people to forget about the show that had been put on by someone else using our Art Expo name. But it was five years later. Also, the exhibitors who had been burned there still followed us to L.A. When you produce business and create trust, people will follow you. We had a great reputation to deliver customers. Many of our better exhibitors became wealthy during my reign. I know this to be true, for later in life, they actually admitted it to me. While I was still running the fair, they didn't want to give up their negotiating strategy (to get a better booth at a better price), by admitting this fact.

It was very important that we establish the date for the next fair, because I had to notify the exhibitors, which is usually done at the end of each year's show so the exhibitors can plan ahead. I met with the people in charge of the L.A. Convention Center who had heard about Art Expo and who very much wanted us. Unfortunately, we were very late in making plans, so the only dates that were available were September 6–9, 1985—right after Labor Day and therefore not a very good time, since (as mentioned earlier), many people are just returning from vacation, and others are busy getting their kids off to begin the school year.

Those dates went against my better judgment, but I didn't want to lose a whole year on the west coast, because we would lose our momentum. So I took a chance and accepted those dates, and as it turned out, LA in 1985 was a good fair. Art dealers always want to see hope for the future, especially artists, who live on their dreams, and this success gave the west coast artists plenty of dreams to live on.

The next thing I had to do was to establish some local representatives, including public relations firms. I don't even remember how I found the group of people I interviewed, but I did what had been successful for me before: I wanted to work only with firms that were well-qualified but small since I wanted the owners doing the actual work and reporting to me, so we'd have that personal connection.

I hired a public relations firm called Baker and Winoker, whose main focus was show- business people, but they wanted to expand and do public relations in the general business area, so they wanted my account very much. The minute I met these two guys, I loved them: they were high energy, they were very good-looking (not that looks matters in most businesses, but in PR, it probably matters), and of course, they knew a lot of show-business people, which I thought would help publicize the show in L.A.

Interestingly, they were both former lawyers. They had met while working at the same law firm and both hated being attorneys, so they left and opened a PR firm. Paul Baker was born in Australia and had moved to L.A. with his parents when he was still a child. Larry was a Californian, born and bred. They really complemented each other: Paul was a down-to-earth business type, whereas Larry was a very flamboyant guy, so I had the best of both worlds promoting Art Expo LA.

We had to decide quickly what kind of public relations we were going to do. After all, Paul and Larry didn't know very much about the art world, and it's very difficult to get the general press or the entertainment press to cover art. We were in between, and many media organizations weren't comfortable with covering us. As history would prove, Art Expo was the venue that popularized art to a much larger market.

Since the show was in early September, we decided to tie ourselves in with Jerry Lewis' famous telethon for muscular dystrophy, which was held on Labor Day weekend and was probably the most-watched program at that time. (This was years before cable took over TV.) We made up a poster that said "Support Jerry's kids: Come to Art Expo." That caption really tickled me (and still does) because my name is Jerry—though of course, it referred to Jerry Lewis's muscular dystrophy kids; but my children would also benefit. We decided to donate $1 out of every $6 entrance fee we received, but because the telethon would air before Art Expo, there really was no way to know what our attendance would be, so I simply donated $10,000. That was a substantial part of our budget for the west coast show, but I felt it was a justifiable expense to let people become familiar with Art Expo, knowing so many people would watch the telethon.

Larry Winoker and I appeared on the telethon, with an eight-foot cardboard check he had created, giving $10,000 to muscular dystrophy from Art Expo. Larry held up one side of it, and I held up the other, while Jerry Lewis talked with us from Las Vegas. The funniest thing about the event was that we dropped the check! Somehow we didn't handle it properly and we dropped it—something no one wants to do on national television. (Larry still blames me, and I still blame him.)

At the end of Art Expo California, which we all considered a great success, Larry and Paul and their wives and some of my staff and my wife and I went to Valentino's restaurant on Pico Boulevard. All night, we celebrated our wonderful first show in L.A. What I didn't know at the time was that Paul was a piano player and somewhat of a singer. His father was a comedian who lived and worked in Las Vegas, and Paul's wife was Marni Meckler, a world-class opera singer. Larry's wife Joann was a casting director for movies, and she also sang. It was great fun, and we drank and had a fabulous evening: we took over the piano as well as the bar, and we sang all night. Some of the people in our group were not always willing to perform, but that evening, everybody performed—even me.

We walked out the door still congratulating ourselves, giving each other high-fives, saying we couldn't wait until next year. Then a homeless bag lady came up the street, with a shopping cart lined with Art Expo posters. To this day, we all kid each other about what a great job they did distributing the posters around L.A. In fact, my wife made a booklet for me for my sixtieth birthday, which all the important people in my life wrote in. Paul and Larry wrote what I great guy I am, a taskmaster who was always pursuing excellence, and that I was the only person in the history of their company who ever gave them a bonus for a job well done. They said this act of generosity toward us meant a great deal to them about the importance of reward. Then at the end, they wrote, "Our business has thrived and grown, and because of our experience with Jerry, we have trained hundreds of homeless people in the intricate art of poster promotion."

Baker and Winoker did indeed do very well. In fact, sometime around 2004, Larry and Paul called to tell me they had sold their business to one of the largest advertising agencies, Ogilvy, for many millions of dollars. I feel great about these guys; they were so proud, they wanted me to be one of the first to know that they had also fulfilled their American Dream. When you have a business that is service oriented, like theirs was, it's very hard to sell since you're essentially selling your own services. But they were really talented people, and they were able to overcome that barrier.

After that first California show, I hired them for New York, and they agreed to open a New York office. I wanted to assist them in expanding. They always worked very hard for me, and later on in life they became my business partners in another venture (which I discuss later).

I worked with both of them directly, and only one other person, Candy Kay, who was (and still is) a beautiful, compassionate woman. Her name sounds like she could have been an exotic dancer (and she could dance and was pretty enough to be one), but she was a very smart, innovative individual who worked side by side with us, and she became part of our Art Expo family. So when Larry and Paul weren't available, we had this top-notch person working with us, so my relationship with their firm lasted through the end of my ownership of Art Expo.

When the LA Expo show finally happened, we had about 320 exhibitors occupying 550 booths, which was just slightly larger than at the Dallas show. The west coast show attracted a different element of the art world: there were many more west coast and southwest artists. Some of those artists and exhibitors eventually came to New York, and some New Yorkers eventually went to California. Also, the building was easy for us to work in: although it was a union building, it was a little less rigid than working with the New York unions.

Also, the exhibitors had good sales, and when they left the building, they wanted to sign up for the following year. That's a terrific response for a first show: getting exhibitors to want to come back is the most important thing.

Bloomingdale's window celebrating Art Expo, 1981.

Art Expo featured in Times Square, 1986.

42nd Street Chorus Line, after dancing with me from Broadway to the Javits Center, 1986.

11

From the Coliseum
to Opening the Javits Center

Before we did the Los Angeles show in September, we held Art Expo New York in April, 1985. It was the seventh year we did the fair in New York. It had already been announced that this would be the last show at the New York Coliseum because the building was closing.

The 1985 show was different from previous years since it was much bigger and many more people attended: we had more exhibitors and international dealers who wanted to make contact with artists and the exhibiting dealers. Art Expo was the place to be in the art world. I filled every inch of the building with exhibitors, all three floors plus the mezzanine. I even had some in the lobby—exhibitors we signed up at the very last moment. We had 380 exhibitors from more than 20 countries, occupying 900 booths. The show was charged with so much energy that it was the success I had always dreamed of. Exhibitors and visitors told me they could hardly wait until next year. We were a world-class event, a part of the New York Celebrity Scene. If you can make it here, you can make it anywhere.

JERRY'S LAW #8: "If it's worth doing, do it right."

This show was also memorable for another reason. I was trying to get a cab from the hotel to the show, and I couldn't get one, when the shuttle bus that ran between our official hotels and the Coliseum came around the corner, so I jumped on. On the bus were about 15 art dealers, so I started chatting with them and I asked, "Hey, where are you all from?" And they said, "We're all from Alaska and northwest Canada. We represent the Eskimo artists." I couldn't believe it: every single art dealer in Alaska and northwest Canada who represented Eskimo (Inuit) artists was at Art Expo.

Then they asked me, "Who are you?" And I said, "I'm Jerry Leberfeld, the director of the show." When I said that, they all stood up and gave me a standing ovation, because I had given them the opportunity to meet people in this part of the world who might be interested in the artists they represented. Also, it was amazing they had even made it to the show, because although April is springtime in the Lower 48, it's still frozen winter in their part of the world. Nevertheless, they traveled on however many planes they needed to, to get to New York, because they wanted to be part of Art Expo.

Also that year, we held a special exhibit of electronic art, which was becoming very popular. We called the exhibit, "An overview of a 21st-century art forms, including computer-generated animation, NASA flight simulation, entertainment, educational programming." The art and technology areas include three-dimensional artwork, such as robotics, holography, and artist demonstrations, and continuous sideshows premiering the work of some 50 emerging electronic artists. I was their first step toward Silicon Valley.

Another special event at the 1985 show was "Broadway Art and Artists," an exhibition of famous Broadway art posters and memorabilia that were distributed by current Broadway performers. The stars signed the posters, and the proceeds benefited a cause called "Save the Theaters." At the time, some real estate landlords were trying to knock down the old but not-yet-landmarked theaters on Broadway. Many of them were saved and eventually landmarked by the city. Many of the old theater posters were fabulous. In fact, I bought a couple of them, including one from *The King and I,* signed by Yul Brynner, and *La Cage aux Folles,* signed by Van Johnson and George Hearn, who starred in the original production.

The electronic art exhibit and the Broadway poster promotions were significant because they were evidence the Art Expo show was changing: we were no longer dependent on people from the fine-art world to conduct seminars and exhibitions. Instead, we were more in the forefront and cutting edge of the future. Also, more of our visitors were new collectors, and they were interested in different types of art. We became an entertainment event, as well as a fine-art forum, which was a combination that had never existed before.

The 1985 New York show was such a success that when we announced our next show in L.A., we sold 60% of the space for L.A. before Art Expo-New York even closed. When you're successful and they're making money, they want to stick with you, so I could do no wrong.

I was still dealing with my partners, Phil and Irwin, but they didn't seem to bother me as much. They were happy running around, talking to exhibitors they were friendly with and playing big shots, which was OK with me and good for them. Art Expo had gotten so big that the pettiness between me and my partners virtually dissolved in the massiveness of the show.

I wasn't quite sure I was prepared for that last day of the 1985 show. The New York Coliseum had been my home since 1979; the place that had changed my life forever was closing. Building a great art fair from beginning to end is an amazing experience: installing carpet, then walls, then lighting and furniture, then the exhibitors arriving and placing their artwork in the space this beautiful city created. It took about two or three days to build and open an event, and only about two or three hours to close it. Not only was it difficult to come down from the high energy and aesthetics to this emptiness of a building with only concrete floors, empty walls, and no people, but that year was the worst.

I was exhausted, and I had this empty feeling, plus I was scared that the place that had produced my American Dream was now empty and eerily silent. I had very mixed feelings: we were going to move into a brand-new building, the Jacob Javits Convention Center, a beautiful building designed by I.M. Pei, the world-famous architect. It was located on 11th Avenue, stretching from 34th Street to 39th Street. But I'm old-fashioned, and I've always believed, *If it ain't broke, why fix it?* In my heart of hearts, I didn't want to leave the Coliseum and move Art Expo to the Javits Center. But I had no choice.

I also had mixed feelings about the fact that Art Expo was going to be the first show and the opening event of the new Javits Center. Being the first show in a new convention center could be a disaster, with more technical and logistical problems than you can imagine. But from a PR standpoint, it was special, because we would be the first in this new glass building, and through the media capital of the world could reap unprecedented results, beyond my wildest dreams. Both of these opinions turned out to be true.

A few weeks after my final show at the New York Coliseum, I attended a Javits Center organizational meeting of tradeshow managers and building executives. The purpose was for the show promoters to give input and ask questions to ensure the smooth opening of Javits. We were promised that in this new state-of-the-art building, new rules would be introduced regarding the operations and the new agreement with the unions.

The show managers gave their opinions of what had to be changed and improved so that more businesses would want to exhibit in New York, which was always considered a difficult place to do business, and the new administration told us they were going to change all of that. So we began listing the union rules that existed at the time that we wanted to change. For example, the union electricians had to plug in all the lights, lamps, radios, etc.; of course, the exhibitors hated that, and it was very expensive. Also, each union work crew consisted of six different union members, all of whom had to be hired simultaneously. Excessive tips had to be given to union workers to get the exhibitors' materials and work orders to the front of the line. We wanted easier move-in for small panel trucks, because there was a long wait behind these large 16-wheelers at the loading platforms, so the smaller exhibitors were always complaining. We also wanted to improve the type of food that would encourage the attendees to stay in the building, thus increasing sales. These were our goals. They wrote them all down, and they assured us that they would be taken care of.

We met periodically to get updates. Since the building seemed very incomplete, I was concerned that it would not be open on time, but down deep, I knew it would; what choice did they have? Not opening on time would be an economic and political disaster.

I hired Howard Rubinstein, Inc.—the most politically connected PR firm in New York—and the infamous owner himself agreed to handle our account personally. His primary responsibility was to assist me with the political aspect, and especially the opening-night party, with the problems of all the dealers and celebrities under one roof. My regular PR firm, Baker and Winoker, would handle the day-by-day operations.

There was no doubt in my mind that the opening of Javits would give me unbelievable exposure. Even though we were very successful in the art world, there were still many people we couldn't reach, due to the control of all things art-related by the New York art critics, who would never write a single word about a commercial show such as Art Expo. But the opening of the Javits Center would be front and center in all news and entertainment sections of newspapers and magazines. No one could stop it, it was such an important event.

My other concern about being the first show in the building pertained to the logistical and technical aspects, and they were very difficult, also beyond what I had ever imagined. As the months slipped by and our meetings at the Center still had many unanswered questions, especially about union rules, catering menus, and assurances that everything would be taken care of very soon, we got closer and closer to the opening. Some of the larger tradeshow people, like the Littles and the Thalheims (who produced such shows as the Gift & Variety Merchandise Show and beauty shows), reduced their pressure on these matters, because their most important issue was obtaining the best and most show dates possible. They wanted the same answers I did, but they could live without them because good show dates supersede all other challenges.

I asked Rubinstein to find out how the labor negotiations were going. He told me they were very close to finalization. Thomas Galvin was the president of the Jacob Javits operating corporation, which had been hired to complete the construction of this building. Tom was an engineer and builder who had partnered with I.M. Pei's son in their own construction company in Dallas, Texas. Tom was well qualified and successful, and he was convinced of the importance of this project, a once-in-a-lifetime challenge. This job would guarantee the future of their firm, so they left Dallas for this so-called opportunity of a lifetime, but it didn't turn out that way—quite the opposite, as I will explain.

Tom was a very nice man, a good businessman, and a top-flight engineer—the perfect hire, it seemed. The problem was he was operating in Texas, a right-to-work state, where entrepreneurs are treated with the greatest respect. In New York, you had to deal with the interfering, uncooperative politicians and other bureaucrats, along with many union problems, work stoppages, absenteeism, long holidays, impossible overtime costs, and continuous disputes. You can never fire or replace anybody: the government won't allow you. Many of the workers who got their jobs were not the most qualified but the best-connected, and his complaint about their lack of qualifications fell on deaf ears. Tom was in charge, but who was listening? He had an impossible job, dealing with incompetent workers and politically connected and corrupt contractors. He tried but was eventually scapegoated by the politicians, who never accepted any responsibility. A few weeks before the Javits Center opened, he was fired for insubordination (whatever that means). That was his reward for a job well done. I was personally upset and heartbroken, but the show must go on.

Problems with the Food Service at the Javits

The building hired Ogden Corporation to run the food operations: Ogden was a large institutional caterer that usually handled large convention centers and sports parks, which are not typically known for the best-quality food at reasonable prices. I finally received a proposed food menu. I was blown away. Nothing the show managers asked for was represented—nothing that would keep customers in the building. No hot dogs or hamburgers. No salads. No gourmet sandwiches. The sample menu consisted of mixed salad, filet of sole with green beans, dessert, and coffee; at a fixed price of $31. The other menu choices were no better. Remember, this was 1986, and our daily entry pass was only $6. These food prices were outrageous. The customers could easily go to one of the thousands of New York restaurants for better food at lower prices.

I asked Howard Rubinstein to arrange an emergency meeting with the caterer and the Javits Center management. This was not the hope and change I had expected. At the meeting were the president of Ogden, the New York State Governor's liaison to the convention center, and an assortment of vice presidents (most of them politically appointed and inexperienced "experts"), Howard, and myself.

I asked the caterer why this menu and why these prices, and he answered, "Because we need to make a profit." To that, I answered, "Nobody's going to eat this. Nobody's even going to order it, so how can you make a profit?" Then one of the vice presidents chimed in and said, "Don't blame them; after all, we had to add 30% on the price for our commission." I asked, "Don't they pay rent for their space?" and he answered, "Yes, but we can't pay off the cost of this building without this extra revenue." How can one argue with the logic of that statement?

Then Howard Rubinstein said to me, "Jerry, be fair. This is the way business is done in the government." I pounded the table loudly and profoundly, explained my position, and subsequently got the menu changed—not to what I wanted, but at least better. So I moved on. There were bigger fish to fry—finishing the building, finalizing the union contracts, and the all-important exhibitor move-in.

Art Expo at the Javits was to become the largest art forum in the world. With our great prior success, plus the draw of the new Javits Center, I sold every conceivable inch to more than 500 exhibitors from more than 25 countries, truly becoming the beacon of the international art world.

That many exhibitors, filling more than 1,400 booths, created a tremendous amount of work. There were floor plans for each exhibitor that had to be submitted, plus we had to have their art photos for the catalogue. Technically, in a new facility, anything can happen. You walk in and the exact space doesn't exist, or exhibitors overlap, so we needed to take care of those situations. It was quite a job, especially with a building that was brand new and not always what it was supposed to be. Then there were the administrative details: each exhibitor had to submit their catalogue pages, order their booth furnishings, and pay their bill in full 90 days out. Remember, I came from a credit and collections background, and I was very strong on this point, so that 90 days beforehand, you either paid in full or you were out. After all, we had a substantial waiting list.

The 1986 show was also complicated because I had encouraged a trade event for frame shops to take place in New York City at the same time as Art Expo. They called it *Framarama*. I always wanted to attract additional potential buyers to the show, so it would grow every year. The framing industry bought some art, but they weren't major customers; still, the benefit of having Framarama in the city at the same time worked for both of us, since the shuttle buses would go back and forth between the two shows. This concept attracted framers from around the country who now had two reasons to come to New York in April. Their show was in a nearby hotel. So that combination of shows worked out very well, and it continued until I left.

Spencer Reese was my #1 man, my tradeshow floor manager, who was responsible for handling all of the administrative details listed above. Then three months before the opening of the Javits show, Spencer resigned. Preparation for that show was chaotic enough, so I was distressed at this news. He told me he got a better job, and, as it turned out, his new employer was one of my exhibitors. I would never stop anybody from getting a better job, but the timing was bad for me, and I didn't understand why he couldn't finish out the year. So I asked him, "Why not stay the three months, be part of this special event, and receive all the accolades from the exhibitors?" He would also receive a large bonus for being my #1 assistant. But in his mind, this was his big chance, and his new boss wanted him to start immediately, so he gave me two weeks' notice.

Who was I going to find to replace Spencer in such a short time? Maybe John Reedy could help: he had worked for me as a floor manager at Art Expo-California, and he had just married Michelle, one of my best exhibitors. I called John and he said, "I'll be on the next plane to New York," leaving his new bride so he could help me, without even asking how much I was going to pay him. It was difficult for John to pick up the slack on such short notice (as it would have been for anyone), but I had a person I could trust and work with, and somehow we got through it together. I'll never forget him: John Reedy was a Vietnam veteran, living with problems acquired as a Marine in combat. He was a great friend who stood with me day and night during this very difficult period. He followed the same credo I did: *"Can't is not an option."*

Meanwhile, Spencer's new job lasted less than a year, which was a shame for him, because when I sold Art Expo the following year, he would have taken over as the director of the entire operation. Spencer and I have talked many times since then, and I believe he realizes he made a big mistake by leaving when he did. Making mistakes is part of growing.

I spent the last months before the 1986 show doing radio and TV interviews, creating an advertising campaign, which included a four-page spread, which we co-oped with our exhibitors in the *New York Times Sunday Magazine* in full color. Everything was good to go, I thought. Again, I asked Howard Rubinstein how the status of the labor contracts were. He said, "They're going great. They'll be resolved momentarily." The fact was that the new union agreements were not signed until 10 days prior to the opening, virtually giving the unions everything they had previously, with a few cosmetic changes for political speak only. In fact, one labor contract was still unresolved—the union cleaners, the ones who cleaned the hall every day and night. (We'll come back to this later.) To me, Howard Rubinstein, who never informed me, had just received strike two. Remember, in baseball, it's three strikes and you're out.

"Man of the Year"

As all this was happening, one of my favorite exhibitors, Robert Young (the largest art dealer to the design trades in New York) asked if I would accept the honor of being the Easter Seals' Man of the Year, at an event to be held at the Water Club on the East River in Manhattan.

I was flabbergasted. I knew it was honorary and a fundraiser, but it was still unbelievable, and I said to myself, *Oh, boy, this American Dream never ends.* Robert Young told me he would contact my friends and business associates, and all I needed to do was show up that night, since obviously I was very busy. The host of that evening was Bill Beutel, the famous New York *ABC News* anchor. Robert and Bill made all the arrangements for that evening.

The only real problem was Art Expo at the Javits Center opening was just two days away, so many of my exhibitors couldn't attend this event since they were frantically setting up the biggest show of their lives. In any event, the Water Club was packed with 175 of my personal and business friends. Robert Young surprised me by producing a special Art Expo poster for the event, followed by accolades galore. Pure adrenaline got me through this, for my head was spinning, and I was getting very little sleep. The next 48 hours were crucial.

Our exhibitors had started moving in. It was difficult to build their booths, since there was still construction material all over the convention center floors. I asked a contractor to get off my floor: "You know it's my floor since I paid for it." But they were still working. So as my general contractor was laying the carpet, building the exhibit booth over it, I instructed my staff of off-duty cops and firemen to push these materials off our floors and dump them anyplace they could find. They borrowed the union forklifts. The Javits union workers were on my side and helped move every piece of extraneous material so it wouldn't be seen.

It should be noted that the Javits Center staff that had been assigned to coordinate the opening had totally disappeared. They fled like Gaddafi's security guards at the time of his demise. It's true. You know how these guys disappear? They were not in the building. They were not on their radios. I couldn't reach them because they had panicked. They didn't think we could open the building. I'm telling you, it was unbelievable.

Apparently, they knew things about the status of the building that I didn't know—for example, the building had not yet received a Certificate of Occupancy—which is needed for any building to open in New York City. Plus, there were all these construction problems. By some miracle, we built all the booths in time for the move-in. There were 25 loading platforms built for our 500 exhibitors to unload their merchandise—until we discovered that only 3 were open! The rest were filled with construction material—bricks, lumber, steel beams, etc. We couldn't move them. So we had to work around them.

Did I forget to mention that there was another show in the building at the time, a little smaller one, but still a major show? Jay Thalheim was producing his International Fur Fair, and he also had to use those three loading platforms. In addition, there was a large demonstration of anti-fur people who were trying to close the building and block access to all of 11th Avenue.

Again, I was using my own men, cops and firemen, who were unbelievable. They helped disperse the crowd and put them on the sidewalk across the street. It was pure chaos. But as I've often said, *"Never give up, never give in."* I really needed Winston's help, at this time.

So we had a situation where some streets were closed off, and two shows were moving in through three loading platforms. Trucks were lined up on the 12th Avenue loading docks as well as double- and triple-parked on all the through streets, thus creating chaos in the city streets.

I arranged to allow us to unload our smaller panel trucks in the front of the building, which was a very wide drive-through made for all the buses and taxis that would be arriving to drop people off once the building opened. They told me it was against the law, but they would look the other way. I said, "Well, it's not against the law to tie up all the streets in Manhattan with large trucks, and it's not against the law to open without a Certificate of Occupancy, but it's against the law to have small trucks unload in the front when there's nobody else there?" They said okay, and we started to unload.

So we were doing the best we could. Of course, unloading those trucks seemed to take forever. We were working around the clock, many exhibitors were complaining because their art hadn't arrived at their booths, and they were upset and nervous. But at the end, all of the artwork was delivered and the building opened on time.

On the first day of unloading in the front, there were many art dealers who had smaller trucks. The head of security for the building—another man who was appointed by the governor's office and knew nothing about the tradeshow business and very little about security—told me that I could no longer have my trucks unload in the front. He said only the fur show could have its trucks, since my trucks were taking too long. I screamed, "What?" He said, "I'm sorry. That's the rule."

Remember, I had all these off-duty policemen and firemen with me, and they know every rule and regulation that existed in New York City. I thought for a few minutes. Then I grabbed two of my men. I walked to the entryway, the street that meets 11th Avenue to enter into the building, and I sat down in the front, with my two men, one on each side. The security supervisor followed me in, and I said, "If my trucks don't come in, nobody comes in." It was a 20-minute standoff. He didn't know what to do. I don't know how I got this idea. Amazingly, it came to my mind.

Eventually, a big black limo with an official flag on it tried to get into the driveway where I was sitting. The security guy went to meet the limo. He came back to me and said, "Okay, your trucks can come in." In the car was David Dinkins, who was, at the time, Manhattan Borough President (and later Mayor of NYC). The only reason he was coming was for a photo op, but that circumstance helped me reopen the unloading process for my exhibitors.

We had so many things going on. We had an exhibit where we lined the front lobby with beautiful sculptures that artists brought in from such faraway places as Israel, Italy, Poland, and all over the world. Everything was going on at one time. Would it all come together on time?

So as we were getting closer to filling our exhibitors' booths with merchandise and it seemed that we were going to open; some of the Javits management people showed up. They were high-fiving me. I said, "Where were you?" and they said they had a meeting. I was probably better off without them.

The next day was opening day: we were scheduled to open at 10:00 in the morning. At this point, Tom Galvin had been fired, and they brought in a new person, Mike Rogers, who was a Harvard-educated African-American who worked in the convention bureaucracy in Washington, D.C. He was a good man. I liked him. We worked very well together. He tried to be helpful. But he left after six months. Nobody with any self-respect could last under those bureaucratic circumstances, but during that time, Mike and I had to solve one major problem: there was still no contract with the cleaning union.

Tex Perrino (my first general contractor) was still president of his cleaners union. It was a city-controlled union. They wanted to bring in a state-controlled union, but he said, "Jerry, this is my livelihood. I need this work. You could hire me just for this one job, because they're going to screw you." So I said, "I don't know, Tex, but let's do this." Two days before the building was to open, I kept asking them, "Where are the cleaning crews? When are they coming? What's going on?" They said, "Don't worry about it."

So I walked through the building with Tex: I thought that would intimidate the Javits managers so they would give me an answer at least on the status of the cleaning crews, because if they saw me with Tex, they might think I would hire his union. But the Javits management wanted no part of it, for whatever political reasons.

As soon as Tex left, the Javits management brought me upstairs for an executive meeting, saying, "You can't do it. You can't bring in Tex. Trust us." (Those infamous words.) "There will be people there to clean your building. There's no problem. Don't worry about it. No problem." I said, "Okay." How could I fight City Hall, at that point? We were about to open this unbelievable building.

So I went home the night before the opening. I couldn't sleep. I was still concerned. So I went to the building. It was about 4:00 in the morning. They were supposed to be cleaning the building. Remember, when you bring in that much fragile material, there's straw and wood and glass and everything all over the place. It was a mess, every aisle. We had told the exhibitors, "Put your debris in the aisle, and we'll pick it up that night." But there I was, at 4AM, and there was nobody there to pick it up.

I called Mike Rogers. I woke him from a sound sleep. I said, "Mike, you've got to get over here now." He lived in Manhattan, at the time, in a hotel. He rushed over. I said, "Mike, what's going on here?" He couldn't give me an answer, so I told him, "Here's what we're going to do. You call everybody who works here, and everybody you know. I'll call everybody I know. We'll bring our home vacuum cleaners—the ones we use in our own living rooms, because the big commercial ones aren't available—and somehow, we'll get this place cleaned."

By 6:00 in the morning, we probably had about 50 or 60 humanoids with small vacuum cleaners and family-owned brooms, plus general laborers who we hired to pick up trash and dispose of everything. We worked until virtually the show doors opened.

It was not as clean as we would ever have accepted ordinarily, but it was clean enough, and there was so much excitement in the building that we got away with it. When the doors opened at 10:00, there were lines around the block of people who were interested in seeing the show—and the new building itself. As soon as all those multitudes of people entered the exhibit floor, you could see no more debris. You saw only the people who were excited about this Art Expo event.

Then who cleaned the show after the opening night? They hired a private cleaning company, like you hire to clean buildings in Manhattan. They hired as many cleaning people as they could, because their union contract was not signed during my show, so they paid them good money. *Bureaucracy at work.*

We wondered how they were able to open this building without a Certificate of Occupancy, which is required for all buildings in New York City. Apparently, the state had negotiated with the City of New York and found a compromise. The state agreed to contract 20 or so New York City fire trucks and firemen to be parked, 24/7, around the convention center, on 12th Avenue and some of the side streets. That way, in case of an emergency, they would be there on-hand, immediately. This lasted for more than six months.

That arrangement cost more than $6 million—and remember, this was 1986, so you have to recalculate it in present dollars to get the true cost! To add insult to injury, the state never paid this bill, with lawyers still arguing about whose responsibility it was. This is the way politics obviously works. The bottom line is the citizens of New York will have to pay for this outrageous mistake through their taxes. The state can't pay it now, because it has new debts. There's no conscience there, but that's another story.

Back to the first day of the show. Before the official opening at 9:00 AM, there was a press conference, not in my part of the hall, but by Jay Thalheim in his entrance, with some politicians, executives of the building, and Howard Rubinstein. He didn't tell me this either. Why did Jay Thalheim need a press conference? His was a show for the trade only, whereas mine was a public show. I could benefit from this media coverage, and my show was a hell of a lot more beautiful than his show. How many different-looking furs can you look at?

So I ran over to the other side of the building, I pushed myself in front of the cameras, and I grabbed the microphone and welcomed everyone to Art Expo. I was shaking with anger and frustration, but I realized that I should be proud of myself, because with all these obstacles, if you can make it here, you can make it anywhere—New York,

New York. The show opened, and it was a smashing success in every way. More than 100,000 people attended, a record that will never be broken, in my opinion, which, for an art event, is astonishing.

Those elite dealers who attended but didn't exhibit told me, "I can't believe you could bring this many people to view art." First time they said it was 1980. We were talking about 20,000 people then; now we had 5 times that number. Now we had this enormous crowd of enthusiastic people buying everything under the sun. This was 1986, and the economy had turned up, so everything, all the stars were aligned properly. Almost every one of my exhibitors couldn't thank me enough. Everybody did business. Everybody was happy.

It was one of those things that perhaps once in a lifetime, and here I was, totally exhausted without very much sleep, still living on my adrenaline high. I'll never forget, I sent my parents and my in-laws a limousine. They couldn't believe it, because they never could understand exactly what I ever did; it was beyond their comprehension. They lived very simple lives. They couldn't understand, *how did our son get to this position?* God Bless America.

Also, since Art Expo was the first show at the new Javits Center, we had planned to hold a great opening party. This is one of the things that my dear friend Howard Rubinstein was going to help us with. What he didn't tell me is that the city and state officials had postponed the party for three weeks, fearful that the building wasn't ready so it would be very bad publicity. Of course, they were dead wrong, since the aesthetics and the energy at the art fair made everything fabulous, and they got great publicity, but they still postponed the party without notifying me. I was very upset. This was my party. Have you ever heard of an opening party three weeks after the opening? Only in New York politics.

Sadly, Jacob Javits died only a few weeks before the opening of the exhibition center named after him. Then his wife Marion jumped ship, and said she was going to the official party, not to mine. Their oldest daughter, Carly, was with us all the way, as was her friend, Brooke Shields. They said, "This is the opening of the center. The party will go on." So we had some dignitaries and lesser politicians, we had some celebrities, and, of course, we had Carly, who gave the most heart-wrenching speech about her father and how he deserved this honor.

Our party was held opening night, and the greatest pleasure I got out of that party was strike three: I was probably the only person in this world to fire Howard Rubinstein. It was mostly ceremonial, since he received his money, but I couldn't take it that he said he was going to do these things for me, and not only didn't he do them, but he didn't advise me what was going on. Shame on you, Mr. Rubinstein.

The Javits Center held its grand opening party three weeks after we closed our show, though not with much fanfare. Whoever heard of an opening night party about a month after the opening? Only in the world of New York State politics. I refused to attend: I was much too busy for such phony nonsense. Apparently, in the political world, it's more important to protect the politicians than to protect the citizens.

You notice I rarely mention my partners, Phil and Irwin? The reason is that they disappeared: the show was so overwhelming that they got lost in the space. People always said about me that when the going gets tough, I can juggle so many different things at one time, and obviously this was a God-given skill that I never knew I had. My exhibitors would ask me, *why aren't you panicking? You look so calm.* Boy, I was panicking, but they couldn't see it.

Phil and Irwin did insist on being part of the discussion of the after-show bonuses I gave to our employees. I had learned, from prior years, to exaggerate what I wanted to reward employees, for which they could negotiate me down, and I would still be able to give my hard-working staff what I thought they deserved. Phil and Irwin never really appreciated the effort that went into such an event, and I was tired of trying to explain it to them, so I used my ingenuity to get what I needed. I listened to some of their abstract advice, but I no longer let myself get aggravated, for this success superseded all their nonsense. They knew the fair had gotten so big that their interference had to be limited.

When the show ended on Monday, April 7, 1986, and the largest art event ever was coming down, I stood there in awe and silence, with a sense of fulfillment that what I accomplished was beyond my wildest dreams. Because of the success of the 1986 NY show, when I announced our second Art Expo-California for October 16-19, 1986 at the Los Angeles Convention Center, we were able to pre-book 70% of the exhibit space in advance, which had never happened before. We also announced that the next Art Expo at the Jacob Javits Convention Center would be April 2–6, 1987. Little did I know that would be my last show.

Before I tell that story, I want to wrap up my involvement with the Javits. When the largest and most successful Art Expo-New York closed at the new internationally acclaimed Jacob Javits Convention Center, I received accolades from everyone. As was my usual custom, I stood in front of the entrance to say goodbye to my exhibitors, who greeted me with high-fives and "greatest show ever: can't wait until next year!"

Within hours, the great hall that had been filled with fabulous works of arts was just bare concrete. The Javits management was thrilled that they survived what they conceived as a potential disaster, because the building was not ready. Only with the help of my unbelievable staff at Art Expo could this happen; I will never forget them.

I took a few days off to unwind and get some sleep, and then I returned to my beautiful new office on 58th Street and 3rd Avenue, walking to work with my head up high. Despite all the roadblocks put up by the New York State bureaucracy, we succeeded beyond anybody's imagination. My good friend, John Reedy, who came to my aid when Spencer left, had returned to California to be with his new bride. We kept in touch, and John was to help me at our next Art Expo, which was held in Los Angeles in the fall. In the interim, I had to hire a new director of operations. His name was Jeff Reilly.

I had to put the finishing touches on our first Art Expo at Javits by evaluating what went wrong and what went right, paying our bills, and answering the mass correspondence that followed a great event.

In the great wisdom of the New York State Governor's office, a new president for the Jacob Javits Convention Center was appointed. His name was Fabian G. Palomino. Just who was this new professional to take over this major challenge? What were his qualifications? Fabian G.

Palomino turned out to be then-governor Mario Cuomo's former law school professor, now retired and looking for a new exciting position. Obviously, that experience made him well qualified to take over the next step in improving services and finding important trade shows in year two of the Javits Center, right?

At our first meeting, I had a list of suggestions that could improve the conditions. After all, everyone who starts something new knows the next year has to be better, and you have to learn from your experiences. So I presented my list, and within minutes, the good professor Palomino had his head down and was sleeping on his desk. I kid you not; you can't make up these things. He had a condition called narcolepsy, a chronic sleep disorder. So besides not being qualified, his medical condition proved to be an embarrassment. How would potential shows be encouraged by this sleeping giant?

The Jacob Javits Center has never lived up to its hype, that it would bring bigger and better conventions to New York City. Instead, its reputation for difficult unions, overpriced food, discourteous service, etc. still exists, despite all the promises. The shows in the building now are generally the same shows that existed at the closing of the New York Coliseum. I don't believe the Javits Center has ever made a profit, and the political structure that runs the building is still incapable of making good business decisions, since most decisions remain political.

Mike Rogers became the new president of the Javits Center when we opened our event, but he lasted in that job only a few months; then he got kicked upstairs to a job with Ogden Caterers, the food concessioner. He was thrilled to get out. At least it was a move upwards, not downwards like his predecessor, Tom Galvin.

Just recently, in the wisdom of New York State convention executives, the governor's office proposed a new convention center that would be attached to the Aqueduct Casino and Racetrack in Howard Beach, a sparsely populated section of the borough of Queens. The Malaysian gambling operators who are running the new casino claim they would open a giant state-of-the-art new convention center on this property. They obviously did this to obtain exclusive rights to gambling in New York.

My immediate response was this is the most ridiculous idea I've ever heard in my life. Firstly, it would be impossible for the Malaysian company to make any profit from this type of venture. No sensible business operation would ever even consider it. In addition, it goes against every basic principle of operating a successful convention center, which needs a great transportation hub, an area where people want to visit with fine hotels and restaurants, such as New Orleans, Las Vegas, Atlanta, Chicago, or San Francisco, the largest convention cities in America. Being in the middle of nowhere with no hotels and restaurants and no excitement is a no-no. People come to New York City because it's New York City: most attendees would never go to Howard Beach, even if they could find it.

It turned out I was right: the Malaysian conglomerate found some excuse to drop the project, but they kept the Aqueduct Casino. New York politics again at work. They never fail to amaze me.

And the Javits Center, which opened some 27 years ago, still hasn't fulfilled its promises to bring major hotels and restaurants, or to improve transportation to the West Side where the convention center is located. It's still an isolated island that was opened in 1986, but never met the expectations it promised. I remember there were no parking facilities built in or around the building, so how did they expect people driving in from surrounding states to easily attend these conventions? When will the bureaucrats ever ask the professionals of the convention business for their suggestions? The answer is probably never. We succeeded in spite of them.

JERRY'S LAW #14:
"Inspect what you expect."

Me with world-renown super-model, Carmen, just before the Javits Center opening in 1986.

Being presented the Easter Seals Man of the Year award by Bill Beutel (Anchor, *ABC News*, NY), 1986.

Wearable Art models at Art Expo, Texas, 1984.

12

Somebody Really Big
Wants to Buy Art Expo

After the 1986 show at the Javits Center closed, the time came very quickly that I had to return to work. A second Art Expo-California was almost sold out. I had to break in a new floor manager, Jeff Reilly, and start our West Coast advertising and public relations campaign.

On top of all the telephone calls and letters I received from congratulating participants from Art Expo, I was thoroughly enjoying my daily 10-minute walk to work. Life could not be better, I thought. Then, less than a month after closing Art Expo-New York 1986, I received a phone call that would change my life.

A man named Bob Edgell was on the phone. He said he was the vice-chairman of HBJ, Harcourt Brace Jovanovich, one of the largest publishers in the world, a Fortune 500 company. What did he want with me? He said he had seen Art Expo and was very impressed, and he just wanted to talk to me. It's always been my policy that I would meet with almost anyone, for you never know what might develop.

Bob wasted no time in telling me that HBJ was interested in acquiring Art Expo. He explained that he himself was a small businessman from Cleveland, Ohio: he had specialized in trade magazines, and his company had been acquired by HBJ. HBJ management respected him so much, they hired him as vice-chairman of the company. His job was to acquire new businesses that would increase their profitability. He told me he had just acquired a plastics magazine to add to the HBJ portfolio, and in reviewing the details of the company, he discovered they had been operating a small plastics industry tradeshow. Almost immediately, something became clear to him—that the plastics magazine provided 6% profit on sales, and the unknown tradeshow was producing 30%. Immediately, Bob heard bells and whistles.

This highly intelligent entrepreneur knew he had discovered gold. Large stock-exchange companies were never interested in buying tradeshows. They didn't represent the kind of business that fit into their large corporate pictures. But Bob immediately understood the potential, and after seeing Art Expo and all its attendees' sales and energy, he knew he wanted in. We met a few times, playing cat and mouse. On the surface, he showed very little real interest, but I knew from the first moment that he wanted to acquire my show.

I told my partners, who were obviously excited, but they were also overwhelmed. They never took direct part in any of the negotiation discussions. They knew this was a big deal and their chance to become wealthy. I allowed HBJ to do some due diligence, but Bob knew, from his own observations, how great the potential was. Coming from his own private trade magazine business, he knew there was only so much financial information forthcoming from our kind of operation. In other words, these are private businesses, so they're not required to have the same rigorous accounting records as a public company.

We played the negotiation game for the next three months, until he made a reasonable offer. I declined it, and he raised it to a level that I could accept. I don't remember how much he increased his offer; I only want to point out that we did have some discussions before I agreed to a price. Nobody ever offers their best price first. To me, coming from my poor roots, it was a lot of money.

The only proviso was we had to obtain tradeshow dates at the Javits Center and at the L.A. Coliseum for the next five years. This would guarantee HBJ the future dates it needed to justify this investment. The L.A. Convention Center quickly returned a five-year agreement, but after some delay, I received a letter from the Javits Center guaranteeing only four years. The Javits managers claimed there was a possibility in 1990 that the Democratic or Republican Convention might be held in New York City, so they couldn't guarantee that year for Art Expo. Obviously, HBJ said no deal unless it could obtain a five-year commitment.

So I had the idea to ask my union friends, *how can I get this done?* It was suggested that I arrange a meeting with the Javits' marketing director and the VP for labor negotiations to discuss a friendly way of working this out. Even in my somewhat naïve and moral mind, I realized this meant a cash payoff.

After some additional consultation with the union people, who knew how these things worked, I arranged lunch with these two gentlemen in a small, quiet Italian restaurant on the West Side of Manhattan. In my hand was a brown paper bag. In the brown paper bag was $7,000 in crisp $100 bills. There was no reason for this number; it was just a number in my mind. Mentally, I couldn't get myself to spend more than this. Why not $5,000? Why $7,000? Why not $10,000? I figured they might really want $10,000, but maybe they would take $7,000. After all, I didn't have a lot of money growing up, so it seemed like a fortune to me.

Nobody told me outright that I should bring cash; I just picked it up from my conversations with the union guys. They told me, *you have lunch with them, you be friendly with them, and they'll understand.* That's baloney. I'm not stupid. Why else would they want to have a lunch in a private place? The union guys told me to bring a brown paper bag. I knew there were payoffs, but I wasn't part of that world. It was a new world to me, but you'll be surprised at what eventually happened.

We had a delightful lunch, and I pleaded my case to these gentlemen. I left the bag on the seat without saying one single word. I wasn't worried that they wouldn't notice the bag, or that it might be left on the seat and the busboy would find it. But I was worried that they would take the bag and just ignore me. After all, there would be no way for me to get my money back: I would have no evidence and no recourse.

But there is honor among thieves, as the saying goes. That's true: in fact, there's more honor among thieves than among politicians. It wasn't easy for me to partake in this type of financial transaction. Strangely, I was a very tough businessman with a high moral compass, and after weighing the pros and cons, it became clear to me that a few bureaucrats and political hacks shouldn't stop me from benefiting from all my hard work. It just wasn't fair. I believed if there was a God, he—or she—would forgive me.

So I went to lunch, I left the bag, and the bag disappeared. Within four days, I received a letter that committed to five years of convention dates, which allowed me to move ahead with the sale of Art Expo, and, once again, live my American Dream.

Then a strange thing happened. This was not the end of this transaction. About two weeks after I had delivered the brown paper bag, I got a call from the VP of labor negotiations, who suggested we meet again to have lunch, just to talk, at the same restaurant. We met, had a pleasant lunch, discussed generalities, and he left, leaving a brown paper bag on the seat next to me. I opened it. I found the same $7,000, in $100 bills, now back in my possession. It was a miracle. How was I the benefactor? Did these gentlemen find religion? Did they think I was just a nice guy and they wanted to return my money? Of course, that was not the reason.

I believe that my reputation of fighting hard for good causes at the Javits Center and being a good citizen in the building led them to eventually believe that perhaps it was a setup. Could these bills have been marked? Of course, none of this was true, but perhaps, as I've said before, if you live long enough, justice will prevail. How about that? I got my money back!

Within a few years, both men resigned their positions at Javits. I guess they were found out for whatever other shenanigans they partook in. Nobody ever gets fired in these bureaucracies. They just resign with a big pension. Nothing has really changed. I read every day in the paper about bureaucrats and politicians being charged for crimes, resigning with large pensions, with hardly ever a conviction. Sadly, the crimes get bigger, the convictions still don't exist, but that's another book. As Yogi Berra once said, *It ain't over 'til it's over.*

So HBJ and Art Expo settled on a number and turned the transaction over to our attorneys. HBJ's main office was in San Diego, but they used an internationally acclaimed major Chicago law firm. Art Expo used a mid-sized New York law firm headed by a friend of mine, Marc Weitzen. Marc's firm had hired my daughter Michelle out of law school into a very fine position. Marc and I became friendly, and I realized that Marc's primary client was Carl Icahn. That's right, the man who's known for multi-billion-dollar, multinational acquisitions. Carl and I had something else in common: we were both graduates of Far Rockaway High School, and only two years apart, so we were in school at the same time, though I didn't know him.

Anyway, HBJ's law firm negotiated every little detail of the agreement to the nth degree, dragging out the final resolution. Perhaps that's necessary, or perhaps it's just a way for large law firms to make more money. This relatively small client, Art Expo, was very anxious that this sale would close promptly. I was pushing Marc to make this happen, and Carl Icahn was pushing for his projects. Guess who got first option?

Then what happened was that HBJ got involved in a $250 million acquisition of CBS Books and threatened to cancel, or at least postpone, my small transaction. At the same time, HBJ received an unfriendly takeover threat from Robert Maxwell, CEO of the English publishing firm, Macmillan. This would seem like a very healthy merger between two international publishing companies, but that was not the case.

HBJ's CEO, William Jovanovich, was an American of Czech descent and a Catholic. Robert Maxwell was an Englishman of Czech descent and a Jew. For some reason, they hated each other. So HBJ's Board of Directors would never let this acquisition happen, and under William Jovanovich's instructions, HBJ took out a $3 billion loan. Remember when this was: this was 1986. That was a lot of money: a $3 billion loan from the Bank of Boston, which led to a $30-a-share cash dividend to its stockholders (at the time, the stock was selling for $30). This doubled the value of the shares.

I had previously been offered a larger sale price if I would take stock, but my gut was to take cash, so I had refused that offer. Since we had already completed our agreement, this option was off the table, but in hindsight, the deal would have been worth twice what I received: $30 per share would have been worth $60. The poison pill chased Macmillan away, but it also put HBJ in an impossible financial situation. Remember, HBJ had to start paying off that debt service, and the $3 billion loan was distributed to the stockholders—which was not a good business plan, to say the least. But the CBS book deal went through, and with much anxiety, so did Art Expo.

I remember I kept pushing Marc, and for some odd reason, we got our money prior to the CBS book deal closing. I sat in Marc's office for more than four hours, waiting for the acknowledgement from my bank that the cash transfer was received, again remembering Yogi

Berra's *it ain't over 'til it's over.* The check was received September 17, 1986, one day prior to my 53rd birthday. What a special gift. My financial future was now secured.

This was also an important date because Art Expo-California was less than three weeks away, and we were able to announce to the world the sale to HBJ, and that I would remain the director of both shows for the foreseeable future. We immediately sent a letter advising the world and the exhibitors, many of whom were unhappy about new owners yet very excited about my personal success. No one likes change. They didn't know what a big corporation would offer them.

My partners received their checks through their banks, but they were not through with me yet. Even I can't believe how they reacted. Not a thank-you, not a bottle of champagne, nothing. But when I received Marc's attorney bill for $56,560, of which $2,550 was for expenses, my new wealthy partners complained and refused to pay their full share.

My partners claimed that since I had received additional money, my legal fee should be $5,000 higher. Their justification was that I was receiving additional money under my new contract as director, plus my bonus due for the two shows from my original agreement, plus the money I got as a consultant to the new owners—all of that additional money should be deducted from their percentage of the legal bill. It was obvious, in the HBJ contract, that there would be no deal unless GL would agree to stay on as director. After all, Harcourt Brace had no experience running Art Expo. This is normal in the world of business, but my partners wanted to get an extra $5,000 out of me. Do you believe that? That was my "thank you."

Marc was always very calm—after all, he had to deal with people like Carl Icahn, who was a high-pressure genius. But in this case, even he got terribly annoyed at my partners. I might have paid the $5,000, but Marc was so angry, he said to me, "You're not paying this." He got tough with them and wrote them a nasty letter. And they buckled and paid their share. Even though I had made them very wealthy, they only saw things in this small way. I was glad I was now free of them and on my own to pursue the rest of my life. I never begrudged them their share, and that was obviously the best $8,000 investment they will ever make.

On my birthday, September 18th, I sent a letter to the whole art world announcing the acquisition and assuring everyone that the staff would remain; we would act as an independent division of Harcourt Brace, and we would all look forward to continuing our successes together. HBJ also sent out numerous press releases to the world, and we were all ready to move forward.

Of course, within a few months, HBJ closed my beautiful new 58th Street office and moved me to a space in its New York office on 47th Street and 3rdAvenue. My new office wasn't too bad, but it wasn't the same. Bob Edgell also maintained an office there, and we saw each other very often. He took me to visit various HBJ locations in the area, and the more time I spent with him, the more I liked him. On every visit, he took time to personally greet member of his staff. He made them feel like they were equals, something I always tried to maintain in my dealings with my staff and the unions. We worked on Art Expo-California together. We discussed the next Art Expo-New York in '87, and we became close friends. He was about my age. We shared the same principles, the same hard work that led to our mutual successes.

Then things began to happen that affected Bob's life and changed our relationship. The ridiculous $3 billion that HBJ had borrowed and declared a cash dividend created the demise of this company. HBJ's management realized they had to reduce their enormous debt, so they put up some of their major assets for sale.

First, they sold Sea World, which had two locations, in San Antonio and Orlando. This was their cash cow, as they called it, for $900 million.

Next to go was the newly acquired CBS book division, into which they had incorporated the trade magazine and tradeshow division that Bob Edgell was now heading. They sold CBS books for $300 million, to a company called Goldman Sachs. Are you beginning to get the picture? They sold it to an investment bank that was looking to turn a quick profit.

Goldman Sachs quickly hired Bob Edgell to head up this company and renamed it Edgell Communications Company, which made Bob feel really wanted. He was angered with the HBJ Board for squandering the $3 billion loan that basically bankrupted the company. He now felt he was in control of his own destiny. Goldman Sachs had promised him a free hand in expanding and also controlling this operation, but this turned out to be a big lie.

In the meantime, my consulting contract ran only through October of 1987, so Bob and I were negotiating to do a joint venture, where Edgell Communications and I would work on projects together. Edgell Communications would finance them, and I would develop them, and we'd be partners. Our joint venture agreement was initialed, and I was excited, not knowing what the Goldman Sachs people had in mind. They were doing things to Bob that he didn't even know about. They were cutting his authority, insisting that Edgell Communications pay them a 13% interest on the Goldman Sachs investment yearly before they made any other expenditures. In those days, interest rates were higher, but still. Goldman had made an investment of $300 million, so 13% interest was substantial.

Goldman's managers were only interested in making a profit; they had no long-term interest in the company. They took Bob Edgell's prestigious name and abused it, which hurt this very good man. Of course, this business approach was impossible for Bob to live with. They actually told him if he didn't like it, he could leave. When they threatened to change the name of the company, he left on his terms. He was a proud and wonderful man, and a good friend, and he was humiliated by these investment bankers who couldn't hold a candle to him, and who were using other people's money.

That was the beginning of a new era that I call the downfall of vintage individualism, of entrepreneurs who created businesses that had built this country into the most successful period since the Industrial Revolution. Bob Edgell left Goldman Sachs and moved out of New York, and I didn't hear from him again. In his mind, this proud man was humiliated in the publishing world and went into hibernation. More of his story later on.

In October of 1987, I finished as director of Art Expo as agreed on in my contract, although HBJ wanted me to agree to a three-year consulting arrangement. However, I knew in my heart of hearts that the corporate world would begin to change the way things were done and that it would be a very disappointing place for me to work. I could have obtained a 3-year contract and most probably been bought out: that was probably the financially smarter thing to do, because big companies always want to get rid of the original owner eventually. But my gut told me to do my duty and move on with my life.

Art Expo had been a success from the start, and the business continued growing every year from 1979 to 1985. Throughout that time, we were in the New York Coliseum. The show grew from 275 booths to almost 1,000 booths—which is tremendous growth, especially in the art world.

As you know, in 1986, Art Expo was the first show in the brand-new Javits Center, which was designed by world-renowned architect I.M. Pei. I was working harder than I could ever have imagined. A new building, new unions, new challenges. But it was so exciting and motivating. I was running a successful business in a world that I had only just discovered, but which, in that short time, I had become a very important part of. There was no time in those nine years to slow down. I was the Director of the largest art fair in the world.

The momentum, coupled with my desire to live the American Dream, and most important (in hindsight) the fact that I had become an important, well-known person in that world was intoxicating. Everybody knew me. I couldn't walk down West Broadway in Soho—which in those days was where all the fine galleries were located—without everyone saying hello to me or talking about me. Of course, today the art world has moved on, and I don't know how many people would recognize me or even know who I am, but in those days, it was beyond my wildest imagination.

For the most part, I loved the celebrity, although there were a few exceptions. I always kept my relationships with the dealers at arm's length. I was friendly, but I didn't socialize with them. For one thing, there were too many other things going on: I wasn't just the front man, I was also the hands-on working person running the day-to-day business operation. I had to balance the celebrity of the art world with the business world.

When I ran Art Expo, I had my heart and soul in the decision-making process: it was part of my being. I had been doing it for nine years, and I seemed to leave every type of work I did after nine years. Plus, I wanted to rid myself of my two unappreciative, envious partners. I did move on to do other projects, but Art Expo was the most important business thing in my life. But I'm moving ahead of the story...

So after the sale to HBJ, I stayed on as director for only one year. After that, Maura Haverly became the director. Spencer Reese would have gotten the job, but he had left (as mentioned) to work for one of our exhibitors. Maura had been our artistic director—and she was indeed the "artistic" type. I loved Maura, but not all the time, for several reasons. One was that she focused on foreign exhibitors who were important to her, and she often overlooked the business aspect. She thought like a museum curator, not understanding that even the fine-art galleries wanted to know how we could help them make money. Also, she always came in late and left early, even though I warned her a thousand times. Nevertheless, I kept her, and she did some very good things for Art Expo. Obviously, my bark was always bigger than my bite, and my employees knew it.

Unfortunately, Maura didn't have the business acumen or work ethic to run the whole show: she didn't know or care about the administrative details. She had the same flaw that many salespeople have: they think they're the most important to the success of an endeavor. But they're not; they're just part and parcel of the whole package. So Maura didn't last very long as director for the new Art Expo owners.

I didn't really keep track of Art Expo after I left; I moved on to other ventures. I do know that Art Expo still lives on, and that it was sold and resold at least five times and now only exists in New York. The new owners tried an Australia-Art Expo show, but that was a dismal failure. They've since cancelled the California show, and now they present a much smaller inconsequential version in New York, where it was once the greatest art show on earth. I never went back to visit until 2008.

It may sound inconceivable, but for 20 years after I sold Art Expo, I never returned to the art fair that made me famous as well as financially secure. Then in 2008, I decided to organize a small reunion with a few of my management personnel who were with me those special years, namely Judy Brightwater, Spencer Reese, and Jim Carney, an off-duty fireman who was in charge of security (and who did everything). We were all excited about getting together again. Who knows how many exhibitors I would be remembered by, or if the new show management would know who the heck I was, since there had been so many mergers and acquisitions within this show? But, for some reason, I decided this was the time.

First, I checked the Art Expo website to verify the dates of that year's show. In browsing the website, I came across an announcement of a new special feature called the Art Expo Hall of Fame. Exhibitors plus artists plus the art world personalities who were instrumental in the success of this fair—the biggest and most successful one in the world—were to be acknowledged. As I browsed the names of those being honored, almost all of whom were personally known to me, I noticed there was one special omission: Gerald Leberfeld, the founder and director. Could this be an oversight? Could they have thought I was deceased, or were they unable to locate me, which is hard to believe, since I'm listed in the *White Pages,* at the same address where I've lived since 1985.

The story gets even more interesting, because Phil, one of my original investing partners, was listed as the founder of Art Expo! The same Phil who was prosecuted for art fraud and then spent a few years in prison. The same Phil who was prominently mentioned in a book entitled *The Great Dali Art Fraud and Other Deceptions.* He sold phony Dalis, Miros, Picassos with forged signatures. He knew they were fakes, but he needed the action, I guess, and when I previously had heard a rumor about it, I told him, "Phil, you can't do this. If you do, you'll jeopardize the whole art world." But he continued doing it; he said, "I have certificates of authenticity on everything. I would never [sell fakes]." He lied. So now this guy was being honored in the Art Expo Hall of Fame. Obviously, the Hall of Fame was a public relations idea to bring more attendees to the fair. This idea of honoring Phil, however, could have reaped the opposite result of dishonoring the fair.

So I contacted the VP who was in charge of Art Expo at the time, who claimed he was unaware of the situation, and he quickly sent me a letter offering to make me part of the Hall of Fame. I declined, with the reason that honoring Phil would put this wonderful project in jeopardy, and my involvement could be considered guilt by association. The end result was Phil was disinvited, though I was still not willing to be part of this program.

It should be noted that this was the first and last time this so-called important Hall of Fame was utilized at Art Expo. I still visited the fair that year and asked my staff that was celebrating with me to meet me at the show management office, where we were offered comp tickets to the event.

It was an eerie feeling to return to Art Expo after all these years, and entering the show's management office in the Javits Center lobby, I bumped into the VP who had claimed little knowledge of how Art Expo originated. He spotted me first and jumped up with a big handshake and hug saying, "Jerry, what a pleasure to meet you. I've admired your work since you first started the show." God's truth, that's what he said to me.

It's a funny thing how, all of a sudden, he remembered me. Anyway, I met up with the rest of my staff. We walked the show, and a great number of people from all over the world remembered us, and we had a grand old time. We went off to dinner and celebrated our fond memories.

The main reason I tell this story is because I believe that history should be in writing. After all I went through to build this great fair, someone was ready to change historical facts, perhaps innocently, but the truth should always prevail.

JERRY'S LAW #14: "Inspect what you expect."

So whatever happened to Bob Edgell? This great man seemed to disappear off the face of the earth, and, sadly, that's what happened in 1995. I found out, to my dismay, that Bob had committed suicide. He was living with his wife in Longboat Key, Florida, and he had jumped to his death from the seventh-floor terrace. He had invited his wife's best friend to spend New Year's evening and day with them, planning his demise and not wanting her to be alone.

His death sent shockwaves through the publishing industry. This still-beloved individual had taken his life, and we all knew he had so much more to give. He was only about 60 years old.

Why did he take his life? It's my strong feeling that this proud man, who had a good marriage and financial security, had so much pride that his rejection by Goldman Sachs and his embarrassment by the corporate world made him feel a failure who didn't have the strength to live with his depression.

Six months after Bob died, a memorial service was held at St. Bart's on Park Avenue in Manhattan. This enormous, world-renowned church was filled with top executives from the international publishing community. Everyone wanted to pay their last respects. Like many in the room, I felt cheated that a man that we grew to trust and respect was taken from our lives and could never be replaced.

There were many eulogies, including from the former CEO of HBJ, William Jovanovich. HBJ is now no longer in business: it went bankrupt because of the actions taken by this one man, who used his $1\text{-}1/2$ % ownership of the shares in a great company to destroy it because of his personal prejudices.

The most unbelievable eulogy was delivered by Bob's oldest son. He looked Jovanovich in the eye and said, "The corporate world killed my father." Everyone in the room was shocked and silent, but they knew exactly what he meant. Personally, I long for people in my life who I respect personally, and I miss them, and I want to hang out with them and sit on my stoop. So please sit on my stoop with me, Bob Edgell. This was a man I will never forget, and I will always miss him.

Bob Edgell's suicide makes me reflect on two other men I admired in my life who also took their lives. Remember Thomas Galvin, who was fired as president of the Javits Center just a few weeks prior to the opening? He had done an outstanding job in spite of all the political roadblocks placed before him. His reward was to be humiliated by being fired, without being able to enjoy the rewards of his tremendous efforts. Some years later, he jumped to his death from his office window in a high-rise building in the Times Square area. Like Bob Edgell, Tom also had a very good marriage and was financially secure. I credit this suicide to the gutless New York political world.

The third man I admired who also took his own life was Robert Young, who had organized making me Easter Seals' Man of the Year. In addition to operating a highly successful art showroom in the D&D Building in Manhattan, he was extremely handsome and financially secure. During a vacation, his beautiful 21-year-old daughter had become paralyzed from an accident while diving off the rocks of the Australian coast. He blamed himself, even though he wasn't there, and this hardship was the main catalyst in ending his marriage.

So what, if anything, was the common thread causing these three accomplished human beings to take their own lives? In my mind, the fault was mainly from them sitting on top of their individual worlds and then falling to a place they didn't want to be, blaming themselves. I think this depression is harder to deal with for people who have been successful than for people who are poor to begin with who are better able to deal with disappointment since they live with it all the time.

People reading these comments might say that I'm a person who praises most of those around me. But those who know me best know that I'm many times overly critical and cynical, and my expectations for myself and other people are probably excessively high. My praise of these three gentlemen is more the exception to my rule. If there is an afterlife, these are the three men I want to sit with on my stoop in the sky. That may be a little corny, but it's how I truly feel.

13

Remembering the Special People and Places of My Years as Art Expo Director

During my nine years as Director of Art Expo, I had a rule of thumb that I would see *anybody* and *everybody* who wanted to see me. I had learned from my days as a Fuller Brush salesman that you don't choose the houses you make sales calls on; you see everybody since you never know what's going to happen. This opened the door for many wonderful experiences and people to come into my life, which I reflect fondly upon today.

The Biggest Poster Dealer in the World

One day, a man named Jacques Athias walked in to my Madison Avenue office. He worked in the French library system but was also a part-time dealer of French posters. He pitched this idea that he'd like to try to sell French posters in America. Considering much of the contemporary art and abstract art looked pretty much the same, I thought it might be a good idea to mix it up. The French posters—which were advertising posters from the '20s, '30s, and later—were very historically interesting: So, he exhibited at Art Expo and later became the biggest French poster dealer in the world.

The Art Expo Documentary Maker

Another person who walked into my office one day was Alan

Epstein, who seemed a bit strange and off the wall. A graduate of Yale University, he had a video camera, and he told me he wanted to be the official documentary maker for Art Expo. I didn't need or want a documentary maker because I didn't see any real practical benefits of having one. But he persisted, so I gave him access to the show, and he scratched out a living doing some PR projects for some of the exhibitors.

The main thing about Alan was that he never gave up. As Winston Churchill said, *Never give up. Never give in.* I admired this about Alan. He knew what he wanted to do, and he eventually traveled to the international art show in Basel, Switzerland, which was the largest and most important art fair in the world. He gained entry to that show because he had been part of Art Expo, and people knew him. He did some wonderful fine-art documentaries.

The most amazing thing about Alan was that he could get into almost any after-party or event. Because there was a video camera on his assistant's shoulder, nobody checked anything; they just waved him in. He'd often invite me along, but I'd tell him I was going home to see my family. Part of what I learned from him is that if you want to get into someplace, just carry a video camera, because it makes you look like you're from the press. *What security?*

Alan was an interesting guy, who sadly died young of cancer, but I'll never forget him. He did a special video for me, and every time I look at it, I break into tears. He had filmed close-ups of some of the work at Art Expo 1983 and set it to the John Lennon song *Imagine*. He had matched each phrase or word in the song to a work of art at the show. It was beautifully done. He was a genius.

He never became famous, but his mother—his Jewish mother—was so proud of Alan, because he had graduated Yale and because of the success of his art documentaries. She wasn't so proud of the fact that Alan had smoked marijuana (and who knows what else?)—as did many of the young people who grew up during the 1960s and the Vietnam War, which was very sad, because I believe that affected their futures. She came to me and said to me years later, "Jerry, you made me the happiest woman in the world, because I see my son actually happy and accomplishing something."

I tell that story, since, in my own little way, I helped Alan believe in himself and make his mark in the art world he truly loved.

A few years ago, I got a phone call from a young woman who asked me, "Are you Jerry Leberfeld? Are you from Art Expo?" And when I said yes, she said, "I'm Alan Epstein's daughter." She asked me to tell her about her father because he had died when she was a very young child. I was happy to tell her whatever I could about her father, since Alan was my favorite type of individual—unique.

The Basel Art Fair

I met other wonderful people during my many visits to Switzerland for the Basel Art Fair. I went every year for eight straight years. The purpose of going was to find European exhibitors that would exhibit at Art Expo and raise the artistic and interest level. The early days were terribly difficult. The art world is elitist, so nobody wanted to have much to do with me, since they didn't know who I was, but I continued to go, and eventually, I got to know many of these important international art dealers.

JERRY'S LAW #4:
"Start at the top and work your way up."

The airport for Basel, Switzerland, is actually in France, since Basel borders Germany and France. In one little corner you can walk in all three countries. That's why there are so many different languages and customs in Switzerland.

Basel is a very beautiful old city. One part is modern, where the convention center was, but I stayed at a very famous old-world hotel called the Drei Konig (Three Kings), in the old quarter.

One year, I went to FIAC (a French acronym that translates to the French International Contemporary Art Fair), another very European art fair in Paris, but I discovered that all the same dealers were at Basel. So I didn't meet anybody new at FIAC.

It was very difficult to get the European dealers to come to Art Expo because they didn't want to pay until they showed up, and I couldn't risk having an open space at the show in case they decided not to come.

I had to convince them to give me 50% down, which was something they never did for the European fairs, and I finally did, after many years of persuading.

JERRY'S LAW #6:
"When forced to compromise, ask for more."

Even though I had never been to Europe before on business, I wasn't nervous or anxious or apprehensive about going; instead, I was excited about meeting people. Plus, most European art dealers and exhibitors spoke English.

The Basel Fair was held during a week of a big German holiday. That's why they hold it in June, because the Germans were the biggest art collectors, and probably had the most money in those days, like they do today, of all the Europeans. I'll never forget this fact about these European exhibitors. I always dressed well, since I knew it was important, especially in Europe, to dress in a suit and a tie, double-breasted, whatever it was that made me look somewhat European.

At one of the fairs, an Italian art dealer was looking at my shoes. "What are you looking at my shoes for?" I asked. He said, "I never talk to anybody if I don't like the way the way their shoes look. If you don't shine your shoes, if you don't have expensive shoes, you'll never buy art from me." He was a snob, but I enjoyed his attitude. He said, "You've got to look expensive to buy expensive."

A few of my Art Expo exhibitors took space at Basel so we visited them first to get guidance. Edmund Newman was one of those people and a good friend of mine. He was an Englishman who was a well-respected French-art dealer—he represented French artists—and he lived in Paris, London, and New York. So he said, "Jerry, let me take you to this wonderful Italian restaurant." Switzerland is not noted for their food, but this place everybody knew, and if you didn't make a reservation for Art Week at least a year in advance, you couldn't get in. It was special, as was Edmund.

So we got in, and there were about ten of us. He always reserved a large table, and Edmund introduced me to the head waiter, who asked me, "Where are you from?" I said, "I'm from New York," and he breaks out in this song, *"I love New York in June, how about you?"* I hesitated for a second and then I jumped in and sang, *"I love a Gershwin tune, how about you?"* And for eight years, every time I walked into that restaurant, as soon as this man saw me, he started singing that song, and I answered. Everything in the place stopped and then everyone applauded. It was something special.

I also remember that everything we ordered was cooked at the table, on little portable stoves. It was a very interesting, wonderful restaurant. If it's still there, I probably still couldn't get in, but if the head waiter was there, we would sing, for sure.

So the Basel Art Fair was a very important show. Once people became familiar with me, I was treated like a king, because I was the director—or *Il Direttore,* as they would say in Europe—of a New York international art fair. Even though I wasn't up to their standards (by their definition), Europeans always respected the title, so they respected me, too. And over the years, I did pick up many great exhibitors.

My Close Friend, Jacques

I didn't become close friends with too many of my exhibitors. I knew them all, but I kept an arm's length. My way of doing business was not to get too close to people because I believed that would not be good for business, since then there would be favors involved. I spoke to everybody, though, and everybody knew me.

And I did make a few close friends. One was Jacques Carpentier, who was one of the first international dealers to exhibit with me: he had a gallery in Paris, on rue du Bac. He was a fine-art dealer, and he had a wonderful family, but the most interesting thing about Jacques (to me) was that he was a Holocaust survivor, as is my wife, Aviva. His family were important antique dealers, and when the Germans marched into France and occupied Paris, his family and a group of their Jewish friends took their very young children and shipped them off to Switzerland to an orphanage. They knew instinctively that their lives were in danger.

So he grew up in an orphanage in Switzerland, and as the years went by, the parent were killed, died, or disappeared. The orphanage closed: there was no more money coming in from France. Young kids were getting older. They ran the orphanage—in a way, they lived there—and they survived. They became a gang of young teenagers, who could only survive by stealing food, goods, money, whatever they had to do, which was amazing. These were very fine people, but when you have to survive, you survive.

Jacques came back to Paris when the war ended and became quite well known and influential in the French art scene. He became a close friend, and I always looked forward to him coming to Art Expo; unfortunately, one year, his sales manager told me he had just died suddenly of a heart attack. We cried together. I had lost a good friend.

Meeting Famous Artists

During my years at Art Expo, I also had the great opportunity to meet many famous artists. I met Salvador Dali, who was in the latter part of his life (he died a few years later, in 1989, at age 84), but he did roam around the Art Expo floor in his own strange way. He still had the big moustache, and it was interesting talking to him, although he made very little sense. He talked about things that weren't relevant to anything that was going on around us, and our conversations were very short, since he always kept moving. I don't know if he ever made sense. He was surrealistic; he was one of his paintings.

Erté was also at the show. He didn't speak much at all, so I didn't really get to know him, but it was nice meeting him. Like Dali, Erté was also in his late 80s or early 90s: those guys just worked forever.

I met Andy Warhol, who was a fascinating character. He created the Brooklyn Bridge 100-year-anniversary poster for Art Expo 1983. As I mentioned earlier, Warhol asked me if I wanted a painting of me in the double image, which he offered to do for $25,000. I thought that was atrociously expensive, so I passed on his offer. Little did I know that his paintings sell for millions of dollars now. At the time, though, I wasn't that interested in a portrait of myself. I was never so egotistical that I wanted to see myself once, let alone twice.

I don't think he was actively trying to commission portraits of just anyone, but he never stopped working, so I assume he did that type of portrait for other people. He didn't go knocking on doors, but if he met people who had the money to commission a painting by him, he would do it. He never met money he didn't like. He came to the show every day: he loved to be with people. He enjoyed his fame. He died only a few years later, suddenly, still a relatively young man: he was only 58 years old.

R. C. Gorman, an American-Indian artist who lived in Taos, New Mexico, attended the show. He's known mostly for his paintings and sculptures of oversized Indian women: the most important thing for an artist is to be recognizable, because if people can't immediately identify a piece of art by the artist who created it, then it's more difficult to make it really big in the art world. Gorman was great technically, and his images were recognizable.

He yearly held a major party during the Santa Fe Indian Arts Festival, and he invited me, together with a couple of women Native American art dealers who exhibited at my show. It was a great time to be there, since all the great American-Indian artists were presenting their work; plus, I had another reason to go, because these two women and I were planning to petition him to let us distribute limited editions of his sculptures. So I went to the party, but Gorman said no to our idea, since he'd had a bad experience in the recent past: some San Francisco dealer he knew had taken some very large sculptures of his to sell, but he had never paid Gorman, so he didn't want to be bothered. It was bad timing for us.

The party was great, though. I drank a lot, and I met a Native American woman who started talking me up; she said there was a full moon that night and that she was going to the desert to dance nude at the full moon, which would be around midnight. And she asked if I would like to go along with her.

I have to admit that was a unique invitation, and I did consider it. But the two women I went with—who knew I was married and were also married—dragged me away. So I never had the experience of dancing nude at the full moon. Still, I did have the experience of the conversation, which was curious because the woman who invited me explained that my life would change if I did this nude dance with her at the full moon. I'll never know how my life might have changed....

I also met Peter Max, which is a story I already told. And Yaacov Agam, an internationally acclaimed Israeli artist, whose life story was very interesting. During World War II, when the Germans occupied Paris, Agam was an orphan who lived on the streets and survived by stealing food and eating from garbage cans. Later, by the time I met him, he was a man of extreme wealth, but that didn't change the way he handled himself. Whenever anyone talked to him, he always seemed like he was desperately trying to sell something all the time. He didn't need the money. I think this behavior was due to the fact that he had come from such poverty. He was an interesting man, and he did wonderful work.

Richard Avedon was a world-famous photographer who also exhibited at Art Expo. In 1958, he had photographed Marilyn Monroe in costumes of famous movie stars of the past—such as Theda Bara, Clara Bow, Jean Harlow, and Lillian Russell—and he had made a series of hand-signed color posters. I have the series, and it's one of my prized possessions. (If any of my heirs are reading this chapter, *don't give these posters away!* I think they have some real value!)

Victor Vasarely was at my show to celebrate his 80th birthday, which was something special. He was a world-renowned artist with style and a heart of gold.

LeRoy Neiman was at every Art Expo: like Agam, Neiman was another guy who would try to sell you anything at any time. This was about their egos, I guess, because they were wealthy people. He just passed on, at age 89, as a famous artist and great celebrity—being able to combine his talents.

And there were many more, too many to mention. Perhaps in my next book.

Making Artwork Available to a New Generation of Art Buyers

The reason famous artists were at Art Expo is because they were willing to produce limited-edition pieces and other pieces that were not one-of-a-kind works of art that would be prohibitively expensive for our show. They knew Art Expo was the canvas that made artwork available to a new generation of art buyers.

For example, Salvador Dali's dealers were selling limited-edition lithographs, which were much less expensive than an original, and were affordable to the people who came to buy at Art Expo. Many of our buyers were nouveau-riche, including many presidents of major corporations and their wives, who bought art for their homes and their offices. Corporate art was really being developed at that time, and we were at the forefront of developing this trend. These were collectors who didn't exist before. They were going through the learning curve and their tastes really matured at Art Expo. Many developed into major collectors who now visit and buy from important New York galleries. For example, one person who came every year was from the family that owned the Alexander's department stores (which went out of business: in fact, the family sold off its real estate properties, which were worth more than the department stores).

Meeting Celebrity Artists

I met many celebrity artists. These were people who were famous in some other field, usually entertainment, but they wanted to be visual artists, too, so they did signed and numbered limited-edition lithographs. Dealers don't want to sell only one painting by an artist; they wanted to be able to sell many pieces so they can make some money. Then, if the artist's work was accepted by the public, there might be a gallery that would want to host a one-person show, which did happen often. But all of the celebrity artists started by doing a lithograph— except for Tony Bennett, who preferred original painting. He was eclectic, and he built a large inventory of originals over many years.

I met Donna Summer, the queen of disco, who passed away in 2012; it was her last dance. She did a lithograph. It was contemporary art, abstract. She was a good artist, not great, but okay. She was a wonderful person, very friendly and not at all full of herself: in fact, she came to one of our after-parties, sang, and socialized with everyone.

Probably the most interesting person I met was Pavarotti. His agent came to me and said, "Luciano has produced some art that he wants to sell. He wants to be a visual artist; what do you think?" I said, "It's alright with me." Then his dealer said, "Luciano wants to come to the show before it opens, to avoid the crowds, and he'd like to look around and see what's going on." Of course, I said, "Great." He came the day before the show opened: while the exhibitors were setting up their booths, he walked through the door, this unbelievable presence: he was a big man, but with very personable characteristics. I walked with him around the show, and he was genuinely excited to be around all these visual artists. I saw a warm, friendly human being with no ego in sight.

Then something extraordinary happened. Within minutes of our walking around, one of my exhibitors started singing an aria that Luciano had performed as the male counterpart, and Luciano answered, in song. We kept walking, and more of my exhibitors who knew opera started singing arias to him, and he continued to answer. This went on for about 30 minutes. It was astonishing. I wasn't an opera buff myself, so I don't know what he was singing, but it didn't matter. It was thrilling to hear him sing. And he enjoyed the experience, too: he was happy that people were singing to him, and he enjoyed singing the responses.

Pavarotti's art was lithographs of Italian landscapes. They were just average, but he wanted to do it; he loved doing it. And since his name was Pavarotti, his lithographs sold out, especially since his signature was on them. Of course, most celebrity artists never came back after doing the show one time: they wanted to go through the experience. They all enthusiastically thanked me, expressing how much they enjoyed the experience, and, of course, vise versa.

I also met Marcel Marceau, the greatest mime of the twentieth century. He produced a series of lithographs of Bip the Clown, which was a character he played from the Paris street scene. The series was very nicely done. He invited me to lunch, and he said, "I always wanted to go to the 21 Club." I had never been there; I was never that interested in the chichi restaurants in Manhattan; I suppose because I stayed true to my roots in Rockaway. But when he invited me, I said, "Great, let's go."

So Marcel, his agent, and I went to the 21 Club. As soon as we started talking, I found out he was Jewish, which I didn't know; I suppose it didn't occur to me that he might be Jewish, since he's from France. Then I found out he loves telling jokes, especially Jewish jokes. For one straight hour, he told one joke after another. Here was a man who never speaks, yet he sat down at lunch and told Jewish jokes with a Jewish accent. I can't remember the jokes, but they were the type of jokes Jewish men tell about their wives and their mothers-in-law, Jewish jokes about their sex lives or their nonexistent sex lives. Marcel was a great character. I asked him a few questions, but I could barely get a word in edgewise. I guess since he didn't talk at all in his work, he couldn't stop talking when he had the opportunity.

I met Anthony Quinn later in his professional life. He was retired and lived in Hawaii, and he loved to sculpt, and he was quite good. He came to Art Expo with his sculptures and his entourage and his dealer, and they took a booth, and we had a chance to talk. I was quite impressed that even though he was probably close to 80, he looked fabulous. The character in his face and words revealed to me why he became famous and stayed famous: there is something unique about him.

The only celebrity artist who exhibited at Art Expo numerous times was Tony Bennett. He had always been an artist, but he never really tried to sell his paintings. He painted under the name of Anthony DeBenedetto, which is his real name. Tony was something special—and he still is—because of the remarkable comeback he made in his career. When I met him, he had lost his voice somewhat, like many singers do, sometimes because of drinking or drugs, even prescription drugs, or other reasons. In his case, he simply didn't take care of himself. He also had trouble with his children (he had two sons with his first wife and two daughters with his second wife, but both marriages ended in divorce), but his children were adults and they started reconciling with their father. In fact, his eldest son, Danny (whose given name is D'Andrea) became his agent and changed his father's life. Tony wanted to paint, and Danny encouraged him to paint. Danny got his father out of his bad habits and back into the good habits of his life, and he got his voice back, and it was even better than before, and he started performing again.

And he started painting. So I made a deal with his son and agent, Danny, that I would give his father two spaces (two booths) if Tony would do a certain amount of publicity for me, which Danny and Tony agreed to. Tony did a lot of publicity for Art Expo; also, just having him in the show in person was worth enough to give him the exhibit space. He went on *The Tonight Show* with Johnny Carson several times and talked about Art Expo and how he was going to exhibit there. *The Tonight Show* was the biggest show in America at the time, and for me to hear him talk about Art Expo was just terrific. This was in 1985, the first year we had a show in L.A. Tony was performing at the Brentwood Theater, and he liked to schedule musical performances at the same time he was exhibiting his artwork.

Tony Bennett had originally exhibited at Art Expo New York, so he followed us to California. He loved what he was doing. I believed this career energized him to the extent it made him an even better singer. His success at the New York show gave him the opportunity to do many art shows in galleries across America. He invited me to his Brentwood concert. I sat down, and then a screen descended behind him, and to my surprise, it showed a montage about Art Expo, in tribute. During the montage, Tony talked about Art Expo and all the artists who exhibit, their art, and his art, and then he went on to do a fabulous singing performance. He also invited me backstage. It was a wonderful experience for me.

Tony did a lot of TV shows and always did what he agreed to do, although he never promoted Art Expo in a commercial way; for example, he wouldn't provide a testimonial or an endorsement; he didn't pitch or advertise it directly. Instead, he simply talked about our show and described why it was important to him and why he thought Art Expo was good for bringing emerging artists and famous artists together on the same canvas. An equal opportunity for talented people. That was an experience I'll never forget. A man of his word.

I also met other celebrities who didn't exhibit at Art Expo but who came to the show as visitors. As mentioned, Brooke Shields came in 1986, because she was a good friend of Jacob Javits's family. She was only 20 or 21 years old at the time, and she looked terrific. She doesn't look much different now, 27 years later: she looks great. And to me, she's a terrific human being.

Gene Simmons of Kiss and Diana Ross (who was his girlfriend at the time) also came to Art Expo. I offered to have a security person walk around with them so they wouldn't be bothered by anyone, but they said, "No, no, no, we want to go incognito"—as if that were possible! Gene Simmons is a big man, easily recognizable: everybody knew who he was even without his painted face, and Diana Ross had the biggest hair I ever saw. And they were both wearing full-length white fur coats! For them, this was incognito.

These stories are all true. You can't make this stuff up!

Me visiting
Theodoros
Stamos at his
studio, 1983.

Marcel Marceau
exhibiting at Art
Expo, 1984.

Peter Max
at Art Expo,
1984.

Me with Tracey Bregman (left) and Kristian Alfonso, famous Soap stars, circa 1983.

Me with NYC Mayor Ed Koch at Art Expo, introducing Andy Warhol official poster celebrating the 100-year anniversary of the Brooklyn Bridge, 1983.

Me with Roy Innis, President of CORE/Congress of Racial Equality at fund-raising dinner for Foundation for Future Generations, 1989.

14

Moving On Up to Manhattan and Other Splendid Places

While I was still director of Art Expo, I was working in Manhattan, in our offices on Madison Avenue and 53rd Street. But we were still living in our East Rockaway, Long Island home, the first home we had bought 18 years earlier. Meanwhile, both our kids had moved out of the house, and we were empty nesters. I thought it would be great to live in the city, so I said to Aviva, "I'm tired of commuting. I get home late every night. I want to live in Manhattan: we're doing well now, and we can afford it. I'll try to move the company's office to a bigger space, where I'll be able to walk to work."

Aviva was reluctant because she felt safe in the community she knew. I believe her insecurities came from her childhood wartime experiences. But she said okay, and we started looking for a place, which was an interesting experience since we had never lived in Manhattan; we were suburban people who had only been to Manhattan to see shows and meet friends for dinner. The first apartment we looked at was in a building directly across the street from where we live now (at 25 Sutton Place South); the building was 20 Sutton Place South, at 56th Street. The apartment was in our price range: under $400,000. So we made a bid, the seller accepted, we got the apartment. We made our application to the board of directors: this was a co-op building, so prospective buyers need to meet with and be accepted by the board. When we met the president of the board, Sam Gershwin, he told us, "You are two great young people, with great credentials: you're just what we need in this building." We went before the board to be interviewed; we got rejected.

We were devastated.

When things like this happen, I know you should just take your lumps and move on with your life, even if you are disappointed; I know the old saying, "What doesn't kill you makes you stronger." But I was devastated by this rejection, so I went back to the president of the board, Sam Gershwin, and I asked him, "What happened?" He told me—off the record—that we had been rejected because the building had a system where any one person on the board could say "no" to any prospective buyer, and we heard that two people on the board had said, "We have enough Jews in the building. We don't need any more."

This didn't surprise me: I had seen prejudice before. But that didn't mean I had to accept it. So I called my friend Jay Greenfield, who was a senior vice president at Paul, Weiss, Rifkind (one of the biggest law firms in New York) and who argued cases before the Supreme Court, which was quite an honor in a firm like that. He was a brilliant man. I said, "Jay, I need your help. I would never ask you for help under other circumstances, but I'm so hurt by this. What can I do?" He said, "Jerry, we could sue, but what are we going to win? You want to live in a building that doesn't want you? Or do you want to collect a few dollars? It's unfortunate, but that's the way it is. You have to move on." And he was right.

So I wrote a letter to Mr. Gershwin, expressing how people feel when they get rejected for no reason at all. I had an important job, plenty of money in the bank, and I had no debt; I was always a fiscal conservative. But that's the way it is in life: not everything is fair, and looking back, that experience made me stronger and a better person. I realized you should never want to go where you're not wanted; you should find a place where you're admired for what you are. I was always a liberal on social issues; more about my philosophy later.

Aviva and I started looking again for our new home, and we visited a half-dozen apartments. We even bid on another apartment, but it was on Madison Avenue in the 80s, which was a very crowded—but exciting—area. It was gorgeous: it had everything we wanted: a giant dining room, a beautiful living room with a fireplace. So we made a bid on it, the bid was accepted, and then we got a call from the broker, in tears.

Gerald Leberfeld

February 26, 1985

17 Sachem Street
East Rockaway, NY 11518

Sam Gershwin
New York, NY 10022

Dear. Mr. Gershwin:

As you may know, our recent application for membership in your coop-
erative was rejected. We are aware that we probably have neither the
legal right to receive fair and complete consideration of our application, nor the right to seek redress for our injuries. However,
after reviewing all the events leading up to this disappointing
action, we would like to ask you, as an individual, to reflect upon
the consequences in human terms of your allowing this decision to
be made in such an irresponsible manner.

After complying with the Board's requests for our financial statements, including tax returns, and for personal references, which
came from highly respected professional people, some of whom have
known us for 30 years, we were astonished to discover the superfi-
cial review afforded our application. Our appearance before the
Board was, quite honestly, a sham. Few Board members were present,
and even fewer questions were asked which would reveal anything
about our suitability as your neighbors. Indeed, one older and
clearly influential Board member left the interview shortly after
it began. It is also our impression that our documents were either
not read, or at best merely skimmed by several Board members. Addi-
tionally, our ordeal was cruelly dragged out for another 11 days
while we were led to believe that the entire Board would be con-
vened to meet with us again. Of course, this never happened.

Whether these events transpired due to apathy or because of some
kind of prejudice, we will never know. However, we ask you to ask
yourself if this is any way for decent people to treat each other.

What was our fatal error? If it was to be married for 27 years, raise
two respectful children, and work hard and honestly to build a
secure and independant lifestyle, then we are guilty. Perhaps we
were merely naive, believing that the American Dream can be realized without giving and receiving favors, and without relying on
"who you know" to get what you dream of attaining.

We believe that this decision has been an injustice to all parties.
Now, upon reflection and without anger, we are writing with the hope
that future applicants will receive fair consideration by the Board,
based on the real issues with which you are justifiably concerned,
rather than upon the capricious decisions of one or two individuals. We are sure that most of you are decent and interesting people, and regret that you will not be our friends and neighbors.

Sincerely,
Gerald and Aviva Leberfeld

235

The broker told us that the president of the board wanted that apartment for his daughter, and he told the broker that he wouldn't approve us, so the seller might as well sell it to his daughter. To add insult to injury, he wanted the apartment for less money than we had offered! But the seller gave in: she was a widow, and she was scared that if she didn't sell it to him, she might not be able to sell it at all. So she sold it to this creep for less money. That was awful, for us and for her, but that's another life experience. "Power corrupts."

Then we looked at an apartment in the building right across the street from the building that had rejected us. The address was 25 Sutton Place South, and it's a lovely building situated on the entire block between 55th and 56th Streets, from Sutton Place to the East River. Many apartments in this building had river views, and we found this lovely apartment, the one we live in now. The apartment was on the third floor, with a partial river view and full view of the 59th Street Bridge. A wonderful extra benefit was that the building had an inside garage: we needed our car, since we had all our family and friends in the suburbs. Sutton Place didn't have all the hubbub that mid-Manhattan has. It had less traffic. It's much quieter, yet we're still close enough to everything.

We bought this apartment from two gay men, which I point out because they did many creative things. They didn't spend a lot of money, but they added a lot of nice features.

When we went to the closing, though, everything was all agreed upon, until the sellers told us they didn't want to sell the apartment to us after all: they had changed their minds! They said we didn't live up to certain conditions, none of which were true. They didn't have a leg to stand on, they had no right to cancel the deal, but they tried everything, even walking out of the room. I've never really had a good real estate closing that I can recall, and in this case, sure enough, we found out they had gotten a bid for $25,000 more than we had offered. But they had agreed to our offer, and they couldn't get out of it. So we bought that apartment after all.

Moving to 25 Sutton Place South was the best thing that ever happened to us! Within two years, I was on the Co-op Finance Committee; within three years, I was on the board; and within five years, I was president of the board. I spent six years on the co-op board, encountering some very difficult and interesting problems. The good in this experience was that I made many new friends. The bad was that I lost many new friends. I treated this responsibility as if it were my own business, which meant I tried to do it right and be very efficient at it. Most people are mainly concerned about their personal building problems, but the board president's job is to be concerned about the overall difficulties of the building.

At the same time, in September 1985, I built a wonderful office in the Architects & Designers Building on 58th Street and 3rd Avenue. Living on 56th and Sutton, I had a wonderful short walk to work every morning, thus fulfilling one of my lifelong dreams. I worked on planning the new office with a very good friend of mine, Don Workman, who was a designer. It had everything we wanted. Everything was functional and beautiful; we didn't need large, oversized offices and workspaces. We simply wanted a functional space where everybody could work effectively and interact. Considering that I had started in 1978 at a broken desk at my consulting office in Englewood Cliffs, this was quite an upgrade. As they say, *You've come a long way, baby.*

Within three months of our moving to Manhattan and my moving into a new office, I got an offer to sell Art Expo, from Harcourt Brace. The first thing they did after buying me out was to close the office—the new office that we had just moved into. I worked for the new owners for over a year, as a consultant, still a good situation.

I still look at that building on 58th Street when I walk by. That office had a beautiful patio: we created a sculpture garden, which is rare in Manhattan. It was the perfect place, but life goes on.

Rockaway Boy Buys a Weekend Home

Around that same time, Aviva and I bought a small weekend home in the country, in a place called Pine Lake Park, in Cortlandt Manor, Upper Westchester County, only about 50 miles from Manhattan. It's a summer community that was built 80 years ago but became a co-op in 1962—an older community of small bungalow-type units. Once a year, we visited friends of ours, the Nussbaums, who had a place there; in fact, a whole group of our friends would go. The park had four clay tennis courts and a small manmade lake, where everyone could swim and row and fish. It also had basketball courts and a fabulous social hall in a big old white barn, with live entertainment on the weekends. The atmosphere was like it was in the 1950s, but we started visiting in about 1970, and it was still like the '50s. Nothing ever changed at Pine Lake. It was in a time warp. It was great if you were the type of person who didn't care about material things and just enjoyed being in wooded, peaceful surroundings. We visited once each summer with our Rockaway friends, and all our children had a wonderful time—so much so that every year, Ruth Nussbaum would ask us, "Why don't you get a place up here?"

So in 1986, I proposed that idea to two of my closest friends, Marty and Paul, and their wives: I asked, "Why don't we buy a place? We'll share it, and sometimes we'll come together, sometimes we'll come separately." The bungalows cost only $15,000, so they agreed it was a good idea. When we applied, though, the board didn't want to approve us, since they didn't like approving ownership to more than one family. I knew that, in general, it's a very risky proposition to buy property with other families, but this was such a small investment, it was only $5,000 a family. Anyway, it didn't matter because eventually, they both backed out, and I ended up buying the bungalow alone.

It was actually only half a bungalow: in fact, it was only 375 square feet in total. The interior spaces of the two halves were completely separate, but we shared a concrete deck with the owners of the other half of the bungalow. We lived side by side with an older couple, the Sidemans, who were lovely people. They had two children who visited occasionally, with their spouses and children. Then their daughter Paula and her husband, Tom Atlas, and their children David and Stephanie started coming up much more often, and we became very friendly with the entire family. At the same time, our kids were spending more time with us, so we needed more room, and we could see the Sidemans also needed more room. So we bought a bigger place that was closer to the lake, and the Sidemans took over our side of the bungalow. We both renovated our larger units, and everybody was happy.

We bought the first half bungalow from a widow named Hilda Chernoff, who everybody said was kind of strange. One thing we found unusual was that once a year, Hilda would come and stand outside our bungalow (which used to be hers): she would stand a good distance away and stare at it for about an hour. Nobody knew why she did that, but we found out that Hilda loved Pine Lake so much that when her husband died and was cremated, she had illegally spread his ashes all over the front of our lawn. Then she came every year on their anniversary to be with her husband's ashes. No wonder we had the greenest lawn in Pine Lake.

We bought the second bungalow at the lake location Aviva had always wanted, because it was gigantic: it was a massive 750 square feet. In that 750 square feet, we had three bedrooms, a small living room, a dining room, and a kitchen. All the rooms were tiny, but we fit in it. It was perfect. We built a giant deck, which we lived on outside: after all, we only went there during the summer. We still love it: in fact, we still go every weekend.

Not only do we go, but our daughter Michelle and son-in-law Scott also come with our two granddaughters, Maxine and Ava. After a few years, they bought their own bungalow. We bought the bigger bungalow with extra rooms so they could stay with us as many weekends as needed, but, obviously, they wanted their own place, and we understand. Both are very involved: Michelle runs the weekend entertainment (among other projects), and Scott has already become President of the Co-Op Board. That's the way it should be: we're passing on the torch.

We bought the larger bungalow from a woman named Natalie Cashen, who was also a widow. She asked $50,000 for it. When I pointed out that it was in terrible shape, she said, "Look, I'm leaving all the appliances!" She had an illegal washing machine, which she wasn't allowed, which she was leaving for us, with all the other appliances. So we said fine, and we bought it. When we went in before the closing and did an inspection, none of the appliances worked. So essentially, she left us her trash.

"But the stove works," she said, when I brought it to her attention. "Not really," we explained. She then said, "Well, one of the burners works if you put a match really close to it." In my famous negotiating style, I got her to give me back $1,000, which was not enough to pay for the appliances, but we wanted the bungalow anyway. And we fixed it up, and we love it.

❖

239

We did look for a summer community before we decided on Pine Lake Park. We went to Southbury, Connecticut, because we knew somebody who was building houses there, on the river. It was lovely, but we would have to drive 35 minutes to buy a container of milk, or 45 minutes to go to a movie. That's not what we were really interested in.

While we were there, though, we visited an upscale retirement community in Southbury, the Overland Park Community. All the people living there were financially comfortable, and I interviewed a few of them about a project I was working on about Social Security. My son-in-law's father, Frank Whitney, had served in World War II and then started a small grocery store business, which he grew into many stores on Fire Island. When he got his first Social Security check, he returned it. In fact, he returned the first six Social Security checks. He wasn't a rich man, but he felt there were people who needed this money more than he did, so he returned the checks. But the government made him keep them.

When I heard about this, I decided I wanted to find out more about what people thought about Social Security. And when I interviewed the retired people I met at this upscale Connecticut senior living facility, I have to write about this, because this really is important to know: Not one person said they wouldn't give up all or part of their Social Security payments if they were sure that the United States government wouldn't waste it. It was interesting to me that most rich people would give up this money if it went to good use; I was very impressed by that. There's controversy today about rich people versus poor people, yet my son-in-law's father and the people in this retirement community were all from different backgrounds. We're all Americans, and, I think, in the right atmosphere, we would all do the right thing. I think we're arguing about the wrong issues in the world today. We politicize everything. Who started the term "class warfare," anyway?

I don't remember how the money was spent at that time, but I know there has always been a lot of waste. The money earmarked for Social Security never really went into a fund. And these people knew that, because they were educated business people. They knew what the Social Security fund was, and they knew that the money was used for the general budget. And who knows where *that* goes? Nothing has changed today: Social Security is broke, and the funds' assets are still nowhere to be found. Perhaps we should let the retired people in South-bury, Connecticut manage the Social Security fund.

Buying Another Home—in Florida

Then in 1987, after I had sold Art Expo, a friend of mine, Marty Holzberg (aka "Pierre"), and his wife, Charlotte, asked us if we wanted to spend some time with them in the winter in Florida. I was still work-ing as a consultant, so obviously I couldn't spend the whole season. We bought a 2-bedroom apartment together for $80,000 in a place called Inverrary in Ft. Lauderdale—not on the beach, but just west of I-95 off Oakland Park Boulevard.

Marty had owned a carpet store and made a good living. He had just sold his house in Fairlawn, New Jersey, which gave him the most money he had ever had in his life: more than $500,000 in the bank. I also had a substantial amount of money in my bank account, since I had just sold Art Expo. Even though we had the cash to buy the Florida apartment, we decided to try to get a mortgage, because then we would be able to deduct the mortgage interest off our taxes. (We didn't think about the fact that the deduction wouldn't really mean that much.) So we went to at least a half dozen banks, and not one bank would give us a mortgage. We said "We'll put half down." Still they said no: they wouldn't give us a mortgage because they didn't want to finance more than one family per property.

That didn't make sense to me, from a credit standpoint. After all, I had been the credit manager of Olivetti for many years, and I knew the more money people have in their bank accounts, the less debt they have and the greater their ability to pay. Moreover, if two families are willing to guarantee the debt, that's as secure as you can get when making a loan. But the banks just wouldn't do it. There were rules that prevented them from giving us a mortgage.

So we said, who cares? And we paid $40,000 each and bought the house for cash.

It makes me wonder how things have changed since 1987: we were willing to put down 50% on a piece of property that was appraised for more, there were two co-signers on the debt, and we still couldn't get a mortgage. Yet in this day and age, where we're having this real estate disaster, how many people got mortgages even though they had no down payment and a lot of debt? Boy, how times have changed, and in only 25 years! It is astonishing. Maybe the government and banks should go back to somewhere in between those two extremes.

We used that two-bedroom apartment for a few years, then we decided we wanted to move uptown, so to speak, to Boca Raton. That's where everything was happening. So we put the apartment up for sale, and we had a problem selling it, since the real estate market in the early 1990s was weak.

Eventually, we found a woman who was willing to buy it, but only under one condition: that we would leave all the beautiful artwork on the walls. The artwork had some real value: I had acquired it when I was Director of Art Expo. The Florida apartment was the perfect place to hang it: there were at least 10 pieces of art that were probably worth $20,000.

The buyer didn't know much about art, but she knew it looked nice. Our friend Charlotte, who co-owned the apartment, said, "Jerry, don't worry about it. We'll replace it with other art, and she won't know the difference." Charlotte was a real estate broker who knew about these kinds of things, and she took us to a flea market where we bought a dozen pieces of art for $4 each. Each piece was framed with a thin metal band that was pressed on to the print. It was hard to hang, since the frame was so thin that there was nothing really to hang it on. We worked hard and finally hung it all over the apartment. Sure enough, at the closing, the buyer said, "Thank you for leaving all the art: it's so beautiful."

After we sold Inverrary and moved up to Boca Raton, we rented a place together. Marty and Charlotte eventually moved to Boca Point, and we moved to a place called Boca West, which are both gated country-club communities. Aviva and I rented several places, until we found a place we really liked. Boca West is a large community with many subdivisions: various builders built big homes, small houses, apartments, and everything in between. The place we chose had standalone apartments and some double-apartments (separate apartments upstairs and downstairs), all separated by beautiful landscaping. This builder wanted to create something special. It seemed like we were in Bora Bora, in a rainforest. It was called Plantation Colony.

This apartment was upstairs, but I didn't mind, since the view is nicer and there's no noise from people above us. We had a little river running behind our unit and were surrounded by trees and flowers and a golf course. When we first looked at the apartment, we noticed a picture of two people we recognized: Lesley Visser and Dick Stockton, who were both famous sportscasters. There were articles on the walls about them and their careers. They were the owners of the apartment, but they weren't there when we saw the apartment, as they were covering the Winter Olympics.

They had decorated the apartment in very dark tones: brown carpeting, dark walls, dark furniture. They called it their "out-of-Africa" home. We loved the way it looked (although we lightened up the décor), and we closed the sale with a fax. We faxed our offer, and they faxed back and said make the deal. It was the only civil real estate closing in our lives.

So here I am: a guy who grew up in Arverne-by-the-Sea and lived in a public housing project now has three homes—on Manhattan's Sutton Place, in Boca Raton, Florida, and in Pine Lake Park, New York. All of a sudden, we had three homes and three addresses. Each one sounds better than the other. This is surely part of the American Dream.

Look what happened to the former president of the Arverne Demons, my teenage social and athletic club: now I had been president of the Sutton Place co-op board, president of the Pine Lake Park co-op board, and president of the board of the Plantation Colony in Florida. Each one of those experiences was wonderful—but also very difficult and ultimately disappointing, because when you're dealing with a lot of people and you're trying to do the right thing, you can never win. But that is another story, for another time.

JERRY'S LAW #8:
"If it's worth doing, do it right."

We still have all three places. We spend the winter three months in Florida because I'm totally retired, and from the middle of May to the middle of October, we spend weekends at Pine Lake Park. So we're really using all three homes, especially since Pine Lake Park is less than an hour driving. We have many friends there, families that we have grown up with—and, of course, our wonderful daughter Michelle, with granddaughters Maxine and Ava, with Mr. Fix-it, our son-in-law Scott. Remember, I'm Jewish, so I'm technically handicapped. Scott must shudder every time the phone rings at Pine Lake.

15

My Semi-Retirement: Traveling the World and Developing New Ventures

So what does a guy who's 53 years old and retired do with the rest of his life? That's a question I asked myself. So let's review the next few years together. Perhaps we can search together to find this answer.

The most obvious thing to do was the traveling that Aviva and I had dreamt about all our married life. So we took two special vacations of three weeks each: one to Kenya, Africa and one to China. The African safari experience was probably my best vacation ever because we viewed almost every imaginable animal in their natural habitats, and we also took a wonderful air balloon trip over the Serengeti during the great wildebeest migration.

In China, we were fortunate to go at a time when the Chinese Communist government was willing to let some tourists explore parts of the country that had previously been restricted by this military dictatorship. As with all China tours, we had an American tour guide and a Chinese tour guide, who was previously in the Red Army—I think they call it the Red Brigade. The Chinese government didn't trust anybody. Our Chinese tour guide was married to a diplomat assigned to the Chinese embassy in Washington, D.C.—obviously a very prominent position. She told us she could visit her husband once every two years, but she had to leave her children in China: obviously, they didn't want the family to seek asylum.

In addition to the regular fascinating itinerary of China, we were treated to two special events. We were the first tourist group to be allowed to helicopter over the Great Wall of China. Everybody gets to walk on one of the walls in a small predetermined town, with a great number of souvenir vendors. This was different. We were taken to a remote military airport and told to wait in the office hangar of the Sikorsky Aviation Company, an American builder of helicopters. It was explained to us by the American technician that all helicopters sold to China required the company to keep a maintenance crew present to secure the helicopters' operational safety. He asked us what we were doing, and stated this was the first time he had ever heard of tourists taking a military helicopter over the Great Wall. A helicopter moved into position to pick us up, and the American technician gasped. He said, "You're not going on that Russian helicopter, are you? You wouldn't get me to go on that thing for $1 million." Obviously, he wasn't impressed with their safety record.

Several Chinese militiamen came to accompany us on this helicopter. They took all our cameras away and angrily told us, "No photographs." I looked around and saw that the airport was filled with nothing but a few propeller aircraft, which the western world had stopped using years ago. We shrugged our shoulders, pocketed our cameras, and boarded the helicopter. There were about 20 of us, accompanied by a fully dressed Chinese military person who sat in the center seat, keeping an eye on all of us.

I noticed that the inside of the helicopter was somewhat unimpressive: the seat cushions were both stained and torn: not a lot of comfort for American tourists. But as typical American tourists in a foreign country, we just went along to get along.

Our fears were well worth the experience of viewing the thousand miles of that winding miracle called the Great Wall of China, one of the Seven Wonders of the World. Fortunately, we lived to tell the tale!

The second experience was seeing the underground city of Beijing. We saw our Chinese and American tour guides whispering to each other, "After all, they saw the Great Wall of China in a helicopter. Maybe the Chinese government would allow them to see the hidden city of Beijing." Everybody said, "Oh, the forbidden city," which is a famous tourist landmark, but that's not what they were talking about; they were referring to the *underground* city. They went to the authorities, who said yes, they could take us there. Both tour guides were amazed and very excited; as far as they knew, this was a first.

We were taken by bus to a large clothing store in central Beijing. We entered the store, and the owner opened up a trap door in the floor, and there was a set of stairs. We walked down those stairs to be greeted by two official-looking men in Mao outfits, those gray jackets with small collars like you see in movies. Then we were taken farther underground in two elevators, then we walked, and what did we see? We saw room after room: classrooms, kitchens, sleeping rooms, all that could enable one to survive under certain dangerous conditions. We continued to walk until we got to another bank of elevators and were taken up to another large store, and then we returned to our bus.

The story behind this underground city is that during the time when the Soviets and the Chinese were close allies, the Russian military had a great presence in China. They were training the Chinese Army, but the governments got into a big dispute, and the Chinese government told the Russians to leave their country within 24 hours. The Chinese thought that the Soviet Communist dictatorship would retaliate with some kind of atomic bombing. So they immediately put a million workers on a project of building a city beneath the city that would house two million Chinese people so that some would survive an atomic attack.

Of course, this was a fallacy, since the gases from those bombs would have killed them anyway. Nevertheless, this city exists. And I have not heard of any other tourist ever seeing it or even hearing about it. In fact, the Chinese people don't even talk about it, so that was a special experience in our lives.

We took many vacation trips over the next five years. During this time, I tried various different projects, including starting a few new businesses. It should be stated that although it sounds like GL was successful in every venture in his business life, this was far from true. I tried different ideas, with some failures. Anybody who tells you they didn't make any mistakes in their business journeys is just lying.

My approach is you come up with an idea that seems to fill a niche that a large company would have little interest in, then (of course) the time comes when you build it up and they want to buy it. I'm going to take a little time to go over projects that I did from 1987 to 1998, some that struck gold again. Some were charitable causes and some were business ideas that just didn't work.

Merkin Project

As I mentioned before, many of my exhibitors wanted to start new businesses with me, and my personality encouraged me to at least listen to their ideas. First, a young lady named Marian who worked for one of my exhibitors told me she had a very close and personal relationship with a fine artist named Richard Merkin. I had some familiarity with this artist and his work. She proposed if I would produce some limited-edition Merkin serigraphs, she would sell them as fast as he would produce them.

I signed on to this agreement, and I invested $35,000 for the first two serigraphs; she would sell the 500 pieces, and we would share the profit. Unfortunately, the bottom line was she sold only 70 pieces. So after six months, I dissolved the partnership, since obviously she did not have the ability to do what she promised. After a dispute with the lady, she finally agreed to return to me the remaining pieces of artwork, all 430. This was the first thing I did after Art Expo. I was embarrassed. I didn't want my art peers to even know about this project, so I put the remaining pieces under my bed and moved on.

Some years ago, I befriended a man who used eBay as a sales tool. We partnered and sold approximately 200 of these pieces. I recouped maybe $10,000 of my original investment—which is why I always say *never give up!* There's always some opportunity around the corner.

IDEAS Tradeshow

In July of 1987, one of my Art Expo exhibitors asked to meet with me about a new idea for a tradeshow. Betty was a dealer in Asian art who had a showroom in the D&D (Decoration & Design) Building in Manhattan, which was the headquarters for all major suppliers and manufacturers to the design trade. Anybody who was anybody was in that building. Betty was enthusiastic about jointly producing a tradeshow for the design trade. She didn't agree with the policies in the design world, which closed the showrooms to everybody who wasn't accompanied by an interior designer. Her idea was to have a show at the Javits Center, which would familiarize consumers to the fabulous products available to them and expand the customer base for interior designers, just as Art Expo had done in the art world.

Betty wanted to be my partner. She would guarantee the sale of space to the major players in the D&D Building, and I would organize and produce the show. We would contribute equally in the startup costs. She said that with my reputation as the highly successful promoter in the art world and her connections in the design world, it was a win-win. After all, most of the important interior designers and home-furnishings manufacturers had visited Art Expo because of the overlap in our interests. Betty was a likeable person, and she had always been supportive of the art fair. So we agreed to proceed and test the market and contributed $40,000 each as startup capital.

The next startup requirements were to choose a name and register it in New York and California, get exhibition dates at Javits, and find suitable office space. We agreed on a name, and I was truly excited about the idea: we decided to call it the IDEAS show, for Interior Design Elements and Accessories Show. The main thrust of the show was to have exhibitors who produced interesting products to complement the couches and chairs and wall coverings that were prevalent in the design showrooms, adding such things as lighting, ceramics, art, antiques, and just unusual accessories that would make their homes more interesting.

We were able to register the names in both New York and California, which were our target markets. Javits supplied us with an acceptable exhibition date of December 1–4, 1988, which is a great consumer shopping period between Thanksgiving and Christmas, and which also gave us a full year to develop the show.

The D&D Building had a waiting list for space, but in a discussion with the building managers, we discovered they had a mezzanine area, which was actually one flight down from the main level. Of course, nobody wanted to be on the mezzanine to show their products, but it was a perfect situation for us since it was a low-rent office in the D&D

Building, which gave us the prestige of the address, and it gave us direct access to our potential exhibitors. So far we were batting 1,000. Everything was falling into place.

We agreed on the same principle as Art Expo, having two trade-only dates, followed by two days open to the public. That would give the designers quality time with their clients and our exhibitors, while opening the show to many new potential customers to the interior design industry. We would have an interior design reference table so the consumers could meet designers, and they could see photos of their work and their references. On the public days, we wanted people to be able to buy sofas, chairs, accessories, and so forth, but we still had to get around this rule of "to the trade only," which meant that the general public needed to work with designers to buy those goods. The manufacturers, of course, wanted to sell to anyone who would buy. So we solved that problem by simply requiring that people who wanted to buy would go over to the designers' table and choose a designer to assist them.

In the fall of 1987, I was on the hunt for someone to run the day-by-day operations and be show manager. At that time, I was attending monthly meetings of the NAEM, the National Association of Exhibition Managers, which was a professional organization for tradeshow owners and their executive staffs. At the November meeting, a young lady walked up to me and introduced herself, saying she visited Art Expo and was very impressed with the operation. She was looking for a job, and she wondered if I could recommend something.

Her name was Bailey Beeken, she was in her late twenties, and she had good tradeshow experience. Bailey was apparently in the right place at the right time, so we made an appointment to meet and discuss the new IDEAS show. After a few meetings, I decided that Bailey would be a good fit, because she was a young, well-educated, ambitious person who I thought would be able to function within my image and work ethic. So in January 1988, we opened our new office in the mezzanine of New York's D&D Building.

On her first day, the first thing she said to me was, "I don't do coffee. You'll have to get your own." This was the '80s. What had I done? Apparently, I had hired a big-time feminist, perhaps a future president of the National Organization of Women! Somehow, we worked out the coffee problem. And I thought I could channel this energy and aggressiveness toward making the show a success.

Unfortunately, from that point on, very little good happened. My partner, Betty, did not have the temperament to sell space for a tradeshow. Her idea to sell space was to take people out to lunch or dinner, but she couldn't ask them directly, "How many booths do you want?" If you can't stand rejection, you can't be in the tradeshow business. So she actually sold zero spaces. *Zero*—that's right: this is not a misprint.

Also, because Betty knew all the major players, she insisted on calling on them herself. That meant that Bailey could sell only to the peripheral of the industry, which, fortunately, she did, and we managed to accumulate about 60 booths in the first four months. Also, Betty developed a quick dislike of Bailey, which turned into hatred. I don't know why—probably because Bailey actually sold space. It created an impossible situation. When you function as I did in developing tradeshows, you have to be both employer and employee: in other words, you need to roll up your sleeves, take virtually no salary, and look to the future for your reward.

So we struggled for four months while we discussed continuing. I told Betty we had to invest an additional $20,000 each for working capital, and we would reevaluate in another 60 days. She kept blaming Bailey for all our failures, while never accepting the reality of her own shortcomings. She said the industry was difficult to penetrate, and our potential exhibitors were saying, "What do we need a New York tradeshow for? We all have showrooms in New York!" But our idea was that we would bring together everybody in the industry, and we would bring in thousands of potential new customers who had never visited the D&D building, since it was to the trade only. Adversity can be overcome, but it takes continuous effort, which Betty was unwilling or unable to do. She said *I* should put up all the additional money, and she would slightly reduce her percentage of ownership, but that wasn't what I wanted. I wasn't so concerned about the money as about her inability to sell space and waning commitment to the show.

I went to option two, which was to find investors. The first people I thought about were Larry and Paul, my California-based PR guys from Art Expo. Within a few days they said, "Yes, we can't wait." I said, "We need $60,000 for the next few months to see if the show is a go." Betty would get $40,000 of that, since that had been her initial investment, and we needed to buy her out. The other $20,000 was the amount I would match for working capital. Larry and Paul agreed, so I went to Betty and offered her money back, and she said, "No." She was convinced we had preplanned this business deal to get rid of her and to screw her out of her interest. She was obviously paranoid. She was really off the wall. How can you not want your money back when the alternative is to lose all your money?

How could I have known that Betty was two different people? I found out later from other people who had done business with her that she could be very difficult.

JERRY'S LAW #14: "Inspect what you expect."

You can't run a business without money. Betty didn't want to invest any more money, and she didn't want to be bought out. Can you imagine? She could have gotten her $40,000 back. I don't know if we would have succeeded if we had gone forward. But we'll never know, because in May, I decided to terminate our partnership. I returned the $15,000 in deposits that we had received from the exhibitors who had signed up with us. I wanted to get on with my life. So I lost $40,000, and she lost $40,000. Plus, I lost an additional $15,000 from the exhibitors' deposits: I paid that back out of my own pocket. Sometimes you've got to just walk away. After all, what was I going to do, argue with her? She didn't understand what I was talking about. So I lost some money on a very good idea, but not all things work as planned.

The good news was that Bailey and I got to know each other, and a few years later, we worked together as partners on another trade show, with great success. What made that partnership even better was that my daughter Michelle and Bailey had developed a close friendship, and Michelle was to be involved in that new tradeshow, along with my PR buddies, Larry and Paul, which was called FunExpo and which was very successful. I'll discuss the development of that show a little bit later.

National Fitness and Sports Exhibitions, Inc.

Within a year, in 1989, I conceived a new tradeshow idea that I was very excited about: I called it National Fitness and Sports Expositions. The plan was to produce an interactive consumer and trade show, where fitness and sports products manufacturers and promoters could set up equipment that would be utilized on the show floor. This would be an exciting venue for children of all ages.

I registered the name with the states of New York and California, my primary markets. I met with experts in the industry. To a person, they all thought it was a great idea. Remember, I had been a successful entrepreneur with Art Expo, and people want to be on the side of a winner. Many of these people offered to invest, but I decided to do it alone. After all, my prior partnership experiences had left a bad taste in my mouth.

It was important to get good dates at an appropriate venue. I eliminated Javits, because in my mind, it was not right for this type of show. Then, bing! It came to me: why not have it at Madison Square Garden? It's the greatest known sports arena in the world, located in the heart of Manhattan!

I always thought the MSG logo should be a national trademark that had never been explored properly. Remember, at the time, all the well-known fashion designers and show business personalities were licensing their names on other products and franchising them as trademarks, so why not MSG? I realized then that the fastest way to reach my goals was to get this type of partner who would accelerate the idea.

One of the experts I had met was a man whose expertise was getting sponsorships for a sporting event, and he knew the MSG executives at the highest level. He said he would introduce me if I would just promise that he could sell exclusively to sponsors of this new fitness and sports show. This was an easy yes. Remember:

JERRY'S LAW #4:
"Start at the top and work your way up."

Don't waste your time with people who can't make final decisions. And he did introduce me to the executive vice president and the financial vice president; they both loved the idea. It was all coming together.

They worked up the numbers. I asked them for $250,000 of working capital and the use of Madison Square Garden as my venue, and they would be 50-50 partners, and I'd be running the operation as director. In the world of these large corporations, $250,000 is an expense item, so it wasn't much to ask for, and, of course, they could offer the venue only when the dates were open, when there wasn't any other event going on at MSG. It seemed to be a win-win for everybody. With Madison Square Garden's name on the show, it would be so much easier to get fitness and sports manufacturers to come on board, and they all had the celebrity sports and entertainment figures under contract to do personal appearances. This was getting to be more exciting by the moment.

We met a number of times. We mutually produced the contractual agreement. We initialed it. Then something strange happened on the way to signing the final contract. They called me and said, "We changed our mind, but we're still willing to rent the space for a reasonable amount of money." But that had the least value of this potential relationship. I was never told what happened that had changed their mind. Perhaps it was someone on the Board of Directors. I asked my sponsorship associate, and he didn't know; he was also upset, because he was counting on this project. There was nothing for me to do but to move on, and without the partnership of the Madison Square Garden trademark, I lost my enthusiasm. With the MSG name, you call on a potential exhibitor, and say, "we're partnering with Madison Square Garden," then almost everyone is likely to try it. It's so hard to get people to exhibit during the first year, but that would have opened the door and put us on the fast track of success.

The only reason I mention this venture is that not all good ideas work out, but in each and every thing that you try, you add maturity and experience, and it helps your future successes.

JERRY'S LAW #18:
"You cannot do the minimum and reach the maximum."

Within the next 18 months, I started what would be my last two tradeshows. Both proved to be a wonderful experience with real excitement, plus the rewards of great profitability.

My United Nations Adventure in Indonesia

In early 1990, I was approached by Irv Koons, whom I had befriended while I was director of Art Expo. Irv had been vice president of a major advertising firm when he retired; since then, he had become a senior advisor to the Director of the United Nations' World Development Program. This was a joint venture between the UN and governments of third-world countries, wherein they shared the cost of sending experts to these countries to help develop new businesses, thus giving employment to their citizens.

Irv asked if I would be interested in going to Indonesia for the UN to help develop small industries and their products and advise how to best utilize international trade shows. Aviva and I had traveled extensively since I sold Art Expo in 1987: we lived out our travel dreams. But I wasn't quite sure I wanted to spend extensive time in a country I knew very little about. Also, this was a volunteer position in which only my expenses would be paid, and was scheduled to last six months.

On the other hand, this opportunity appeared to be the kind of exciting challenge that one only dreams of. Yet I couldn't get myself to grasp the idea of being away in a foreign country, separated from my family for that period of time. My daughter Michelle, who knows me very well, encouraged me to push the edge of the envelope: she said "This will be an experience that you will never forget." And she was right.

Knowing that six months was out of the question, I negotiated with the UN that I would go for four weeks and then increase the time on this assignment, if required. In other words, I guaranteed to complete the job to their satisfaction.

Of course, everything had to be negotiated. They wanted me to fly commercial; I wanted business class. They wanted to put me up in a four-star hotel; I wanted a five-star. This was the normal procedure for them, but they easily relented. I was to leave on October 16, 1990, and Aviva was to follow me a week later if I found everything suitable. But I knew that my darling wife would not want to be away from her family for that much time, especially in hot humid 90° weather, while I was away all day, working.

To get a better concept of my tale, let's go back for a moment to some history of Indonesia and how the presidency was established. In 1945, General Sukarno led a military coup to take control of Dutch Indonesia and turned it into an independent country. It had been a Dutch colony, and the Dutch government officials left peacefully, but to this day are still involved in the commercial aspect of the country. Sukarno controlled the country by the rule of force. During the years of his control, many people were assassinated and many thrown into prisons, never to be seen again. In 1967, he was overthrown by another military coup led by General Suharto, who controlled the country with an iron fist until 1999, when the presidency became an elected office, which it still remains today.

When I left for Jakarta, I had in my possession a letter from the UN to a gentleman named Casper Kamp, who was the director of the UN office for Indonesia. The letter was to introduce me and advise which company I would be working with, which was PT KIT. The UN's responsibility was to watch over me, protect me, and support me in every way. I was given the name of the director of the company I was working with and a check advancing my expenses, in the amount of 2,457,000 rupiah—which in American money was a grand total of $1,321.

When I arrived, very jetlagged, at the Jakarta airport—which was a beautiful, modern facility—I was greeted by three signs that said, "Welcome, Mr. Leberfeld." I kid you not: there were three limos waiting for me! One was from the hotel, one was from the United Nations, and the third was from the company I was consulting for. My logic told me to go with the young lady who was an employee of the company I was consulting for. Her name was Yetty Sutlanto.

My adventure was just beginning.

This was my first day, and Yetty and I agreed it should be a time for me to relax, see this new country, and settle into my new hotel for a good night's sleep. It was early in the day—much too early to sleep—

so Yetty offered to guide me through my first day in Indonesia. So pay close attention and travel with me for perhaps the most fascinating and unusual four weeks of my life.

Yetty suggested that we first visit an historical amusement park, with areas that reconstruct some of the many cultures of this archipelago of more than 13,000 islands and 180 million people, and view the enormous diversity of the peoples of Indonesia. The best way to enjoy this adventure was to ride the tram over these different sections, which showed their homes, customs, and daily way of life. Yetty explained in great detail what I was viewing. Riding across the sky with this lovely young woman in this transparent cable car was a great beginning. Or so I thought.

Within 15 minutes, in 100-degree temperature, the cable car stopped moving. We had a breakdown of the system. No one panicked; we just sat for almost an hour, sweating, until the local engineers decided they could not fix the electric power plant. Thus we had to be manually cranked back to the other end. That was when it first hit me, *this is not America, this is a third-world country.* These misfortunes were a way of life: nobody panicked, everybody stayed friendly, and so I discovered that the next four weeks would be different in every way.

It struck me, by the way they dressed and by the Friday prayer schedule, that almost everyone in this country was a Muslim except for me: I was Jewish, but nobody seemed to care. If you were to tell me that all Muslims hate Jews, I wouldn't believe you. My personal experience was quite the opposite. In this poorly educated country, I saw virtually no covered faces, no disrespect—only warmth and friendship from everyone I met.

After leaving the amusement park, I was driven by car to see the ultramodern city of Jakarta. Could it be that all the streets were paved, all the largest hotel chains were represented, grand high-rise office buildings and wonderful-looking restaurants and shops? This was more like New York City, and I thought this trip was going to be easier than I originally thought. But this was not the real Indonesia.

I checked into my Western-style hotel, which was modern, and my room was adequate. The only thing left for me to do that day was to have dinner and go to sleep; tomorrow was the first day of my new job. Yetty offered to have dinner with me so I wouldn't be alone, but I knew she had a family and she had been wonderful to me all day, so I thanked her and said I would see her tomorrow in the office.

The next morning, I was picked up by driver in a Volvo. I mention this because I found out that ownership of certain cars designates status in Indonesia. I discovered that these cars are rewarded by the government for special service: for example, the President of the country and that level received Mercedes-Benzes, the next level received BMWs, and then still a very high level received Volvos. I found out over the next few days that the man to be my steady companion, called Soekaryo, was a former admiral in the Indonesian navy as well as former Minister of Health of the entire country; when I met him, he was Managing Director and Chief Operating Officer for this company that I was sent to advise. The automobiles seemed to be a status symbol for those with certain government service and business accomplishments.

Also, they were given drivers not only for status but for practical purposes. There was a shortage of jobs for young citizens, so the idea was that each person of influence would be expected (if not required) to hire the unemployed. In our case, three young family members shared this responsibility, so that each driver would share each day and thus feel they had a job and responsibility as a person and not just sit around and do nothing. Those at the top of the Indonesian society would have to succeed in military service, then government service, and only then could they enter into the business world. Almost everyone I met at this level had followed the same procedure. It was a way of life for the few thousand families who would ever reach this level of importance. (More on this later.)

When I arrived at the office, I was greeted by Yetty and Soekaryo who were kind and gentle to me from the day I came to the day I left. They never left me alone unless I requested it. We spent the first day getting to know each other—we talked about our families and ways of life, our personal opinions, our value systems, and more. It was a great day.

I had been apprehensive that although I had been very successful in my life, coming to this foreign country with different people who have different ways of thinking and different habits, I might not be able to communicate in a way that would enable me to be successful in this venture.

Soekaryo asked me what I like, and I told him I enjoy tennis, good food, and interesting people. He said he didn't play tennis but he had a good friend who works for the health department and loves playing tennis, and he would arrange for a game anytime I wanted. Of course, we could play only at 6 or 7 in the morning, since any later in the day, the temperature was brutally hot.

We also talked about our wives. I found out his wife was a senator in the Indonesian legislature (remember this was a Muslim country)—a famous person in her own right. I had the pleasure of having dinner with her twice.

We went over our objectives, and he explained how these companies are organized. They are conglomerates of presidents of other major companies in the country. The Indonesian president requests that they form these conglomerates to create new business ventures that can then hire the young unemployed. Nobody says "no" to the president, and each board member participates at least monthly in meetings to discuss the future.

I was told on my first day that everyone on the board would like to have lunch with me, to get to know me better. I was astonished, but you know something? I had at least 12 lunches with Indonesia's most fascinating and accomplished people. Some of the board members were mainly interested in America, some in my business background, others in my personal background, and several of them were interested in developing a joint venture on projects that I could perform for them in the good old USA. They all wanted to have business interests in America, because they all believed that America would secure their futures. Almost everyone had sent their college-age children to American schools. Most of them went to universities in the Houston area, obviously for the oil connections.

But back to the reason I went to Indonesia for consulting to this conglomerate, for the purpose of expanding their factories with products that could be exported. Soekaryo and I spent the first few hours in getting to know one another, then he took me to the showroom, where he explained the array of products they were attempting to export. The product lines ranged from woodcarvings of traditional Indonesian figures to poorly labeled canned fruits and vegetables and everything in between. Essentially, they took what they were making in the country and put it in a showroom. And their product line was virtually worthless in the Western world. The quality of the products they produced was above average for that part of the world, but those products were all wrong for the markets that they were interested in penetrating.

So from the first day, it was clear what my goals and objectives were: to select a line of new products for export; to train their factories to produce these products; to repackage these products in an exciting way; and to create an international marketing program using trade shows and other vehicles to reach their sales objectives. Knowing what your goals and objectives are makes it much easier to succeed.

Yetty and Soekaryo were there for me all the time: I could call them or be with them even on the weekends. They introduced me to their spouses and friends, and I felt always part of their social circle.

The work week was Monday to Friday from 8 to 4 and sometimes longer. I traveled to the countryside, where the product factories and farms that produced the fruits and vegetables for canning were located. I traveled to Bali and other rural places where they did woodcarvings and other tourist-type products were produced. Discussing my day-to-day workings is not very interesting, but the only way I could get to my final conclusions.

On November 6, 1990, I submitted my final report, with copies to the United Nations' Development Organization and, of course, to the company I was working with. How I got to these conclusions will be explained as I further describe my Indonesian journey.

This country's economy is supported almost entirely by its natural resources—mainly oil, natural gas products, rubber, coal, tin—as well as pharmaceuticals and medical equipment. I discovered almost immediately that the country's labor force consisted almost entirely of well-educated and important family-connected management types or unskilled laborers. However, it is impossible to succeed in manufacturing and distributing of this type of products without a strong middle-management team, yet this type of employee was virtually missing in this country. Therefore, I suggested they hire a Singaporean marketing company to train some Indonesian college graduates to learn these middle-management positions. Singapore, a neighboring country, is very well advanced in international marketing and is the most success-ful Asian country in developing Western markets. But Indonesians are very slow to accept this type of assistance from outsiders. I kept ham-mering away, and eventually, they agreed.

For my first weekend in Jakarta, I told my host that I would be okay by myself and do the tourist things. On Saturday, my first stop was the world-famous Indonesian Puppet Museum. I paid my admission fee and started to walk down a flight of wooden steps, when I tripped and fell down the stairs. I remember bruising my arms and mainly landing on my backside. The museum attendant rushed to my aid, and I assured him that I was fine and continued to view these extraordinary puppets.

But as the day moved on, I began to feel some discomfort, so I went back to my hotel. The first thing I did was drop my pants, and to my amazement, I had the largest and darkest black-and-blue mark covering my entire buttocks. I did not know what to do, so I called Soekaryo and asked him to find me a good doctor: after all, he was former Minister of Health. He told me the best doctors in the country were assigned to the Western hotels, for tourism purposes, and he would come over and ask the hotel doctor to join us. In the meantime, I took a Polaroid photo of my buttocks and for some reason, I express-mailed it to my wife in New York. I was actually wondering if should I fly back home for medical assistance. After all, this big brave international traveler was in a foreign country and scared.

A short period of time later, my new best friend Soekaryo showed up and comforted me until the doctor knocked on my hotel door. I answered the door, and the doctor was a thirty-something gorgeous Indonesian woman with a black medical bag. She asked me what was wrong and then said, "Drop your pants," and with some reservation, I followed her instructions. She studied my problem and I asked her, "Will

I ever be able to play tennis again?" How stupid was I! She laughed and said, "How about tomorrow morning, with me?" I was in shock. She told me all I had was a deep bruise, nothing broken. She handed me an ointment and told me to periodically rub it into the injury.

I was still skeptical, but I read the label to find out where this medicine was produced. To my relief, it said West Germany, and to my amazement, within 2 days, this unbelievable medication had almost 100% cleared up my black-and-blue mark. To this day, I still look for this medication to be accepted by our FDA for American usage. Whatever happened to globalization?

Once I solved my medical problem, I enjoyed the rest of the weekend touring Jakarta. On Monday morning, I was off to work. I explored the operations, staffing, and all the other details, gathering the facts to allow me to move forward.

By the middle of that week, I moved to a new hotel called Borobudur Intercontinental, a beautiful old-world facility with an indoor/outdoor walking track, swimming pool, and tennis courts. I finally found the perfect location to make the rest of my stay very pleasant.

To increase my learning curve, I planned a trip to the most well-known place in Indonesia, the island of Bali. When most people say they've traveled to Indonesia, they probably only visit this beach resort, for its beautiful geography and people. It's like another world made up of people with their own customs and religion. This is perhaps the only place in Indonesia that doesn't practice Islam exclusively.

Yetty was going to accompany me, and we were to leave on Friday morning. She would leave Bali on Saturday afternoon; I would stay through the rest of the weekend enjoying this paradise, which I had visited with Aviva about 10 years earlier. We visited many carving factories, tourist shops, and export showrooms, because in all of Indonesia, Bali created products that were well received by the tourist trade. We made many connections for a future product line and therefore accomplished our goal.

Yetty returned to Jakarta on Saturday afternoon and gave me a plane ticket that was to leave the Bali airport at 6 PM Sunday. But when

I arrived at the airport about 4 PM, I was advised that there was no Sunday evening flight to Jakarta and I would have to wait until 6 AM Monday morning. I was a little annoyed, but I realized this was the third-world way. I just accepted it and did the best I could. I decided going back to a hotel and getting up at 4 AM in the morning to get back to the airport didn't work for me, so I chose to hang out at the airport and sleep in the lounge so I would be there for my 6 AM departure.

The Bali airport was an interesting place: it was very large for the number of people who were using it, and it was white tiled, from ceiling to floor—probably because the tiles were available locally and easy to maintain. Very few people were there at this unusual time, and I kept dozing off when I noticed that the visitors in the middle of the night were mainly roach-type insects, which I easily observed as they traveled across the white-tiled floors.

I survived this experience and returned to work that Monday morning, where I was greeted by Soekaryo and Yetty, and I made no big deal about this airport adventure. We continued my work study by taking more day trips to factories and farms in the countryside. Soekaryo and his wife, the Senator, took me to dinner that week, which was a special experience because I learned how Indonesian government functions. I spent additional evenings with Soekaryo and his male friends going to excellent restaurants. Chinese restaurants are among the best in Jakarta, and the bigger the facility, the better the restaurant is considered. That's different from the Western world, with our small, intimate restaurants that are owned by famous chefs. Everything important was large in Jakarta.

My new friends knew I loved music, so they took me out to see the nightlife of their beautiful city. Most of the bands were from the Philippines and played American music, and disco was in fashion. So after making the rounds of the live music scene, I was taken to their most-famous supersized discotheque. Because I was with these prominent gentlemen, we were given a special table. Within minutes, I was approached by a beautiful young Indonesian woman who asked me to dance. The strange thing was that I was the only one asked. So I danced. Aviva will tell you that I'm a good dancer, and disco was my passion. Before the evening was over, I had been approached by at least 30 Indonesian women to trip the light fantastic, and they all wanted a picture with me. What a great ego boost!

But I discovered that they were motivated by something else. In many countries, age is not a factor in a man's importance; *status* is the major factor in his desirability. In other words, I was a 58-year-old executive sitting with some of the most important people in Indonesia, and everybody wanted to dance with me and take my photo. I now believe there are more than 30 photographs of me with a young girl, hanging in 30 middle-aged Indonesian women's living rooms. How many Jewish men from Rockaway can make that claim? It was a great evening, and I returned to work the next day dog tired but exhilarated.

I spent the next week developing new ways to maximize Indonesian business potential and ways to find and train middle-management Indonesians, and preparing my final report for K I T (which stands for *kias inter trada*, the International Trade Development Company). I also continued to have lunch meetings with board members, where I met some of their gorgeous wives, with their beautiful long black hair and perfectly sculpted tan faces and peachy complexions.

Then a funny thing happened on the Friday of that week. Soekaryo approached me and said next week would be a short one since he and the rest of the board members would be leaving town to attend the royal wedding. Then he asked me if I would like to go! The Prince of Malaysia was marrying the Princess of Indonesia. This was a very important event for the region as well as the country; everybody was talking about it, and Jerry the Jewish boy from Rockaway was invited! He handed me this gold-leaf-engraved invitation with my name on it. I'm holding it right now in my 79-year-old hands.

My first thought was I had nothing to wear, only the few suits I brought with me. Obviously, I thought I needed a tuxedo. But that was not the case: Soekaryo and his buddies took me shopping, and we selected a beautiful Indonesian-style shirt, with traditional Indonesian colors and patterns, and they said it was perfect for the three-day occasion. It appears that it's appropriate for the men to wear beautiful shirts, but for their wives, it's a totally different story: the wives were very excited and were either acquiring new dresses or cleaning old-family ritual outfits that they would wear at different times during the three-day ceremony.

I flew, together with members of the KIT board of directors and their wives, on a small jet plane to the city of Solo, which has the closest airport to the Mangkunegaran Palace of Surakarta, in central Java. There would be numerous ceremonial and family events on Thursday and Friday, climaxing with the President's arrival for the official wedding on Saturday evening. And here was Jerry, formerly "Benny the Book," being included with the official royal party.

After arriving at the airport, we checked into a small motel about 20 minutes from the palace. I shared a room with Soekaryo; other important friends, including an Indonesian Prince, shared other rooms in the motel. The wives did not stay with their husbands; instead, they stayed either at the palace or at private homes.

So there we were, a group of 50-something successful men saying, *Let's go into town and have some fun.* There were 12 of us, so we hired four trishaws (three-wheeled bicycle taxis, driven by men), and we explored the possibilities. One of these gentlemen remembered that in this small town, there was the greatest massage palace in the country, and he said he would take us there. It was evening, and darkness had occurred, and his trishaw was the lead vehicle weaving in and out of secluded streets, and still the massage palace was nowhere to be found. He said perhaps they had moved. We continued our search for approximately two hours, laughing and chatting away. Twelve men, all age 50-something, having a great time just by being together.

It was about 11:30 PM when we gave it up and decided to go to what they called the greatest outdoor food court in the country. We arrived at a small public park and spotted a dozen food carts, each displaying items that I had never seen in my life. The others were all very excited and hungry and proceeded to order all their favorite delicacies. They said "Jerry, let us order for you," and they delivered an array of food of which I could not identify anything. Again, my mind flashed back to my Puerto Rican Montezuma's revenge experience. I realized I needed to find a way to be courteous but avoid eating what I considered to be dangerous materials. So I sat myself in front of a bush, and slowly and methodically so as not to be noticed, I disposed of the food my friends had given me, mainly in the shrubbery behind me.

Between the plane ride and our in-town experience, we were all very tired, so we returned to our motel to rest for the following morning's experience: we were to visit the Royal Palace.

◈

Wives of my Indonesian Business Associates all dressed up
for Royal Wedding Reception, 1990.

My UN Indonesian Consulting project office staff, 1990.

The following morning, at approximately 8 AM, there was a knock on the door. We opened the door and found a tray of unusual looking food. It looked to me like what we would call a wrap, consisting of large green leaves with a variety of other things inside. All of the room doors were opened almost simultaneously to hoots and howls of unbelievable excitement. My friends were screaming that the palace had delivered a special breakfast. They sent us something that sounded to me like *hoombala*. Whatever this breakfast was, they were singing and dancing as though their wives had just delivered their firstborn children. Again, I was conflicted with the choice of eating stuffed green leaves or being discourteous to my gracious host. I decided to take the middle ground and told them that my stomach was a little queasy from last night's late dinner, so I wanted to be cautious and just go to the motel restaurant for toast and coffee. They were probably very pleased, for they were able to eat my portion of the special treat. The restaurant had scrambled eggs and toast, so I was very happy, too.

On returning to my room, I noticed a little sign at the lobby's front desk that said "blind massage." I thought, what in the world did that mean? So I asked. The desk clerk told me that in rural parts of the country, newborn girls are considered a burden—similar to what the Chinese do by eliminating newborn girls at birth. But the Indonesians found other inconceivable ways of dealing with their problem. Apparently, to get a massage from a blind female was considered a special treat, and it was a way for the girls to make money for their families. The theory was that a blind person would have special sensibilities in performing the massage. In any event, it was a turnoff to me, not imagining that anybody could treat an innocent child in that way. This was part of my third-world learning experience on how they learned to mix a society with Western-educated executives and rural, old-world cultures.

About 9:30 AM, a bus with the wives arrived to pick us up and take us to the summer palace and be greeted by the royal family. We arrived with much fanfare following my friends. Inside, I felt very out of place; after all, I was, in my mind, a total stranger.

The palace interior was, of course, magnificent. I found a hardback chair to sit by myself, to avoid all the friends and family hugging and kissing just to stay in the background. But after the initial greetings, I become the centerpiece and was greeted and welcomed by the entire royal family. They said to me, "We'd love you to meet our daughter, the Princess bride." So I followed them to another room in the palace, where giant French doors were open, and there sat the Princess and an elderly woman surrounded by a potpourri of Indonesian cultural items. They explained to me that this wise old woman was with the Princess for seven days and nights, for the purpose of sharing her wisdom and counseling and to answer any questions she might have.

They virtually had to push me into the room, since I felt uncomfortable, like an outsider. But the Princess hugged me and welcomed me, just like another member of the family. We spoke for a while and were then served a magnificent lunch in the royal dining room.

I can't remember every event because but they were numerous and continuous. But I do remember on the following morning that the official ceremonies began. The first day, the ceremony was at the Summer Palace, which was an oval-shaped, enclosed arena that seated perhaps 3,000 people. The first day was a small crowd of perhaps 500 family members, both Malaysian and Indonesian, and close friends. Of course, I was invited. Being included was a very important part of the Indonesian culture: they are very respectful of their guests, always inclusive, and never letting me feel like an outsider. That day's schedule included song and dance in ancestral costume, which were all very fascinating.

Then we had lunch, and then tea at 3:00. Each person was given a clear glass with a metal holder, in which very fine tea was poured. There was a table in front of us, which included some pastries, and a place for us to put down our glasses. What astounded me was that there were 20 glasses on the small table, all looking exactly the same, yet each one of those people knew which glass was theirs—except for me. I got confused all the time, and I probably drank someone else's tea.

So for our group, the wedding festivities were a three-day event of 500 people the first day, and each succeeding day, the number of guests grew, and our seats at the Palace arena went from the front row to further back. The reason was that each day, more dignitaries arrived from around the world, and they were politically more important. So by the third day, when the presidents of both countries arrived with their official entourages, we were moved even farther to the rear. On Saturday, when the royal couple was officially married, the building was filled with more than 3,000 of the most important people in that part of the world.

The ceremony was to get even more elaborate and built to a crescendo on Saturday evening, when the royal couple, surrounded by family, took their marriage vows.

On Saturday, November 4, 1990, President Suharto and his official party arrived to take their place at the royal wedding. Every media outlet in the country was absorbed by this important social event. Even though royalty in both these countries are ceremonial positions, there was much importance to this wedding for its economic and political value.

So on Saturday, the day the President arrived, a private bus arrived to take us to the palace. As I was walking toward the bus, one of my new friends spotted a camera around my neck and said, "Jerry, there's no way you can take a camera into an event where the President is." The rule in both Malaysia and Indonesia was that at official occasions, there would be only one appointed government photographer from each country, so that they could completely control the news from this internationally reported event. I said I would take the camera anyway, and if they didn't let me bring it into the ceremony, I would just leave it on the bus. Nothing ventured, nothing gained. But they still said, "No, please, you cannot do it," and there was fear in their voices.

But I was an American, free to do whatever I wanted. So when we arrived at the palace and exited the bus, there were soldiers all over the place, inspecting each and every person. A machine-gun-toting, tough-looking guard ran up to me and grabbed my camera. But he said nothing; he just aimed my camera at the ground and snapped it twice. He smiled, returned my camera, and said, "Have a good day." My important companions were astonished, and I was the only person at the wedding who took pictures, with the exception of the two official government photographers. I have an album of the wedding in my home, and the only other photo I ever saw was on the front page of the November 5th edition of the *Indonesian Times*, the largest newspaper in the country. This photo shows the married couple with their immediate families and of course, the President. I don't know if I was stupid or naïve. All I can say is:

JERRY'S LAW #4:
"Start at the top and work your way up."

Sunday, we flew back to Jakarta, and on Monday at 8 AM, I was back in the office. It was my last week of this amazing adventure. The only things left for me to do were to finish my report and say goodbye to the wonderful new Indonesians friends, especially Yetty and Soekaryo. It was time to go home, and I realized how much I missed my darling Aviva and the rest of my wonderful family. When you get caught up in a whirlwind adventure like I did, there was little time to feel homesick.

On the day of my departure, November 9, 1990, I received a phone call from Mr. Casper Kamp—remember, he was the head of the UN office in Jakarta. He wanted to have lunch and see how I was doing. I said I was doing fine and had just returned from the royal wedding, and I said sarcastically that I couldn't have done it without him. The United Nations might have some good ideas and some money, but obviously no real value. The fact that I was an executive dealing with the highest level of Indonesian society and this man was still not motivated to do his job just proves again and again that the UN is made up of high-paid worthless executives.

JERRY'S LAW #15:
"Bureaucracy is a challenge to be conquered with a righteous attitude, a tolerance for stupidity, and a bulldozer when necessary."

Upon reflection, my daughter Michelle's insistence that I go is very much appreciated. I could have gotten financial gain out of this trip, for the connections I made would have given me unlimited opportunities with the good friends I made at the highest levels of Indonesian commerce. They feared that their time at the top of Indonesian society could come to an end very abruptly, and the old guard needed and wanted

270

some business connections in my grand old USA. Even today, with our changing government and attitudes, we still remain one of the only truly free society in the world. At this stage in life, I decided traveling back and forth to Indonesia was not what I wanted to do. So I never pursued these opportunities—and stayed home to develop some new trade shows.

Creating FunExpo: The International Family Fun Center and Miniature Golf Show

In the spring of 1990, my daughter Michelle and my former IDEAS show manager, Bailey Beeken, came to me with a new show idea. They were both around 30 years old, at that time, and they had developed a close business and personal relationship. Michelle was still working as an attorney, but only part-time. By choice, she had left her big corporate law firm. Bailey was working at the time as a show manager for a large trade-show companies. Both had caught the entrepreneurial bug: they wanted to leave the corporate world and develop their own business. They had explored many different options but decided to zero in on a trade show for local amusement centers, such as miniature golf.

In the '50s, miniature golf had become an important part of family entertainment in most of America. But as soon as the real estate boom started later on in the '50s, the small businessmen who owned miniature golf courses started receiving large financial offers for their valuable property. So most of them cashed in and secured their futures. Then in the '90s, there was a recession, which again caused many buildings and lots to become empty in suburban American. So the number of minia-ture golf courses began to spring up again.

However, when I personally studied the potential of this market, I realized there were not enough locations or product needs at the exist-ing locations to justify a successful tradeshow. So we dug deeper and found an array of family amusement businesses that were springing up around the country, including waterparks, go-cart tracks, electronic game rooms, skating rinks, etc.—in fact, many of these businesses were beginning to combine some of these attractions into substantial indoor and outdoor facilities. These stand-alone amusement centers were growing quickly, and they needed to acquire products such as electronic games, amusement rides, and food products at a very fast pace to keep up with their growing demand.

At the same time, because there was a recession, it was very expensive for parents to take their children to large parks, such as Disney and Six Flags Great Adventure. It was also a time when many parents were both working and often felt guilty that they needed to make their children perpetually happy. These stand-alone fun centers filled this need.

The owners of these fun centers went to a giant tradeshow called IAPA: the International Amusement Park Association. This association was sponsored by the large amusement parks and therefore had very little to offer in product and educational seminars for this new growing concept.

So in the fall of 1990, the three of us attended the IAPA show in Las Vegas, interviewing potential exhibitors and attendees to see if they'd be interested in our new concept to give this industry their own show. We learned that nobody wanted to be a small fish in a big pond. We did the groundwork to establish a name, get a venue with appropriate dates, and start developing what might be a new tradeshow. After much discussion, we decided on the name FunExpo, with the official corporate name being the International Family Fun Center and Miniature Golf Show, using the slogan, "Where family fun is serious business."

We formed a committee of established family-fun-center operators from around the country who would advise on the development of this new project. We had to develop a Board of Directors, to gain respect within the industry. We reserved the dates of October 24–26, 1991 for our first event to be held in the Market Center in Atlanta, Georgia.

The exhibitors would be manufacturers of various electronic games and those of rides for smaller children (not the big massive rides), as well as go-cart manufacturers. Then, of course, new-concept people who make the most unbelievable electronic and interactive games: they're inventors. There were a lot of these people—more than we had ever imagined.

Before proceeding any further, though, we had to prepare legal agreements to establish a three-way partnership: one-third for me and my daughter, one-third for Bailey, and one-third for our California PR partners and friends, Larry Winoker and Paul Baker. Michelle and I would work for a small salary; in addition, we contributed $25,000.

Larry and Paul would be responsible for all the promotion and public relations campaigns; in addition, they contributed $60,000. Larry and Paul were very excited about being part of this new venture. They had seen me build Art Expo from scratch with much amazement. It was now their business, and they put in the effort well above the value of their $60,000 investment.

Then I asked Bailey to contribute $5,000, just so she would have some skin in the game. She would be the show manager, but I knew that having a financial investment—even just a small one—was critical, to get the level of commitment we needed to make this project work. Bailey rejected this idea with a passion, because this was something new for her. She had always had a salaried job, and she was angry at me for pushing that envelope, but after much discussion, she finally relented. And she will be the first to tell you that I was right, and she enters into no new business relationships unless the other party has some skin in the game.

Soon thereafter, Bailey told us she had a business relationship with a man named Scott, who was the owner of a magazine in the industry called *Tourist Attractions and Parks*. Bailey suggested that it would be very helpful if we could establish some kind of joint venture with him, since she believed a trade magazine sponsorship for a new show was important.

So the three of us visited Scott's office in Philadelphia, and Scott agreed in principle to our arrangement and initialed a piece of paper. Then, to our shock, based on our conversation about the initial idea, Scott announced his own show called Leisure Expo 1992, which he scheduled for Orlando in the February. Scott was a sleazebag: his handshake meant nothing. But he got his reward: our show was scheduled for October 1991, so we had the first shot at the brass ring, and we were successful, and his show failed. We were three hardworking professionals who had dedicated enormous hours to make this project work. He was a lone individual who thought he could succeed by the seat of his pants. He lost his money and his reputation. That's why you've got to be careful.

JERRY'S LAW #14: "Inspect what you expect."

JERRY'S LAW #18:
"You cannot do the minimum
and reach the maximum."

My formula was to build the right coalition of hardworking professionals while still limiting our cash investment. We opened our office in August outside of Manhattan, in White Plains, New York to keep our costs down and still have easy access from where we all resided. I was director, Bailey was the show manager, and Michelle was director of seminars and special events. But, in fact, we all did whatever was necessary.

Losing the other magazine sponsorship was a blessing in disguise: we ended up with a wonderful relationship with a magazine called *Amusement Business*, which was the most well-respected magazine in the industry. Their staff did everything for us: they prepared our catalogues and programs, and assisted by connecting us with important players in the industry.

We founded a trade association called IAFEC, the International Association of Family Entertainment Centers, and appointed some of the most successful family-fun-center owners and equipment suppliers to the Board of Directors. The board members signed an agreement that they would be the official trade association for FunExpo, and they agreed to sign a restricted covenant clause that would prevent them from starting a competing show. This clause was necessary because associations usually want to control their industries. The association was excited to be a functioning part of this new industry event, and this protected us from any future board members pressuring us to do things that were not good for FunExpo. The IAFEC board also received an option that if we were to sell, it would get first rights to match the price, so it could decide if it wanted to become the owner of FunExpo.

And later down the road, the IAFEC did become the owner, much to its joy. We were successful from the first show, with more than 250 booths, and we kept growing over the next several years, where we grew to more than 1,000 booths. That was quite a success for an industry with restricted potential growth. We held our shows in locations like Orlando and Nashville, and eventually to our permanent home in Las Vegas, which is the ultimate home for the entertainment industry.

We did six annual trade shows before we sold it. We drew 10,000 attendees, all potential buyers, at this trade-only event. Almost all of the attendees were entrepreneurs who owned small amusement parks or similar entertainment centers or who were interested in starting a new business.

Something amazing happened at these shows. Many young entrepreneurs operate these centers, and many had small children. After the first year, both the exhibitors and attendees realized they could take their families to attend the show. So picture the small children of our industry participating in the exhibit by trying all the games and rides. Picture this: buying games and rides that their own children were recommending! That created unbelievable energy on the exhibit floor and made parents happy. In addition, we had free soda and cotton candy. That was before the arrival of the healthy food police. We were also the first trade show to develop a babysitting day camp for parents who needed someone to take care of their very young kids while the parents were trying to do business. Each year got better: the number of children participating increased every year.

Our sixth year was 1996, and we had 1,000 booths, which was extraordinary. The IAPA had well over 3,000 booths, but that was a much bigger industry, so of course it was a much larger trade show. Still, we reached an extraordinary level for our industry. The contractor for the IAPA's trade show was Shepard Convention Services, which was based in Atlanta and run by a man named Carl Mitchell. We had our first show in Atlanta, and we also contracted with Shepard, since his company was very familiar with many of our exhibitors, which facilitated the transition to our show. Carl was my kind of guy—a family man running his own small business while being totally hands-on. We had a lot in common, and everything worked out just fine. He gave us a very fair contract, knowing it was our first show. Like me, he was there all the time to make sure that both the exhibitors and the management were satisfied.

Bailey and Michelle were in the forefront. They were both about 30 years old and they were both beautiful and intelligent; I was around 60 and probably considered over-the-hill by some in this young industry. But I was happy to be in this position, letting these two special young women capture the imagination of the new industry. I was behind the scenes and thrilled to be there.

So from the years 1991 through 1996, we produced FunExpo, and every year it grew larger. Then something happened after the 1996 show in Las Vegas. Bailey received a phone call from Kerry Gumas, who was at the time the vice president for acquisitions for Reed Exhibitions Corporation. Bailey said, "Jerry, you remember Kerry from NAEM? Well, he visited our last FunExpo and might be interested in acquiring this show for Reed." I didn't remember meeting him, but I knew Reed was a giant publishing company; moreover, it was only a division of an even larger company, Reed Elsevier, a truly major international corporation, based in The Netherlands.

We were excited, so I said, "Let's talk." At the same time, I thought to myself, *"I start shows so I can sell shows."* So we started negotiation with Kerry and the president of Reed to acquire FunExpo to be part of Reed's tradeshow division.

Easier said than done.

As usual, it was difficult to supply the financial information of a privately owned company. This was not the biggest deal Reed ever did; nevertheless, top corporate managers are always over-cautious, to protect their butts. This was the case here. We met in their corporate offices in Connecticut, and then again in our offices in White Plains, and we met, and we met, and we met. Finally, they made us an offer—which we declined. So they made us a little better offer, and we accepted it. Then they made us sign documents saying we could not negotiate with anybody else for at least four months, until we finally resolved this deal with a signed contract.

Opening Fun
Expo with
our children,
1991.

Fun Expo Motown Party, 1992.

It took virtually to the end of those four months for them to finally agree to buy FunExpo. Later, Kerry explained that they couldn't find any fat in our balance sheet, and they were shocked that we were operating on such a low budget and at full efficiency. Apparently, when they acquire a company, they usually find waste, but this was my own company, and there was no waste or fat. This was a negative to Reed. In the world of big business, I guess that makes sense, but in the world of GL, there was no other way to operate than lean and efficient.

So on June 11, 1997, Reed announced to the world the acquisition of FunExpo. Bailey and Michelle would continue to manage Reed's new acquisition, and GL, as planned, would disappear into the sunset and go on with his life. Shortly thereafter, I got involved in another new venture, the New York Coliseum Antique Show (which I'll discuss later). Larry and Paul received one-third payment—more than $1 million, which was quite a payback on their $60,000 investment. In addition, since 1991, they also received dividends of more than $100,000 each year.

Larry admitted to me that because they lived in the L.A. area, they had invested in many projects, all from California high rollers—and none of those investments had made a profit. They lost money on all those prior investments. Out there, everybody has a deal. So GL was their hero, since he was the first in their lives to ever live up to his commitment to his partners.

I'll never forget working the '97 FunExpo, which was now owned by Reed. I committed to work that show so it would be an easy transition. Reed must have sent 40 employees to work that show, whereas we had a grand total of five. Their people kept flying in and out. What could they possibly learn in one or two days, being on their own and just observing? But I was not going to challenge their management style. After all, it was a major international corporation.

One thing I'll never forget: I said to myself, *"What can I do to actually help them succeed in the future?"* My answer was to introduce Reed's VP of Operations to eight to 10 of the major exhibitors, so he could have personal contact with these important players. I said, "Let's walk through the show, and let me introduce you to these large, important exhibitors." His answer to me was, "I'm not really interested. I've seen enough. I'm going to lunch." This was the VP in charge of tradeshows, and he was at this show for the first time, and he wasn't interested in meeting the people from Pepsi-Cola, Zamperla (which designs and manufacturers roller coasters and other thrill rides), and other big exhibitors. These were exhibitors who came to every one of our shows, and they typically took six booths or more. These are people you want to meet! Because in this type of business, personal contact is essential.

When I heard that he wasn't interested and just wanted to go to lunch, I couldn't believe my ears. But I shrugged my shoulders and said to myself, *"This is why I succeeded, whereas many of these management guys keep changing jobs and have little pride in what they do."*

Sure enough, Reed's investment in FunExpo turned out to be a dismal failure. After just a few years, they threw in the towel and sold the tradeshow for 30 cents on the dollar in promissory notes to the trade association, the IAFEC. It was a great story, because the International Association of Family Entertainment Centers became the proud owner of their tradeshow. Reed did not have the management skills and/or the ambition to make this show work.

JERRY'S LAW #18:
"You cannot do the minimum and reach the maximum."

Even though trade shows were part of Reed's business, they weren't successful with FunExpo because what big companies (like Reed) do is buy companies on the basis of their sales, and if they can't maintain the sales up to a certain level, they sell those companies. This is their way of hiding the bodies, meaning burying their failures. What's $3+ million lost among corporate management?

The people we dealt with were all entrepreneurs, small family businesses, so you had to give them personal attention. In contrast, when they do a tradeshow in the large corporate world, they have different corporate guys doing many different jobs. They come and go; they have limited personal involvement or interest. I knew all my clients as individuals, and they treated them as corporate entities. This is what I meant by finding a niche—in those areas that the corporate world can't compete.

The IAFEC still runs the show; it merged with another association, and I don't know the details of their arrangement, but together, they are still going strong. Michelle and Bailey left the show, not that year, but the next year. Even though Reed bought the show and said something like, "We need you. We want to hear what you have to say," after a while, the new owners want to make their own decisions, good or bad.

ARTE—Art Resources' Trade Expo

In addition to FunExpo, which started in 1990–1991 and ran through 1996, I also pursued another venture in 1991. When I sold International Art Expositions (which was the formal name of Art Expo) to HBJ in 1987, I had a restricted covenant that said I couldn't run another art-related show for five years. But that didn't mean I couldn't *plan* a show. Many of my friends and former exhibitors were complaining about the diminishing success of the present Art Expo in New York, and they pleaded with me to start a new show. I discussed this with my daughter Michelle, who was working with me, and with our Fun Expo partner, Bailey Beacon. Fun Expo was another tradeshow that we had just started, and I discussed splitting my time to start this new art fair.

They encouraged me, and I announced ARTE to be held on September 19–22, 1992 at the Jacob Javits Convention Center. ARTE stood for Art Resource Trade Expo. This show would be open to the trade only, something that dealers had always wanted. The early '90s were tough economic times. Many dealers were encouraging, but not all were willing to give up Art Expo, which, after all, was a known entity. They took a wait-and-see attitude. We scratched our way to get enough exhibitors to proceed and financially reach break-even, but I was not encouraged about the future because of the economic environment.

Then a funny thing happened on the way to the art fair: HBJ had sold Art Expo to a company called Advanstar, whose managers began to panic when they heard I was putting on ARTE. They called me at the beginning of August 1992, a little more than a month before ARTE was to open, and they offered to acquire my new venture. It was a miracle. They were worried that I would destroy them, so they decided to buy

ARTE from me. They promised to continue the shows for at least three years and give it a chance to succeed. They paid me more than $900,000, which I shared with my partners, Michelle and Bailey, and we received the contract to run the show through 1994. Imagine them being scared and paying me off to go away! Obviously, they made me sign another restricted covenant for seven more years, but I knew in my heart of hearts that this was my last art fair.

ARTE proceeded, but it was not very successful in this business environment. In tough economic times, art sales suffer first. Advanstar never announced a second show, and I believe they never intended to proceed, even when they signed the contract with me for three years. So I wrote them a letter asking, "Where's my money for our contract to run it?"

At first, they didn't respond to my letter, so I had my attorney send a letter. At this, they claimed they never received my original letter. But their response to me was, "Well, we're not running the show, so you don't get paid." I always wrote pretty good contracts (or my lawyers did), and that provision was never mentioned, so I disputed their claim. And we settled. It was a win-win and an ego-ego for GL.

Enjoying our
Majolica garden
seats, 1990.

Visit to Nic Boston Antiques,
London, England, surrounded
by Majolica Pottery, 1997.

Africa Safari, Aviva weighing
her 90-pound Nile Perch, 1990.

16

Antiques Become
the Answer

So once again I was pondering *what can I do to replace these important business activities in my life?* I was no longer director of Art Expo, but the reality was that my life and Aviva's life were now filled with great diversity. Besides venturing into new business ideas, we also were financially able to travel the world.

As mentioned, back in 1984, Aviva and I had visited the renowned art fair in Basel, Switzerland to find new Art Expo exhibitors. Then, as was our custom, we took some vacation time in Europe, and we always ended up in London. It was during that time we decided that we both enjoyed antiquing. We knew that Wedgwood was a famous English potter, and we had the opportunity to visit the Wedgwood factory and museum in Stoke-on-Trent, in the English countryside, about 130 miles northwest of London.

We decided to collect Jasperware, with its variety of pottery shapes and sizes, for many functional uses, that was created by Wedgwood since the 1770s. We knew virtually nothing about collecting, so we decided to start this learning adventure together. Jasperware came in many colors, but we took a liking to the dark blue, on which white emblems of different figures were etched, usually on the center of the piece. Following my usual modus operandi, we started collecting at a fast and furious pace, and within a one year, we had almost 100 pieces of Wedgwood.

JERRY'S LAW #2:
"When given a choice, take both."

But as it was when I started in the art world, I had a learning curve that was slow but sure. Within two years, I had developed some expertise, and I began to realize that there were different levels of quality, rarity, and condition, which are the fundamentals of building a good collection. Aviva and I spent much time in antique shops, learning as we were spending.

In 1985, we took the same travel route as the previous year, again ending up in London. It was there that we began to qualify our search, looking for the best antique shops and malls, so as not to waste any time. In London, Grays Antique Market was recommended for the quality and quantity of fine antique shops. We roamed the aisles, but we couldn't find any Wedgwood, so we asked one of the dealers. He said, "Rita Smythe has a booth on the lower level called Britannia," and she specialized in English pottery and, of course, Wedgwood. So we headed down a spiral staircase, and before we even reached the bottom, our eyes were immediately drawn to a booth of highly glazed, extremely colorful objects, featuring many sizes and shapes, including combinations and varieties of animals, fruits, and flowers, in addition to the usual classical figures. We were greeted by this charming middle-aged English woman in full accent who introduced herself: "I am Rita Smythe. Can I help you?"

We said, "You have a lovely space, but we're looking for Wedgwood, and we can't find any." She said, "Of course you can. Many of these pieces are Wedgwoods." At that moment, our collecting was to begin to reach an important level. She introduced us to English Majolica, which was a type of highly glazed, lead-based pottery that was introduced by the Minton Pottery Company in 1859 and quickly produced by the other fine English potters, such as Wedgwood, Holcroft, and George Jones. This was the great Victorian period in England, which created the Industrial Revolution and a burgeoning middle class. This pottery was made primarily for the middle class, and for functional use, in the form of plates, tea pots, game dishes, cheese bells, jardinières, etc. In addition, these English potters also created specially commissioned Majolica pieces for the royal palaces, as well as for important private homes and institutions.

Rita pointed out a beautiful stick stand (for canes and walking sticks), which we could use as an umbrella stand at our home; it had glorious colors, with fruits and flowers on its body, and it was marked *Wedgwood*. This was the beginning of Jerry and Aviva developing one of the most important Majolica collections in the world.

As soon as we discovered Majolica, we started disposing of our Jasperware and building our Majolica collection. At present, we have more than 400 pieces, all displayed in our 2-bedroom New York apartment—and we still have room to sleep!

So starting in 1984 and continuing to the present, we have developed several different collections. One is Winston Churchill memorabilia, as well as ceramic Uncle Sam-style pottery, which proves we are equal-opportunity patriots. We also have a collection of 200 items that we keep in our Florida apartment, most of which are ceramic turtles. They have hard shells, and they walk very slowly. (That's a joke. . . .)

We started collecting turtles in a very humorous way. In 1990, my daughter Michelle and her husband Scott and their two daughters, Maxine and Ava, were visiting us in Florida for the Christmas holiday. We were sitting at the community pool, and my son-in-law wandered off to a body of water nearby, where he found a turtle. He picked it up to show his children, but he discovered there was another turtle under this turtle. He tried to reattach the two turtles, but without success. He felt terrible. So we laughed, and we said to him, "Scott, that's *tortoise interruptus.*" And after they went back home, we found a small ceramic turtle for about $3, and sent it to Scott as a cute reminder of this humorous event. The next year, when they returned for Christmas holiday, they brought the ceramic turtle with them: Scott said, "Florida is a much better place for turtles than New York." This started my new obsession for collecting all things turtle for our Florida apartment.

The Churchill and Uncle Sam collections were a great passion, since they reminded me that America is the greatest place in the world, and that Winston Churchill was perhaps the greatest person of the twentieth century and America's greatest ally. I never forget how much we owe to all the people who fought to make our country special.

Creating a New Show for Antiques

All of this is to give you some background how Aviva and I spent our free time visiting antique shops, shows, and malls. And that's how I met my next business partner, Irene Stella, who ran the most successful and largest antique show in New York City, at the New York passenger-ship terminals. She called them the Triple Pier Shows, which ran twice a year in November and in March. There were some 600+ exhibitors, displaying everything from museum-quality antiques to collectibles that expand your imagination. Every year from 1986 to the present, Aviva and I have attended these events.

Irene and her husband Andy had also visited Art Expo, and, as show manager professionals do, they visited the show office to chat and to congratulate the managers for their successes. Andy had a great love of art, and we had so much in common and much respect for each other, and became very friendly. We all talked many times that someday, we might do an antique show together.

You may wonder why the Stellas would need me, since they were already running antique shows. The answer is simple: although Irene was already producing the Triple Pier Antique Shows, she could get only certain dates at the Piers, since most of the time, the passenger ships were docked there. That meant she couldn't expand beyond her present schedule. And of course, she wanted to do more. She had attempted a new antique show at the Meadowlands Arena in New Jersey, and she described it as her greatest nightmare. The disaster was because of the unions, where everything went wrong. Many of her exhibitors were crying, screaming, or both: they were miserable. She said that experience was the worst in her life, and she would never again work at a highly unionized building again. She considered partnering with me because she knew I was a person who could be able to negotiate with the city, the unions, and the contractors.

The idea of doing a show together was just idle chatter until I came up with the idea of doing one at the New York Coliseum, which had closed at the end of 1986 but was still standing in 1991. When it closed, it was announced that New York builder Mort Zuckerman (who is also publisher of the *New York Daily News*), had entered into a contract with the MTA to demolish the building and rebuild on that site. But five years had gone by, and Mort disappeared from his commitment; nobody else stepped into his place, and the building was still unoccupied.

In my mind, the New York Coliseum was the best venue for an antique show, since it had easy transportation choices as well as parking in the building, and was always considered the heart and soul of Manhattan. So Irene said, "If you can get dates for that building"— which meant reopening it—"and be totally responsible for the union contracts and the general contractors," she would give it another try. She knew that I had dealt with these unions successfully with Art Expo.

I was confident that I would be able to negotiate a deal with the owners of the Coliseum, the MTA. I met with their vice president of real estate and said, "Look, while the building remains standing, we would like to rent the convention center for one show at a time, and we're willing to accept 30 days' notice of cancellation based on your final plans to demolish the existing site." They said, "That's impossible. We don't really have enough staff maintaining the building. It would be very difficult."

So I asked him, "Are the lights still working? Is the electricity working? Is the heating system functioning? Is the escalator working? Do you have a resident superintendent currently on site?" and the answer to all these questions was *yes*. I said, "We need nothing. We'll bring our own carpeting, walls, lighting. You don't have to put in any real effort. Just receive our rent money." These agencies are always running out of money and therefore raising tolls and subway fees, so we thought this was a great way to increase their revenue.

These fruitless discussions went on for months, but I didn't give up. As Winston Churchill said, *Never give up. Never give in.* Finally, the MTA agreed to allow me to use the building one time, and one time only, for which I agreed to pay them $60,000. This would bring even more revenue to the city than just the rental income; it would also bring in money for hundreds of union workers, general contractors, local hotels and restaurants, taxis, the trade-show caterer, and the parking garages. Our antique show was to become a financial boon for Columbus Circle, which had become a place for homeless people and all their shadowy activities.

So from 1991 until the Coliseum closed again in January 1998, Irene and I had 20 successful antique shows. Our ability to keep the building open created much additional interest from other entrepreneurs, and in

1997, just prior to the final closing, there were more than 40 shows in the building, including the New York Roadrunners Club (which runs the New York City Marathon); Black Expo U.S.A.; College Fest; the New York Yankees Extravaganza; the Gay and Lesbian Show; and state law examinations, just to name a few. There was a combination of commercial ventures and city- and state-run programs, which saved the government money since the Coliseum was virtually a free venue for them. Re-opening the Coliseum was a win-win for everybody, so it seemed.

The New York Coliseum Antique Shows were extraordinary! By our second event, we had a waiting list of exhibitors. And hours before opening, the attendees were lined up around the block. There was great energy and excitement in and around the building, which always makes for good sales. I would stand behind the ticket sales booth in amazement as the crowds were growing impatient to get in; I saw many celebrities attending. The show had become a happening.

We discovered, to our amazement, that the best time of the year to hold this event was New Year's Day, and the days around it. Remember, in the early 1990s, there was another recession, and people were concerned about their future. The idea of welcoming in a New Year gave them hope for better times, and they would reward themselves with the purchase of antiques of various values. The sales were unbelievable, because everybody wanted to start the next year with something positive.

Also, I was one of the first in the building, so I could find treasures before the lines of collectors attacked the exhibition floor. That was a special perk of being a partner.

The Stellas and the Leberfelds celebrated many New Year's Eves together at some great New York hotel or in Times Square, because we were blessed with this great success.

But even with all this success, things are not always what they seem to be. The devil is always in the details, so I want to explain some of the interesting events that went on before and during each and every one of these antique shows.

In 1991, we were preparing to reopen the New York Coliseum. Even though the building had closed in '86 and the state had contracted with different unions for the Javits Center, I decided to take the safe route and rehire the same union members who were operating the building when it closed in 1986. I met with the leaders of these different unions and told them of my decision. They were thrilled and revitalized. After all, the state unions had pushed out the city unions at the Javits Center. Moreover, they made it clear that my loyalty deserved their loyalty—so there would be no shenanigans, no billing for deceased former union members, and an honest day's work for an honest day's pay. They all high-fived me and promised to live up to that commitment.

So Stella's organization sold all the available space, and we were on our way. Unfortunately there were some glitches on the first set-up day. We found each and every entrance filled with homeless people who collected cans and bottles to turn in for the deposits. This area had been dark for five years, during which time it became a major distribution center for those deposit bottles (and for some drug dealing). The distributors were a convenient way for the homeless to cash in what they collected, since the supermarkets had not yet become the depositories that they are today.

So I went to the head of this business conglomerate, where 50 or so people were operating, and I said to him, "Let me give you a few hundred dollars so you can move your business for five days when we're in the area running this show." I could have gone to the police and probably created chaos, but instead, I decided to go to the homeless operators. He took my money and lived up to his word—and for every one of the 20 shows we held at the Coliseum, I gave him $200 and he moved his business operation.

The next major problem was to make certain our exhibitors could unload their antiques in a safe and timely manner. Many of our exhibitors had small items and brought them in panel trucks, and there wasn't even enough room at the loading dock for all of the bigger trucks. We needed the front of the Coliseum so the panel trucks wouldn't create chaos at the loading dock.

In typical New York style, the police started threatening to arrest our exhibitors who were trying to unload the smaller trucks in the front of the building. They didn't care that we were bringing all this business to New York City. It took much negotiation between our off-duty policemen and firemen and the local cops, but we found a way to accommodate each other. Remember, as the song says, *If you can make it here, you can make it anywhere.*

So after much chaos, we finally had the building filled with antique dealers exhibiting their wares, and the place looked fabulous. We dressed up the lobby. We had welcome signs in seven different languages. It was going to be a real New York happening, opening at 10:00, when the crowd started pounding on the door. I couldn't find the Coliseum management to open the door. Finally, I located an individual who opened some of the doors, and the show was on. Within 15 minutes, the show floor was filled with buyers, and this was the start of my next great adventure—another chapter in my American Dream.

Even though the unions promised to be on their best behavior, this was never truly a reality, and as the show was getting bigger and more successful, they all wanted more men, even some fictitious ones. I periodically gave them a little something—a few additional men—but it was always about their egos and looking good in front of their union employees.

One year, Andy Stella and I went out for a quick lunch. When we came back, Irene was crying. "What's the matter?" She said, "I found the union guys spitting on the loading platform and on the show floor. When I asked them to stop, they started cursing at me." Irene was a lady, and she couldn't stand the whole idea of these guys spitting and cursing at her. They had also stopped working. So I put on my double-breasted jacket, I called a meeting of the union supervisors, and I talked to the men, who agreed not only to go back to work but to apologize to Irene. This may seem like no big deal, but union guys don't apologize, so this was a major accomplishment. It's true that some men don't like taking orders from women, but it's also true that, to them, I was a guy in a suit who never talked down to them, which is very important in all areas of business and life. They also knew I worked hard, and I was always there on site to handle whatever problems came up. And they respected that.

As we became more successful, the general contractors were pushing me for more revenue. Of course, I was fighting back. One year, I was approached by two men who previously had been supervisors for a show contractor. They were starting their own business, and they wanted to bid on the next contract. We had been using Freeman (another national company) as our contractor, and these two men came in well below Freeman's price. They assured me that they had the capital investors, and it was no big deal because everybody hired the same union guys, and all the carpet, furniture, and pipe and drape were available for rental.

We were in constant contact with these gentlemen, and they gave us their floor plans, and all the arrangements were made, but, again, a funny thing happened on the way to the Coliseum. Sometimes I seem to get a premonition that something is wrong—like the time that nobody cleaned the floors of the Javits Center before our first Art Expo show opened there. Here I was again, using a new contractor, so I had a hard time sleeping. So I went to the Coliseum at 6 in the morning. To my amazement, the floor was empty! The only thing I saw was the two new contractors I had negotiated with, standing in the far corner. I asked them, "What's going on?" They said, "We don't have any money," and Freeman, who they were renting the equipment from, was demanding payment upfront. I said, "Why did you not tell me?" This was the morning of the setup of the show, and they had created an impossible situation.

I had the name and telephone number of the manager of the Freeman operations, because we had been using them. I woke him up and I said, "We need this equipment." He said, "Well, they didn't pay us." I said, "You know me. You know my reputation. I guarantee full payment," and I convinced them to load those items up, and within three hours, the material was at the New York Coliseum. Of course, I never used those people again. I went back to Freeman, so everybody won. I've never, ever experienced walking into an empty building the day before the show's opening. We had one day to set up, and we did it.

JERRY'S LAW #1:
"If anything goes wrong, fix it. (To hell with Murphy!)"

The irony was the show was a big success, and I lost a lot of sleep, avoided a disaster, and saved a lot of money. Fortunately, Irene had no idea what was happening; when she arrived at 10 AM, everything was humming. Having the right partner can avoid a nervous breakdown.

For every show we held at the New York Coliseum, the MTA had to send me a new contract. We had to renegotiate our contract for each antique show. Usually, no response was followed by "We need a little bit more time," followed by "I don't think so," followed by GL eventually getting one additional contract. Sometimes they sent me the contract, I signed it and sent it back with a check; then it would take them months to sign and return it. This was bureaucracy at work. I can honestly say I never had a good experience dealing with these types of government bureaucracies.

But in the fall of 1995, after we had held 14 antique shows, this didn't happen. I kept asking them, "Where is the contract?" and they finally told me: they had decided, this year, to rent the building to someone else. I said, "Who?" They said the Burlington Coat Factory. Burlington Coat Factory! They wanted to rent it from Thanksgiving to New Year's since they wanted to have an outlet sale in the center of Manhattan. We were doing three shows a year! And had revitalized the area: it was now vibrant and safe. The West Side residents loved us.

So when I looked into the proposed new arrangement with the Burlington Coat Factory, I found out a couple of interesting things. First of all, we were paying $20,000 a floor each day that we were there, whereas Burlington Coat Factory was going to pay only $3,000 a day. I asked them, "Why would you rent them the place when I'm paying seven times more?" But they gave me some lame excuse that they were using the space for a longer period of time.

Then I found out that part of the arrangement was they were not willing to use union labor. This was my entry to saving the situation. I arranged a meeting with the union leaders. I said, "I don't know if you know about this, but the show that we're prepared to do at the end of the year is going to be cancelled because of the Burlington Coat Factory, and their contract states they don't have to use union employees. So if you somehow agreed to it, I will let all your union guys know that you knew about it, and if you don't know about it, you'd better go to the MTA and threaten to strike, or whatever you have to do to get me that building."

Within a week, I got the building. I guess I had to fight fire with fire. So why did Burlington have the building? Obviously somebody paid off somebody. Somebody was a friend with someone at the Burlington Coat Factory. This was the bureaucracy that I had to live with, even though I was the guy who reopened the building and made millions and millions of dollars for the MTA and the city. After all, it was not only my shows renting the space; there were all those other events that were now in the building—a building that previously was a blemish on the neighborhood.

So after five more shows, we got a notice that the MTA was closing the building again, on December 31, 1997. But our show extended into the first two days of 1998, so they reluctantly agreed to keep the building open through January 2, 1998.

We considered the idea of moving the show to Javits. But Irene and I agreed there was something special about the New York Coliseum, and the exhibitors would never be happy with this change of venue.

The saddest part of the MTA saga is the building stayed empty for an additional three years. Eventually, the site of the Coliseum became the Time-Warner Center (of high-end shops, a hotel, restaurants, and residential condominiums), but the negotiations between the real estate people took another three years before they demolished the site. That delay cost the MTA additional millions. The West Side community was up in arms when the Coliseum closed. There were signed petitions to keep the building open until a real demolition date was established whose names included Mayor Giuliani and Congressman Jerry Nadler. The local community activists marched in front of the building during our last Coliseum Antiques Show, to force the continued opening of this building. The building was again closed down but not rebuilt; the area once again became a site for the homeless who slept in the doorways of the Coliseum.

Light can turn dark very quickly.

I found out later on that almost all of the MTA and Triborough executives whom I had dealt with had moved on and became management with big New York real estate companies. I wonder what that means: my guess is "One hand always washes the other." Why should the people who run the transportation system in New York City be involved in large real estate ventures? It seems to me it's a conflict of interest.

Irene and I remain friends; Andy has since passed on. I visit her ongoing pier antique shows every time I can. The Stella organization is still run as a family business. I truly believe that Andy and his Italian immigrant parents and Irene and her Irish immigrant parents and Jerry with his Eastern-European Jewish immigrant parents' background succeeded together because we learned from our families that hard work and trust was the best formula for success. This was another chapter for all of us living our American Dreams.

Every time we meet and talk about the wonderful memories of the New York Coliseum show, Irene admits that many of her present exhibitors say that the New York Coliseum Antique Show was the best show of their lives. I never get tired of hearing those words.

The Triple Pier Antique show is still successful, and it's one of the few major events left in this industry. The fact of eBay's presence in this world and younger people losing interest in putting in the time to collect has caused a disappointing downturn in the antique world. But I believe that events where people meet in person and share knowledge, plus the excitement of physically touching something special and developing personal contacts, will someday return to the antique world and bring back its glory days.

JERRY'S LAW #1:
"If anything goes wrong, fix it.
(To hell with Murphy!)"

17

How My Medical History Impacted My Life

No one gets a free pass with medical issues. Nobody goes through life without being affected by their own medical condition as well as that of their loved ones. I'm going to try to review my life here in terms of how I think my own medical issues affected me and how they made me a better and smarter person.

My first memory of being sick is when I was 2^1/$_2$ years old, when I had chickenpox. In those days, there were limited vaccines, so everyone got childhood diseases. I particularly remember having chickenpox, because I had to get glasses.

The only other medical thing that I remember from my young age is that polio no longer existed. It was one of those childhood diseases that was deadly, but fortunately, Dr. Jonas Salk found a vaccine for it. That fact has stayed with me all my life, because Jonas Salk graduated from the same public school and high school that I went to in Rockaway Beach: P.S.42 and Far Rockaway High School.

Overall, as a child, I was fine. I had all the usual childhood illnesses, nothing different from anybody else. Then, when I was 12 years old, I went to Boy Scout camp, on a big piece of land in a faraway place called New Jersey. In fact, it was Alpine, New Jersey, which is now a beautiful upscale community. Back then, though, it was one of the places where

Boy Scouts went to spend two weeks learning how to be on their own and grow up a little bit.

When I came back from Boy Scout camp, I found out I had developed something that was very prevalent in those days—pneumonia. Thank God that penicillin had just been developed, since before penicillin, many people died from pneumonia. I went to the hospital and stayed there for about a week, and every hour, on the hour, they jabbed me in my buttocks with a shot of penicillin. By the time I was finished with that treatment, I couldn't sit down for a month! Today, of course, you can take a pill, and it does the job. It's amazing in my lifetime how much penicillin has done to make people healthier.

About a year after recovering from pneumonia, I had just been bar mitzvah'd, when I developed pains in my legs. I complained to my mother that they weren't going away, so we went to our regular doctor. He sent us to a specialist, who said I had "growing pains." And the treatment for growing pains was they put me in bed for six months. I never left my bed, except to go to the bathroom, during that period. The idea was if you stay off your legs, they'll get better. Of course, this was ridiculous.

One good thing came out of it, though: while I was bedridden, the school sent a teacher to my bedside every day to help me keep up with the class. In essence, I was being homeschooled by a public school teacher! And when I got out of that situation and went back to school, I was a 90+ student. I don't know if I can directly credit the homeschooling for this, but whatever the reason, I was happy to have good grades.

When I was ready to go back to school, though, I didn't go back into my regular classes. In those days, if you were ill for a period of time, the school system sent you to what they called "a fresh-air class"; they didn't like to use the word "handicapped" or anything like that. These were classes for students who were either in wheelchairs or who had some kind of affliction that the schools didn't want other kids to see. There were kids whose heads were turned to the side, others were shaking; there were kids with all sorts of medical problems. The school systems were protecting other kids from the real world. Ridiculous.

I was in that class for six months, and I have to say it taught me an amazing lesson: those disabled children were happy, in spite of their illnesses, and they worked very hard, especially to overcome their afflictions. That taught me you should never feel sorry for yourself, since there's always somebody who is worse off than you are, yet they get through it, so you're going to get through it, too. These very important lessons you learn as a child will benefit you for the rest of your life. Many of today's parents protect their children from reality. Take it from me, that's not helping them.

JERRY'S LAW #20:
"Winston Churchill said, 'Never give up.'
I say, 'Never give in.'"

I went back to a regular class at 15 years old. Kids that age can be brutal, and they made fun of me because I wore glasses and I was cross-eyed. Even with the glasses, one of my eyes would move all the way over to the other side. Most kids, at that age, make fun of other kids, for anything that's different: kids can always find something to poke fun at. And it can do real psychological damage.

My mother found a doctor who claimed he could cure this problem. However, you need to remember that my parents were *very* poor. There was no medical insurance in those days. There was no Medicaid. There was no government assistance they knew of. It wasn't life or death; it was just something that affected me mentally and emotionally. She found a way to pay, though I never found out how.

My ophthalmologist called the doctor we found a quack. Anyone trying something new is often called a quack. This doctor told me, "Look, your eye muscles are weak, so your eye moves all the way to the bottom and to the side." So he developed exercises that made me stretch my muscles up and down and to both sides, as far as I could. And what was I doing? I was simply strengthening the muscle! I did this for a number of months. And what happened? A miracle! My eye has never crossed again.

So I learned something valuable from that experience: that if something sounds right and it's not dangerous, you should try it. My mother was not well educated, but she was very loving and smart, since she knew this problem was affecting me emotionally, and she did what was right. I don't know what happened to the doctor, whether he was ever accepted professionally. But I'm very grateful for how he helped me. The medical profession is not always looking out for you. I learned to trust my instincts and walk away from a doctor that I didn't feel totally comfortable with. It's worked so far.

At 20 years old, I went into the Army, and the only thing wrong with me was that I wasn't very physically fit, but the Army took care of that. I came out a much stronger person, both physically and mentally. I believe that all young people should do military service: it makes them learn about themselves and the world around them. In other words, it develops maturity.

I got married when I was 24 years old and my wife Aviva was 21. I had grown up with something that really bothered me, emotionally: I had overly large breasts for a man, so I never wanted to take off my shirt. The Army had made me fit, in the best shape of my life, but I still had extra fatty tissue in my upper chest, and it bothered me.

So my wife encouraged me to find a doctor who might be able to do something. Sure enough, there was something that was relatively new, in those days, where the surgeon would cut out the breast tissue underneath and reduce the size. So I tried something new and experiential, and I never looked back. I had the courage of my own convictions, something I would practice for the rest of my life.

Unfortunately, the doctor didn't do a great job. One of my breasts is inward a little bit, and the other one is not quite perfect. Today, surgeons do this type of surgery regularly, so they're much more skilled and experienced than they were back then: now, they'll cut your stomach (for a "tummy tuck"), they'll cut every part of your body to reduce it. But in those days, that type of surgery was considered quackery.

Today, it would be called plastic surgery.

It didn't quite solve my problem, but I guess it made it better, and again, I believe if you don't try, you can never succeed. So if you think something is really going to bother you for the rest of your life, you've got to try to do something about it.

Then I went through a number of years where I was fine, until I was about 40 years old. Our family was living in East Rockaway. I got terrific pains in my stomach and groin area, and I went to a number of doctors. To make a long story short, it ended up being kidney stones. Getting rid of them, though, wasn't easy. I went to a urologist in the next town, Rockville Centre, who was supposed to be the best doctor around, and he just put me to bed. The pains got worse and worse, so I called him again and said, "You've got to come over. I can't even go to your office. You've got to come over."

So eventually, he came and looked at me, and I asked him, "Can't you give me anything for this?" He said, "No. I've had five kidney stones. Be a man. Just take the pain." Now if anybody knows the pain from kidney stones, I've heard it described as being like the pain experienced by a woman giving birth, but a woman doesn't give birth for seven days—which was how long I was in pain, literally. So this guy was ridiculous.

Today, doctors either give you something to induce the kidney stone to dissolve quickly, or they give you strong medication to tolerate the pain until the stone passes. But this guy made me suffer like I had never suffered in my life: I was screaming in pain; my wife had to hold me down. So I learned that never mind reputation: your gut and your instincts, and of course, your own intelligence, have to tell you what's right or wrong.

Don't be afraid to fire your doctor and get a better one. If they're first in the class or last, they're still called "Doctor."

So I found a new doctor, a good doctor. How I found my new family doctor is interesting: I was looking for a local doctor, and I found one who lived a few blocks away; I didn't know anything about this person: I just saw a new shingle. The doctor came to see me—doctors made house calls, in those days—and I almost fell over, because it was a woman! She was Filipino, and from her name, I wasn't able to tell if the doctor was a man or a woman. And for a man to be examined by a woman, in those days, was unheard of! Today, I have no problem with it. But she was the total opposite of my previous doctor. She was warm. She was sensitive. And she gave me something to relieve any discomfort. I went to her for the entire time we lived on Long Island in East Rockaway.

When I was growing up, I had all the typical childhood illnesses, and my doctor lived next door. And in those days, doctors made house calls. This was in the 1940s: they came to your house, and you knew their families, you knew their kids, they knew you, they would actually be friends. They knew all their patients personally. And they knew their economics: sometimes a doctor would walk out and say, "Pay me later." Can you imagine that today?

The doctors carried a little black bag, and when they opened it up, it had so much inside it: a stethoscope, wooden stick tongue depressors, thermometers, and so forth. And they very rarely said, "Go to the emergency room," or "I'm too busy to see you now," like today. Those doctors would come anytime, day, night, or weekends. They loved their jobs and their patients, and we loved them. That's the way it was. So I'm not sure about all these new medical improvements. Certainly, the new procedures and drugs are good, but I don't know about the medical profession as a whole. It's perhaps corny to always say, "the good old days were better," but it's true. We expected good service from our doctors, and the relationship we had with them was special. Not like today.

While I was working for Olivetti, where I became the credit manager, I became very friendly with a man who had a private collection agency. We both loved tennis, and one year, he invited me to go to the U.S. Open tennis tournament. We brought our wives. Aviva and I were in our early forties, and they were at least 10 years older, and his wife was gorgeous: she was blonde, with a beautiful complexion, everything about her was beautiful, inside and out. There was just something special about her, she glowed. She was a nurse-nutritionist, so I said to her, "You look great: is there anything you do in your life that helps you look so good?" She told me, "Yes: I take daily vitamins."

I was surprised, because in those days, virtually every doctor would tell you that you're throwing your money away, that vitamins are just quackery. I think they felt threatened, in a way, by the fact that maybe vitamins could help you, that vitamins were competition, which was ridiculous! And today, of course, there are doctors who believe in vitamins as supplements to good health.

I asked her if she could recommend some vitamins for me, and she gave me a whole list, and to this day, I take 15 different vitamins every day. I've made only a few adjustments over the years, because my needs changed, but I always feel better in the morning after I take those supplements.

Whether they really make me feel better or if it's the placebo effect, I don't know. But it doesn't matter: I believe these supplements have helped me be stronger in my life. One of the things I did was play tennis at a high level until I was 70. Generally, I'm a high-energy person, at work and play: I could even dance all night. My wife has always said I needed two wives to keep up with me—I have to push her a little but she has done great.

I take many individual vitamins. As I've said before, when something works, it works; if it ain't broke, don't fix it. I don't know how many more years I'll have, so I'll keep taking my vitamins. Perhaps, in the end, I'll take them with me.

So a number of years went by, and it was not until I was 68 years old that I had any other major health issues. By this time, we were living in Manhattan. One day, I was walking up from Sutton Place to 1st Avenue, which is a little hilly, and I was feeling shortness of breath. I thought I was in good condition at the time, since I played a lot of tennis, singles mainly, and I could play for hours. I didn't have any chest pain, but the shortness of breath concerned me. It wasn't as though, one day, I felt a sudden pain; it was a few weeks that I had this condition. Of course, we're always in denial. On the other hand, some people might say, "I think I'm having a heart attack." My position was that I had a little shortness of breath one day, so I thought maybe it was a cold, or something minor. It took several weeks before I really pushed myself to go to the doctor.

So I went to see my local doctor, Howard Adler, and it was only a matter of minutes when he gave me an electrocardiogram and said, "I want you to go to the hospital. Let me see if I can get you in without going through emergency; I don't want you to go through all that procedural rigamarole if you don't have to."

So he got me into the hospital. Within the day, they gave me an angiogram and found a 90% blockage in my main artery, and some lesser blockages in smaller arteries. There I was, lying on the table, looking at the pictures of my blocked arteries, and the doctor asked me if I wanted the surgery: "Do you want to do it now?" What was I going to say? It's a little difficult to say no, so I said yes. And they put me through this procedure—the angioplasty—and the next day I was out of the hospital and on my way home. They give me a picture of what I had, which showed where they put the stents—the devices to keep the arteries open, kind of like straws made of metal mesh. It's amazing how much better I felt, once the blood and oxygen were flowing again. One year later I developed scar tissue over the stents, and they had to be redone. Ten years later, I'm feeling fine.

Within a week of being home, I was back playing tennis at the Sutton tennis courts, under the 59th Street Bridge. They had a doubles program where you could just show up and they would match you up. I had never played much doubles, but I decided to go, to just see how I felt, since the surgery. I went and I played well. Then my opponent hit an overhead ball to me at the net; as I went down to return it, I heard this popping sound in my leg. I didn't know what it was, but I knew it wasn't good. I stopped playing, and I limped home.

I knew there was an orthopedic surgeon one block from where I lived, since I passed his office all the time. But this was the day before Thanksgiving. I called his office. Of course, he was gone for the holidays, but there I was, in pain from whatever I had done to my leg. You never want to get sick over a long holiday weekend. So I was relieved when the woman who answered the phone said, "We have a new associate doctor here, and he's still in the office. Would you like to see him?" Of course, I said, yes, then when I talked to the doctor on the phone, he said, "Don't come to me; stay off your leg. I'll come to you. You live very close." His name was Ron Noy.

He diagnosed accurately that I had some sort of damage to my quad muscle, which is the muscle that's over the knee that gives you the flexibility to bend your knee. He lent me an icing machine, which he said would help keep the swelling down. He said, "There's really nothing we can do until we get the swelling under control so I can take an X-ray."

Where was I going to go on a holiday weekend? I was surprised that any physician whom I did not have an established relationship with would agree to see me that day; I thought they would all send me to the emergency room at the hospital. I suppose he agreed because he was a young man, and either he was looking to get experience or new patients, or he simply thought it was the right thing to do.

Then, on Sunday of the Thanksgiving weekend, he called me and asked, "Can I come over and check on you? I want to see how you're doing." He didn't come on Saturday, since he was an orthodox Jew. On Monday, Dr. Noy sent me to take all the usual tests, x-rays and an MRI, which really tells specifically what's wrong. Eventually, he told me I had a total quad tear, and said this is extremely difficult to repair, and very few surgeons have experience with this surgery. The other doctor in Dr. Noy's office, who was older and more experienced, said, "If I do two a year, it's a lot." But Dr. Noy said, "I did a couple and I assisted on a couple of these when I was in medical school." He was confident he could do it.

I wasn't quick to do anything, because you can live with a quad tear. Of course, I was limping had difficulty walking. I went down to Florida for a few months, and before I left, my regular doctor told me the best orthopedic surgeon he knew had moved to Florida, and he suggested I go see him. He was at the Cleveland Clinic in Weston, Florida. Cleveland Clinic was a beautiful state-of-the-art facility, but this doctor said to me, "You know, we don't do this type of surgery often. I'm not sure if you'll ever be able to do the things you want to do, so you'd better think about whether or not you really want to go through with this, at your age." In other words, he was not very encouraging.

So I did nothing until I came back to New York, and I decided to let the young doctor do it. I'm not sure what made me make this decision.

In my gut, my instinct was that this guy knew the procedure, that I was willed to him by something or someone. He did me right, so I trusted him. And he was confident that he could get it done. So I went through with the operation.

After surgery, I went home in a cab: what a mistake! My leg was twice the size of normal, so getting into the back seat was excruciating. In fact, for years afterward, I sat only in the front seat of taxies with their additional legroom, remembering that terrible pain.

Afterward, the swelling was enormous, and the discomfort was great, and the rehab was unbelievably difficult. I rehabbed every day for three months. One of the exercises was on a bicycle, and when I first tried to turn the pedal full circle, I just couldn't do it; it wasn't even close. During the course of my rehab, though, I was able to move it a little bit at a time, more and more. It took me three months before I could get the bike pedal to turn around completely, and when that finally happened, it was one of the happiest moments of my life. It proves that if you stick to something, it pays off. And I'm glad I had the surgery and went through all this: it was important to maintaining my quality of life.

I also want to mention something that Ron Noy, the physician, said to me after the surgery. He said, "You know, Jerry, you taught me something. When I saw you and your age..."—he was only 40, so of course, my age, 68, seemed ancient to him—"I said to myself, *I don't want to put this guy through surgery. What's the point? Let him live out his life limping.* But you know what you taught me, Jerry? That if somebody wants to go through with surgery, to improve or maintain their quality of life, I will never discourage them, never." That made me feel good, since he saw that somebody like me could do it. And I did do it. And that made him not think of an older person as somebody to simply cast off, and let them limp or wheelchair their way to their demise.

The next year, I tried to play tennis again. It was difficult, but I persisted. And by the second year, I was competing in the tournament again. I couldn't run as well, but I had the determination to compete— and to win. I was about 70 at that time. When I had played three years earlier, I had played against a guy named Paul Foreman, who is 10 years younger than I. I play a very steady game; I keep the ball in play forever. I always studied my opponents and had a game plan: I attacked their weaknesses. And I had great stamina: keep in mind that these singles games on soft surfaces can last three to three-and-a-half hours. Paul had beaten me badly the last time. He did things like I did, but better. After all, there's always somebody who's better.

After my surgery and rehab, I struggled to get back into the tournament. Somehow I made it back into the finals against Paul, and I won the first set—maybe because he didn't expect me to play at the level I did. I think the score was 6-3. Then he beat me 6-4 in the second set. So we had to play a third set, to decide the tournament winner. I quickly jumped ahead in this set 4-0, then all of a sudden, my game went downhill. It's very hard to finish your challenge since the pressure gets to even the great players. Anyway, he made a comeback, and it was now 4-4. At that point, I was sure I was going to lose, because typically, at the end of a long match, if you start playing poorly, you can lose all your momentum, your adrenalin, your energy, everything.

However, the day before, after I played the semi-finals, I had gone to see a show, *The Man of La Mancha*. Everybody pretty well knows the story about Don Quixote and his Impossible Dream. So when the score was 4-4, I turned away from our audience and faced the back fence and started singing *To Dream the Impossible Dream*, for maybe 20 or 30 seconds. Then I turned back around with new energy, and I won the next two games. I won the set, 6-4. And I won the championship. I lived the Impossible Dream. And it happened to be my last singles tournament.

I believe there are things that push you toward greater success. There's always adrenalin, of course, but your opponent has adrenaline also. There's also your emotions. And at that moment in my life, thinking about this man, Don Quixote, gave me motivation to finish this match and win.

JERRY'S LAW #20:
"Winston Churchill said, 'Never give up.' I say, 'Never give in.'"

Unfortunately, the next year, I injured myself again. I wasn't a big doubles player, but I had played mixed doubles with a friend of mine on occasion, and she encouraged me to start playing doubles tennis again. So I started playing mixed doubles with her, and we did well. We got into the finals, and somebody hit a very hard shot. I tried to hit it back, and the ball bounced off my racket, and, oh, my God, I couldn't move my arm.

To make a long story short, I tore my rotator cuff. I guess after so many years, your body parts begin to deteriorate, and the muscle injuries start piling up.

So I went to see Ron Noy again. Of course, he knew I would want to somehow rehab my arm, even though I was in my seventies. Obviously, each time you have an injury like this, as you get older, you don't really know which is the main course, so to speak. My ability seemed to lessen, but I still enjoyed the game, and that's really the idea. So I did surgery and rehab again. I did great, and I started playing tennis again.

Meanwhile, I was a grandparent by now, and we had two young granddaughters, who were maybe 2 and 5 years old, at the time. My wife and I were in Florida, and my grandkids were coming down to visit, when I developed a very bad cough and congestion. Everybody said would go away. But it didn't go away. Finally, it was the weekend before my grandkids were coming, and I didn't want them to catch whatever I had, so I went to the emergency room. I waited five hours, because if you're not having a heart attack, you have to sit there forever.

Eventually, some doctor examined me, looked at my throat, and said, "There's nothing wrong with you. Just go home. It'll go away." He gave me some cough medicine to take, but my cough and congestion didn't go away. So I found a local doctor, who I still go to, who I love. His name is Alan Melotek, and he is the most thorough, fabulous doctor in the world. He looked at me and said, "Let me take an X-ray." He looked at the X-ray and told me, "You have walking pneumonia." That's serious! You can die from it, if you don't treat it. But if you treat it with antibiotics, in a week, you can be back to normal.

So, from that point on, Dr. Melotek became my doctor in Florida, and I continue to see him whenever I can, because, in a way, he saved my life. He's the type of doctor that knows my medical history inside and out. I've been going to him for eight years now, yet every time I walk into his office, he's either reading or has just finished reading my entire file. This is the kind of a doctor we should all have! He's what you call a "doctor's doctor."

JERRY'S LAW #11:
"Perfection is not optional."

I'm afraid for the future, because I have developed a group of four or five wonderful doctors whom I depend on, and I feel like they're my trusted friends. Who knows in the future world of Obamacare, or socialized medicine, or whatever it's called, will this type of medicine totally disappear? After all, what the government bureaucracy promises is never exactly what ends up happening, for several reasons. First of all, the people who make the promises are probably no longer in office, even if they meant what they said. And second, they don't have the ability or the skills or experience to know exactly the cause and effect of all the things that they promised initially. And of course, the costs go up, and the payments to the doctors go down—not a winning formula.

My concern is that medicine should be kept simple. We should all know our doctors. We should also follow our instincts not to simply accept what a doctor says. My question is whether my children can keep or change their doctors under the new government medical systems. Politician promises can very rarely be taken to the bank: it doesn't smell right to Jerry, and I'm very skeptical and concerned.

JERRY'S LAW #14:
"Inspect what you expect."

Myasthenia What?

After my rotator cuff rehab and after I had recovered from walking pneumonia, I was feeling pretty good. Then in 2004, my wife and I were back in New York, when I woke up one early July morning, and the room was spinning, and I couldn't stand up without falling down. The whole world was turning around me; I didn't know what to do.

I started seeing a series of doctors. The first thing I thought I might have was vertigo, so I went to see an ear doctor. He said, "This is not vertigo. I'm sending you over to Columbia Presbyterian Hospital [as it was called in those days; it's now New York Presbyterian], to the head of the neurology department. If anything, you're having a stroke, or you have a brain tumor." I was horrified and scared, as they say, shitless. But on the surface I stayed calm, so as not to panic Aviva. Just like my exhibitors used to say, "How do you stay so calm?" It's all just on the surface.

He couldn't get me an early appointment; the recommended doctor was very busy. I waited a few days, and my ear doctor called me and said, "I got you an appointment with another doctor. She's very good. She's not the head of the department, but she has a fine reputation."

So I went to see this doctor. As I waited to see her, I realized I was the only person in a very crowded waiting room who was not speaking Spanish. This was in upper Manhattan, and the doctor was Hispanic. I realized she was taking care of poor Hispanic people, probably Medicaid patients. I was grateful to her that she squeezed me in between her regular appointments.

When I finally saw her, she told me very little; instead, she said, "We can't find anything wrong with you. Our neurology department is two floors up, but I don't know when you'll be able to get an appointment." So there I was thinking I was going to die any second from either a brain tumor or from a stroke. I was still dizzy and couldn't even walk without holding onto my wife. So I did what I think everybody should do. I said, "Let me go up to that main neurology department on the second floor. Maybe I can talk to somebody."

When I got to the second floor, there were no patients waiting there—in stark contrast to the floor I had just come from, which was mobbed with people, all waiting to see this one doctor. Here, this floor was newly decorated. The woman behind the information desk was very nice, and she said, "Let me see if I can find somebody to talk to you." A few minutes later, a young female intern sat down next to me and asked me everything that was going on with me. She said, "Let me see what I can do." Within an hour, I got to see the head of the department—which just shows you that if you just accept being pushed around like cattle, you will be treated like cattle. You've got to take care of yourself—without being obnoxious or pushy. But don't just stand around and wait hours for somebody to care about you. That's another concern I have about the future of any kind of large-scale government medical program: will we all be taken care of, at all ages? If it sounds too good, be wary.

Anyway, the head of the neurology department and another his associate examined me and began a series of tests: I had MRIs and MRAs, and many other tests, everything under the sun. I had never even heard of an MRA before, but I learned that it's Magnetic Resonance Angiography, is used to examine blood vessels in various parts of the body (in my case, my brain). Finally, about five days later, I went back for a follow-up appointment, and the doctors told me they had found nothing wrong with me. They believed I probably had a stroke, which they couldn't do anything about, so they told me, "Either your symptoms will go away, or you'll live with them for the rest of your life." Needless to say, that was not very encouraging.

When I went back home, I called my regular doctor, Howard Adler. Unfortunately for me, when I was first struck with this condition of dizziness, he was on vacation. I went to see him and I explained what happened and how discouraged I was about my condition. And he said, "I have a local neurologist who I always recommend, not the head of the departments of these hospitals, but he's very experienced. Why don't you go see him?"

And a strange thing happened as I was going over to see him. I was still dizzy, and also my eyelids began to close, every 20 or 30 seconds. I would rest my eyes, and they would return to normal.

When I went into his office, Dr. Snyder looked at me and immediately said, "I know exactly what you have." I said, "What do you mean, you know exactly what I have?" He didn't even look at my medical records—all my MRIs and MRAs, all my doctors' reports and X-rays, everything. But he said again, "I know what you have. And I'll eat my diploma if I'm wrong."

Then he told me, "You have something called myasthenia gravis." The closing of the eyelids is the #1 symptom. I was relieved that I finally had a diagnosis. But what bothered me was that I had not only gone to an ear doctor, but also an eye doctor; I had seen so many neurologists, and even my cardiologist—yet none of them ever thought of giving me the tests for myasthenia gravis.

Myasthenia gravis is indeed what I had. "Myasthenia" comes from the Greek words for *muscle weakness,* and "gravis" is Latin for *serious* (or *grave*). What happens is that the antibodies attack the muscles and nerves: although antibodies usually protect the muscles from disease and other things, in this case, they get a false signal and attack these muscles so that your nerves and your muscles really never connect, which then makes your muscles weak. I was so atrophied after these few months of trying to find out what was wrong that I had no muscles anymore, no strength.

Then Dr. Snyder administered several tests. One was a blood test; another was an EMG (electromyography), which I call the Frankenstein test, because he connected electrodes to my body so the doctor could test my muscles and nerves to see the connections between them. That proved, without a doubt, that I had MG.

We don't know how many people have myasthenia gravis, although in America, it's estimated to be between 20,000 and 100,000. I discovered that some famous people had it, including Sir Laurence Olivier. Some people go into remission; some get medication that stabilizes them. Fernando Ferrer also has it: he was the Borough President of the Bronx and he also ran for mayor of New York City: he's a terrific guy, and he came to our fundraising walk last year, and fortunately for him, his condition seems to be in remission. Also, most doctors believe Aristotle Onassis had it, because he died of muscle weakness, which was never properly diagnosed.

If you don't treat myasthenia gravis, you're going to die, since your mouth and throat muscles become weak and don't function, so you can't eat. That, of course, makes you become weak and emaciated, and eventually, you die of malnourishment. Or you may not swallow properly, which can make you choke to death.

Currently, it's treated with a variety of medications. One that most patients take is called Mestinon.® I take this every four or five hours, but only at mealtimes, and it gives me a boost that makes me feel better during that time period. The miracle drug for most of us is Prednisone, which is a steroid that's used for many things. Prednisone wasn't discovered specifically to treat myasthenia gravis; instead, it was developed to be effective for organ transplants: it made the transplanted organs' success rate better. It reduced the amount of organ rejections that occurred.

In my case, I started out taking 60 milligrams of Prednisone, and now I'm down to five milligrams every day. Prednisone itself can kill you if you overuse it for long periods of time. Also, many people get very bloated faces and bodies. I'm not bloated in my face at all, at least not that I know of. If I am, it's probably a good bloat, because it basically got rid of my wrinkles. Everyone tells me how good I look, thus very few people realize how negatively the disease affects me. No sympathy for Jerry.

Both those drugs, Mestinon and Prednisone, have normalized my life. My weakness is mainly in my legs. My doctor thinks that it's a combination of the myasthenia gravis, linked with spinal stenosis. At present, I'm in the process of determining if I can receive medical assistance on this issue, short of a serious spinal operation.

I can't play tennis anymore, since I can't run. In Florida, I still live in a place that's one flight up with outside stairs. I refuse to sell it, because I think those stairs are forcing me to do certain exercises that help me. I go to the fitness center three times a week, exercising for about an hour-and-a-half. I have actually rebuilt my leg and arm muscles from my atrophy. I'm to a point where my muscles look almost normal.

Anybody who thinks they don't need to exercise is wrong. I tell everybody, no matter what you have, don't believe that you can't exercise in some manner. I believe that exercise, vitamins, and generally taking care of yourself, add years to your life. Many people down here, in Florida, who are younger, are totally out of shape, having difficulty walking and breathing, and they don't even have any medical conditions like myasthenia gravis!

I got involved with the Myasthenia Gravis Association. They just started to have a walk/run to raise funds. The whole idea is to make people aware of this condition, especially doctors. In fact, after I learned that's what illness I had, I called every one of my doctors—my eye doctor, my ear doctor, my regular doctor, the other neurologist, my cardiologist—and I said, "You know what I have?" When I told them it was myasthenia gravis, they all said, "Oh, my God, I learned about that in school; why didn't I think of that?" They don't think about it, because it's a condition you don't normally deal with. I called them all so that when another misfortunate person with MG comes to see them, they will not have to go through the uncertainty that I did.

The idea behind the Myasthenia Gravis Association is to get the word out, and that's why I'm involved. We need to get the word out not only to patients, but even more important, to doctors so they'll be aware of the symptoms of this condition. Young children can get it, teenagers get it, people of every age. When I go to these support group meetings and I see younger people, I feel terrible, since I realize that they will have this condition for the rest of their lives. Whereas in my case, I didn't get it until I was in my seventies and I had already lived a very good portion of my life. I've had some good times. I've done a lot of things, so I can live without playing tennis or doing some other physical things now. But when you're very young and you know that you're going to be weak for the rest of your life, that's very difficult to deal with. Many younger MG people can't hold a regular job; there are days they are so weak, they can't even get out of bed.

I still get very weak and take a 20-minute nap almost every afternoon. My biggest problem is walking. I have continuous pain, but I'm not a big complainer. I'm happy where I am in life, and I try to do whatever I can to inform people, so I go to support meetings both in Florida and New York City.

I'm obviously going to be living with this for the rest of my life. After six years, I don't believe I will ever be in remission.

I do want to make one more point: people should not be afraid to change their doctors. Let every staff person and doctor know your medical history every time you go to a new office. Repeat to them everything that's wrong with you, everything that concerns you, every drug you're taking. Do not assume they're reading your records or checking everything.

And always listen to your gut. If you don't like a particular doctor, or office, or hospital, change it. Your gut is probably right. You should always keep going until you find the right hospital, the right doctor, for *you*. After all, nobody's going to take care of you better than you.

So here I am, writing this chapter about my medical history. For what it's worth, I want anyone who reads this to know that I'm not dying. That's not why I'm writing my life story now. I don't want people to say, "Well, I know that he only has a few months to live." My reasons are nothing like that. I'm writing this now because I want to share my life story. If anybody gets anything out of my experiences and what I've learned in the course of my life, then writing this will be well worth it. I know so many things are very simple, but the simple things are the most important things. Often, things are not as complicated as they seem.

JERRY'S LAW #20:
"Winston Churchill said, 'Never give up.'
I say, 'Never give in.'"

JERRY'S LAW #14:
"Inspect what you expect."

18

Retirement Roller Coaster:
The Bad, the Good, and the Ugly

In the beginning of 1998, I closed what was to be my final tradeshow—the New York Coliseum Antique Show. It occurred to me that I was then in my 65th year, approximately the same age that my father was when he retired. On his 65th birthday in 1968, he closed the doors of his small business, living his dream of collecting a Social Security check and enjoying retirement. In the '60s, most seniors were not expected to live much longer than their 65th birthday, but today our life expectancy is well into our 80s. We're much different than our parents in our lifestyles, with our physical activities and our general health. We want to continue our retirement as if nothing else has changed. This is easier said than done, because when you leave your business or job, you begin to lose contact with the world and the people in that world. You have to gain new knowledge of what's in store for you and develop a new game plan in this world called "retirement."

I was in a better position than most because my business successes had given me financial security, but all the money in the world can't buy good health or friendship or help in developing new interests. You become more isolated than you can imagine. You must work extremely hard to start this new phase of your life by developing activities that will maintain the quality of life you strive for.

So in January 1998, a cold winter in New York City, Aviva and I moved down to our apartment in Boca Raton, Florida to enjoy the weather and to begin to develop plans for my full retirement. The first difficulty was that Aviva had always had time on her own, but now she had to put up with me full-time. This was like our first year of marriage—a major adjustment period.

Within the first month, I was nominated and elected to the Board of Directors of my Florida community. For some reason, I don't have the ability to go with the flow: I always get into trouble by jumping in feet first. I just don't stand back and let everybody else talk.

Sure enough, within a short period of time, major issues came to the Board's attention, and I was elected to be the treasurer. Remember, in the early 1990s, during my presence on the New York co-op board, there were a number of serious issues (involving dogs and washing machines, believe it or not!), which created an environment wherein I was either loved or hated by my neighbors.

It appears that I am not a very good politician. But I *am* a person who gets things done. In the worlds of condos and co-ops, this is a dubious honor, for most people who claim to support you are primarily interested in their own needs. Knowing this did not deter me from getting involved or learning my lesson, for I would, once again, later (in 2006) find myself in the middle of another neighborly controversy when I became president of my summer community at Pine Lake Park. But that's getting ahead of my story.

Back to Florida, in 1998. This community's name was Plantation Colony, and the original builder had constructed one- and two-story buildings with the concept that they were simple bungalows surrounded by lush trees and bushes, giving it a special feeling of living in the faraway tropics. To make this happen quickly, the builder had used certain fast-growing plantings such as Brazilian pepper trees, schefflera, and ficus trees. In 1998, the current president of the Plantation Colony community became obsessed with reducing the number of trees in our subdivision, and he replaced them with what I call "the Long Island landscape look." That means he wanted to have shrubs and bushes around each house. His justification for cutting down these trees was that he claimed they had been planted illegally and had to be removed within a year by law of the state of Florida.

We started seeing parts of our development looking very barren, and nothing like what most of us had bought into. The community was outraged. There were calls for a special election, and all the Board members were thrown out and replaced with myself and other advocates of a lush, tree-lined community.

We found out the law against these trees was nonexistent. The idea of the Florida legislature was simply not to *increase* their population and to plant slower-growing Florida-style trees for new plantings. To make a long story short, our new Board developed a five-year plan to replace some of these trees and developed a yearly maintenance program to control any excessive growth. It has worked beautifully, and the community remains appropriately landscaped.

Then, some months later, I woke up and walked to my terrace, which overlooks a small body of water and land that had been covered with an assortment of beautiful shrubs, flowers, and trees, which had beautifully separated my view from the community golf course. To my amazement that day, it looked like a hurricane had torn up the area. I was shocked. I toured the rest of my development and found this condition existed throughout. The peace and tranquility of Plantation Colony had been destroyed overnight by construction vehicles developing a new golf course.

That started a year-long battle with the Boca West Country Club, which was in charge of the management and development of this new golf course. The landscape, which was there when we bought our unit, was an important part of our lush and serene view. Obviously, we didn't want to look at the golfers going by at 7:00 in the morning, or hear the noise of their carts, and their talking while they were looking for their balls or whatever they do on the golf course. All of a sudden, without notice, they had ripped out all those shrubs and said, "We're not responsible to you. We have our own rules and regulations."

But I fought them. I wrote dozens of letters and had numerous meetings and much aggravation with the country club board members. And finally, the golf course association agreed to replace all the greenery that had separated us from the noise of the golfers and their carts. So, once again, I was able to go back to my terrace and have a wonderful morning cup of coffee and enjoy the tranquility.

The land belonged to the golf course, but when you buy into a community with subdivisions, you don't expect them to rip out the landscape surrounding it. The same is true, for example, if you pay $1 million for an apartment in Manhattan, and then somebody builds in front of you so you have lost your cityscape or river views. The builder probably said, "Nobody's going to build here, this land is earmarked to be a park," so then when someone builds a building, you realize you've been duped, and you're stuck with a million-dollar apartment with no view.

I held my board position for three years. During that time, even though the Florida apartment was only our winter home, the various projects became somewhat of a year-round effort. When you're retired, the idea is to keep busy.

My daughter Michelle suggested I do some volunteer work in my areas of interest. I located a New York State program, where retired businessmen mentored minority entrepreneurs who needed advice on the best ways to start and succeed in their new businesses. This was right up my alley, helping someone young and energetic succeed in starting a new business while remembering and drawing on my own personal experiences. I visited the closest office, which was on 34th Street and 5th Avenue, and I met with a gentleman who was responsible for matching up retired businessmen with the appropriate applicant.

I visited this office at least six different times, but for some reason, the guy who was running it never connected me to anyone—and there were hundreds of people out there who needed help! This was another bureaucracy at work, where someone had a great idea but didn't know how to set it in motion properly.

So I left this project in frustration and moved on to my next volunteering idea, which was to help an environment-friendly charity, the World Wildlife Fund. I called them on the phone; someone took my name and address and phone number and said they would get back to me; within a week, I got a telephone call. But the call was for only one purpose: they asked me to donate money to their organization! They claimed they did not need any volunteers, but they would really appreciate my money. This was another waste of time, and I concluded that no good deed goes unpunished. Seriously, it was very frustrating. I really tried to find volunteer work; I was looking for something to keep me busy by helping a needy charity. Easier said than done.

JERRY'S LAW #19: "Verify to clarify."

Meanwhile, I was still struggling to fill my life with gratifying activities, which is difficult when all your life you've been going to work every day at jobs you love, and then, all of a sudden one day, that all stops. We traveled at least twice a year, which filled some of this void. Then the birth of my two beautiful granddaughters, Maxine and Ava, became the #1 blessing during my retirement. I finally had the time and the finances to enjoy every special moment that I had with my granddaughters, something that I was unable to do with my own children. I was upset at myself for not spending more quality time with my own family, using the excuse that my work schedule didn't permit it. To this day, not seeing my children grow up as much as I would have liked is one of my biggest regrets. I believe many people have that same regret, but hindsight is always 20/20.

In 2001, the tragedy of 9/11 occurred. I actually saw the second plane hit the World Trade Center. I had my regular doubles tennis games scheduled for 10:00 that morning on Roosevelt Island, and I had to walk over to the tram. When I exited the elevator and entered the lobby of my apartment building, the man behind the desk said to me, "Do you know that a small plane just hit the World Trade Center?" Then he said, "If you go out on the back terrace, you can look downtown, and you can actually see the smoke from the twin towers."

So I went out to see what I could see, and at the moment I looked south from the terrace, the second building got hit. I knew immediately that it was not an accident, that something bad was happening.

I went over to the tram, which was already shut down, to tell my friends that we couldn't play, and we went back home to deal with the situation.

After the terrible events on 9/11, I volunteered to help process the victims' claims at the West Side Piers. Many people came to make claims, and the city needed qualified people to sort things out. It was amazing to me how many phony claims there were from creeps trying to take advantage of this American disaster. We processed the paperwork of those who really needed help and assisted them in filling out their forms, and hopefully they got some help. Unfortunately, the enthusiasm of assisting the victims has waned over time. Thirteen years later there are still victims waiting for help. As bureaucrats will tell us, "The wheels of justice grind slowly." That's bullcrap in this situation; that's not justice at all.

Foundation for Future Generations

Through my experience at Art Expo, I met some extraordinary people. One was Rabbi Bernard Mandelbaum, President Emeritus of the Jewish Theological Seminary, the organizational branch of the Jewish conservative moment. He had retired from his position and was still yearning to help others, so he created an organization called Foundation for Future Generations. Its ultimate purpose was to award scholarships to young scholars to study the Holocaust, and in his words, "To create a living memory of the children."

He put together a group of powerful, prominent individuals, including Norman Cousins, Sam Goody, Charlie Kramer, Roberta Peters, Senator Abraham Ribicoff, Theodore Sorensen, and now Jerry Leberfeld. Rabbi Mandelbaum was a warm and sensitive human being, and we became close friends. In fact, when my father passed on, Dr. Mandelbaum walked miles with me to the synagogue every day for a month to pay respect to my dad. The rabbi and I stayed friends until the day he died.

Of course, the Rabbi's cause appealed to me for many reasons. One was my darling wife, Aviva, who was a Holocaust survivor. For me, it was a difficult task, since I had no experience with fundraising. In addition, most of my closest friends from my youth—remember the

Arverne Demons?—had limited finances. But between the existing board members, Dr. Mandelbaum, and myself, we created more than 100 scholarships.

It's important to note that charitable giving is also trendy, but raising money for the Holocaust was a situation where people said, "Well, everybody knows about it. Why do we have to keep reminding them?" So this wonderful organization lasted only three years, to the great disappointment of Rabbi Bernard Mandelbaum.

Fast forward to 2013, when I asked my grandchildren, who are 12 and 16 years old, what they have learned about the Holocaust in school. Unfortunately, the answer is very little. Their schools don't spend much time on it. Bernard Mandelbaum was 100% right with his concern about remembering the children and the destruction of six million Jews and making sure what happened will have a permanent place in our history books. In other words, who knows what the world will remember in another 10 years? Will civilization remember the expression, *Never Again?*

I don't think that's cynical. People go on with their lives. I hear it from my own children: "I don't want to talk about it," they say. What do you mean, you don't want to talk about it? It was the greatest tragedy of the twentieth century, for God's sake! It's not the Roman Empire or the Crusades. It's Jewish history! We should learn from the Roman Empire. We should learn from the Crusades. And we should learn from the Holocaust. It could happen again—and within our grandchildren's lifetime.

In 2002, I still wasn't satisfied with the fullness of my life's activity. I continued to search for something special that would be my challenge at the grand old age of 69. I continued to ask questions of myself: *What do I enjoy doing that I could eventually convert into a time-filling hobby?* I remembered I had developed a reputation for public speaking, so I became the master of ceremonies at many different events, including the International Majolica Society. Remember the Victorian Pottery Organization that met yearly at different geographical locations? I organized and developed their annual meeting, which included a Saturday night speaker and some additional programming. I enjoyed speaking in front of this group, and as emcee I was able to create an entertaining evening since I was very familiar with the membership and the pottery.

We had about 500 members, and about 150 people attended the meeting. The purpose of the event was to share our experiences. We sometimes brought special pieces or photos of the pottery we owned. We had speakers from around the world, mainly from England, who were familiar with this project. It was nice to get to know other collectors, and it was fun to travel the country and visit each other's homes— you can have a wonderful collection, but most people look at it and say, "What is this?" People who aren't familiar with Majolica think it's just a lot of stuff, but when you get a collector in your own house, there is energy and enthusiasm beyond anybody's imagination. When we had a meeting in New York, I had up to 50 people in my home. My collection is considered one of the top 10 in the world.

Of course, I know other major collectors whose homes I've visited privately, and I befriended many interesting people who collect Majolica and share our enthusiasm.

Also, part of my retirement calendar has been speaking at group functions, which I helped develop, such as public school reunions and the Arverne reunions of all my childhood friends. I also organized some charity dinners.

Then I got this brainstorm: since I liked to speak in front of people and feed off the audience, why don't I take up acting? It was a crazy idea: I was almost 70 years old! That's when people *retire* from acting, but I thought that because they retired, maybe I could get some of their parts. And that's how I embarked on the next adventure of my life: my acting career.

Broadway Is Calling

Everyone around me said it was crazy: "You're 70 years old. Why are you going to start an acting career?" I didn't know why; it just sounded exciting to me. As mentioned, I thought of acting since I remembered how in business, I was very comfortable speaking at meetings and feeding off the crowd. Of course, I found out later that acting was totally different since you have to isolate and immerse yourself into the part. In fact, the audience is blacked out in your mind, and you don't see anything.

First, I searched *Backstage,* the theater newspaper, to find someone to give me private acting lessons and see if there was any real compatibility with myself and this new career. My parameters, as always, were that the cost was reasonable and the location was convenient.

I found a teacher on the West Side. Her name was Naomi, and she was a professional actress. She was maybe five years younger than I was. The first time I met with her was at her apartment. She lived on 89th Street and Amsterdam Avenue in a lovely, pre-war West Side apartment building. She had been in Broadway theater and on television, but was now an acting teacher.

I walked in, and we started my new adventure. We begin with screams and gyrations. Many acting teachers begin this way: they want you to be able to release your inner self, which was an experience for me. So there I was, running around her living room, screaming and jumping on one leg, and stomping on the floor. I don't know what I was doing, but that was the first part of my acting exercise.

Then she said, "You'll have to excuse me for a minute. I have to go in the other room and check on my husband." She came back out, and we did some more exercises, some readings, whatever you do when you're first starting to become an actor. So I went to her three times, and every time was somewhat similar, and she always said she wanted to go check on her husband. The third time I was there, I had to go to the bathroom, and, for some reason, she told me it was through the bedroom, and I discovered that there was no husband. I figured it out: I was a man, walking into this lovely single lady's home, so she was protecting herself.

I liked her, and after a few lessons at her home, she told me she taught a class at Michael Howard Studios, which was in the 20s, between 8th and 9th Avenues. There are many professional acting schools in New York City—mainly for young actors, since people my age don't typically do this. So I thought going to the school might be better than private lessons, since I would be with other students. She suggested I join her class, which I did.

I found out you have to be vetted to get into the school. I don't know how they vetted me, because I didn't have to audition, but I had to be interviewed. I suppose they want to make sure that I wasn't some pervert or weird character.

So I was in this class, and there were at least a dozen students, all young. The oldest person, other than me, was probably 25. Each was more beautiful and talented than the next. They were young people from all over the country who wanted to become actors; they were all striving to reach their impossible dream called *Broadway*, and there I was among them. The 25-year-olds were saying, "We're over the hill. We're too old." So imagine how *I* felt, this 70-year-old man: I was terribly uncomfortable in this new environment, with nobody within 40 years of my age, yet I shared their ambitions. But I went through with this experience.

Anyway, we played roles. The younger people were mainly learning how to make out with each other, how to do love scenes. It was interesting to see how they were very shy in the beginning, and eventually they got into it. It was a learning experience. They did not give me one of those parts. I don't know why; they just didn't.

The most interesting thing I learned is that you have to keep rehearsing; you really have to work at your craft. It's very hard to be an actor. You have to get out of your own skin and be somebody else. It was, for me, challenging. I did the best I could, and it was great because of the young people I worked with, because we were all equals, learning together. The class was only once a week, so in between classes, we rehearsed in public parks, coffee shops, street corners, anyplace we could find that was mutually convenient, and we didn't care if the people around us thought we were crazy, because we were rehearsing our parts. Somehow, in the last week of our class, it all came together when we performed.

It was nerve-wracking, but it was also exhilarating. As things go, I eventually got comfortable with my younger fellow thespians, so this is how my next and exciting new profession started.

The first role I did was Rappaport from *I'm Not Rappaport*, which is about an aging man who's very independent. Naomi asked me to choose a role that I would be comfortable with, and I chose this one. Judd Hirsch originated the role on Broadway. In the play, Rappaport wants to continue living on his own, but his daughter, who's married to a doctor and lives in Great Neck, on Long Island, wants to put him in an assisted-living facility near her. It was a wonderful part and my first acting experience, and I'll never forget it. The girl who played my daughter was a beautiful Italian woman who came to America to take up acting. She was beautiful in a lot of ways; I don't mean just aesthetic beauty; she was a very kind person, too. So we rehearsed in coffee shops and every other place, and we both struggled together.

That class lasted eight weeks, and when it ended, I decided to take another class with a different instructor. I wanted a little different approach, so I signed up for another beginner's class with a former actor named Diane Shalet. Like Naomi, Diane was also close to my age, though we didn't talk about age. I asked her if she had ever been in the movies; she said, yes, she had made a few. She was a very shy person; she was very attractive, but surprisingly shy. She told me the best-known movie she had made was with Steve McQueen: she had played a prostitute in the old West. In the westerns they made in the 1950s and '60s, there was no explicit sex; all they showed was the girl at the top of the stairs, and the cowboy would walk up the stairs and then take off his gun, and then maybe his hat. You get the picture? So she played the part of the prostitute, which she was kind of embarrassed about. Being inquisitive, I rented the movie, and I thought she was very good.

I don't remember the name of the movie, but I'm looking at her resume right now, on Wikipedia, and I see she had a recurring role as Miss Hawkins in the television drama *Matlock,* and she did many guest appearances on *The Monkees* TV show. She was also in *Bonanza* and did hundreds of guest appearances on other television shows.

When I took lessons from her in her class, I tried to befriend her, but I couldn't get close to her. There was something about her that was closed off. I used to drive her home from the class with other students who lived on my way. She lived on Central Park South, in a one-bedroom apartment, which she also must have had for 40 years.

She had been married to an actor, Michael Strong, who was the founder of the Manhattan Actors and Writers Lab. Apparently, he had died a few years earlier, and she had lost her way, so to speak. She was shy already: after all, just because you're an actor doesn't mean you're outgoing. But I think she became even more withdrawn after her husband died. I had the sense that something was going to happen to her. When I started to write this book, I again looked her up on Wikipedia, and discovered that she died within months of the last time I saw her, on February 23, 2006, the day of her 71st birthday. And I'm convinced she took her own life. It's very strange that somebody should die on her birthday. I had known something was wrong in her life.

Anyway, she was a fabulous teacher. She gave me a totally different approach to acting. Each teacher is so different: even here in Florida, my acting instructors are different from each other; every one teaches something different and has a different approach. For example, Diane told us, "I don't want you to see a movie that you're going to do a role in, because then that actor's interpretation of that role will throw you off when you try it yourself." Yet another one of my acting instructors said, "Go see the movie, because it'll show you how your part is played." Different teachers have totally different opinions on how to approach acting. I took only two classes at Michael Howard Studios, one with Naomi and one with Diane.

In 2004, I decided to try to expand my horizons by auditioning for Broadway and off-Broadway plays. This was an ambitious undertaking that was short-lived by a series of injuries and illness that restricted my strength and agility. I tore my quad muscle and my rotator cuff, and in 2007, I was stricken with myasthenia gravis, a condition that sapped my strength, but not my enthusiasm. It could affect my physical abilities, but not my brain and desire.

In 2005, when I went to Florida in the winter for three months (which my wife and I have been doing since 1987), I tried to find an acting group down here. I made a list of every playhouse within a reasonable distance, and I called each and every one. Being as persistent as I am in most things, and remembering *can't is not an option*, I finally hit pay dirt. Somebody at the Delray Beach Playhouse told me, "We have a group of seniors down here, and our resident instructor is a retired actress who works weekly with them. She also teaches a group of high school students." Her name is Dolly Workman, and she obviously teaches people at both ends of the age spectrum. The Delray Beach Playhouse was considered a very fine regional theater.

I immediately joined this group; in south Florida, men are always in demand, especially older men. And I'm still with them today, eight years later. The age of the other actors is anywhere from 60 to 90, and, truthfully, Mildred, who is now 95, is our best overall performer. She has great stage presence. When you see people like that on stage, you say, *Oh, my God.* She is so inspiring.

Acting has taught me about when you get old: everything slows down, including your brain. But at 79 years old, my ability to memorize my parts has gotten better. Almost everyone cannot believe that people of my age can remember all those lines, but take it from me, we can remember. Of course, like many other people, I occasionally have what they call "senior moments," but I work hard to get through them. It's amazing: the adrenaline seems to move me. It makes my brain work better. I can't explain it; I guess it's true that *you lose it if you don't use it.*

We perform once a season, usually at the end of March, in front of about 200 people, many of our friends and relatives, but others, too. Retired people in Florida love the theater—especially when it costs only $10 and includes refreshments. That's a deal—even better than the early-bird special.

So I have three months to rehearse and memorize my part. By some miracle, and with much effort, I've developed the ability that I hardly ever drop a line. My little secret was that every time my granddaughters visited me, their reward was to read my script with me, and, of course, there was always Aviva to help me. When I'm doing a play, I rehearse maybe an hour a day, every day, in my house with my wife: that's when I try to memorize my lines and develop the character. Every time I read the script, I get something more out of it. When I start doing a play with a group of people, for the first four or five weeks it may not seem funny or interesting. But by the time you get to be on stage, it is either hilarious or interesting (depending on the type of play, of course), because it takes that much time and patience to develop the characters and to understand your part.

Here are some of the plays I've been in, all of which were originally done on Broadway or off-Broadway. I played the carny husband Wilbur in *Hairspray.* I played Lawrence in *For Whom the Southern Bell Tolls:* it's about a mentally challenged teenage boy—which I played, and I loved that part. One of my favorite parts was in a play called *Sylvia*, where I played Greg, who's a dog owner. The dog is played by a woman with fuzzy hair who performs on her hands and knees; Sarah Jessica Parker played the part on Broadway. It's hilarious. Greg takes the "dog" to the park, and the dog runs off with this macho dog named Bowser. Greg has fallen in love with this dog, and he becomes jealous of Bowser's relationship with Sylvia. That's basically the story—sounds stupid, but you laugh from beginning to end.

I also did something from vaudeville called *Flirtation*. And I played Harry in a show called *Blackout*, which is about a grumpy old Florida husband who complains about everything, and his elderly wife wants to have him think about things other than being unhappy about everything around him. So she tries to seduce him, and that's the blackout part. The woman who played my wife in the play had been married to one man for 57 years, and she told me she had never kissed another man in her life. So think about her transition into acting, where she had to be somewhat physical with me—or rather, with my character in the play. We didn't take our clothes off, but, at the end of the play, there's a scene that's simulating intimacy.

My real-life wife, Aviva, didn't mind my doing these scenes at all. In fact, she loved it. After all, the love scenes weren't real; they were nothing serious. And I was so proud of Alice, who was my wife in that play: after all, you can feel when somebody is stiff, if you're holding that person and she's keeping a little distance between you; you can tell when she feels uptight. So our transition together was a beautiful thing.

My wife comes to all my shows, along with our friends. Every one of our shows is sold out. It is amazingly great fun for people of our age group. We perform in a regular theater, which seats about 250 people. We know we're getting better year after year. People ask us about our next performance. If they were suffering, they would find an excuse not to attend.

At the end of each performance, at our after-party of tea and cookies, people always come up to me and say, "You were great! How do you memorize all those lines?" And that makes me feel good, that I'm still able to do these things. I think that's very important for other people to know: that just because you get older doesn't mean you stop doing things that you enjoy. *"Can't is not an option."*

I also played George Burns in *Burns and Allen.* That was great. I researched it, and I worked with a woman, Jane, who was great as Gracie. With George, it was all about timing. And I had to use the cigar theatrically, which was a great prop during George and Gracie's performances.

I also played a character named George in another play. This George was a henpecked husband whose wife didn't want to sleep in the same bed with him anymore, which hit home with some in my age group. It was sad, but funny. It was called *I Can't Hear You When the Water's Running.* It had also been a Broadway show.

I played Ray in a show called *Lone Star:* that was the first part I ever played here in Florida. Ray was the younger brother of two country bumpkins: I really played a hick. My brother went off to war, and I was too young to go. I stayed at home, and he let me use his Cadillac. When he came home from the war, he told me how great we were together as brothers, and I had to tell him something that he couldn't live with, which was that I slept with his wife when he was away. The rest of the play is about how we deal with this information.

One interesting thing happened while performing in that play was that a young woman who was part-time in our acting group, Janet (who was also a professional actress—and a waitress, of course) started a conversation with me at our post-performance party. She joined us periodically, and she could memorize her lines in one day. She just jumped in and did her part. She told me, "Jerry, I did that show off-Broadway, and you were as good as or better than the guy I played it with." I didn't really believe her . . . but it was still very encouraging to hear her say that. That was my first play. She still encourages me to this day. I still enjoy acting.

I also played George in *Same Time, Next Year* and Al in *The Sunshine Boys,* which was hilarious. I did something else called *Abraham Lincoln's Letters,* which I really loved. We did this in another theater (because we were asked to leave the Delray Beach Playhouse, for ridiculous political reasons that I won't even go into here). So we found another place to perform, and the woman who ran the new theater in Boca said to us, "I don't know if I want you to do scenes from Broadway. I'd like you to do letters, famous letters, and, well, not-so- famous letters." After we did it, I have to admit that it was one of the most well-received performances we had ever done: it was astonishing. It proves that you're never too old to learn.

This past year, I performed the role of Harry in Neil Simons' *The Prisoner of Second Avenue.* So you can see, for a guy who has been doing this for only a few years, I have a pretty nice resume. My acting has become a wonderful part of my life, and for those who are reading this, I want to say it's important, as you get older and you're retired, to find something challenging to do.

I especially enjoyed performing scenes from Neil Simon's plays. In fact, a wonderful thing just happened to me on the way to the Palace Diner on 57th Street in Manhattan. You're not going to believe this, but I was introduced to Neil Simon, who I've admired for so many years. A friend of mine who goes regularly to the Palace Diner asked me to join him one day. Neil Simon was there, so the owner asked my friend if we would like to meet him. Of course, I'd like to meet him! What a thrill. We chatted, I explained my career, and I suggested that we exchange telephone numbers and autographs, and he gleefully agreed.

I've also performed in a commercial, which I got paid $150 for; in fact, I think I took a picture of the check. It was from a Japanese company that was doing a short documentary about elderly people who take in dogs that become their companions and make their lives better. My character was in an old-age home with a whole group of seniors. This company wanted to show the film to an elderly Japanese audience, because Japanese people don't understand this concept. The funny thing about doing this commercial, though, was that they took all us elderly senior actors in a minibus from Manhattan to a small park on Long Island. It was summer and blisteringly hot and humid, about 95 degrees. It took hours to set up the scene, and we all had to sit on the ground, outside, and wait, while the dog was kept in an air-conditioned trailer. I guess it's harder to find a good, trained dog than it is to find elderly actors.

I also perform in our summer community, Pine Lake Park. Every other year, we do a theatrical performance. I'm like most elderly actors: it's hard to find regular work. My acting career has consisted of two commercials and more than 15 live performances, both at Delray Beach Playhouse and on the stage in Pine Lake Park. Which just goes to show, if you keep wishing on a star, you can still become one.

Striking Gold

In general, retiring sucks if you're an active person. Every part of your body slows down, including your brain. Connection with the real world leaves you year by year, and most of the people you worked with and knew in your industry, leave your life. You must find a way to reconnect. We live longer now. And we're a lot more capable of doing things than we think we can. So if I could give any advice to anybody, here it is: Find a hobby; help somebody, either as a volunteer or a mentor or a teacher; do *something*. It's amazing how much you can do, physically and mentally. Personally, I'll keep acting as long as I can. What we all need in retirement are new friends with similar interests.

JERRY'S LAW #18:
"You cannot do the minimum and reach the maximum."

When I was in my fifties, I thought it would be exciting to be part of this great event celebrating the year 2000, the New Millennium. I wondered if I would be fortunate enough to be still alive at the ripe old age of 67. Well, another dream came true: I made it! I was excited, and then I began thinking about my next chronological goal, my next milestone. When you get older, it seems important to reach certain milestones.

In my mind, the next most important day in my life was to reach February 15, 2008, when I would celebrate my fiftieth wedding anniversary with my one and only bride, Aviva. This was something that in my parents' generation would be few and far between. In the fall of 2007, Aviva and I spent many hours deciding what would we like to do for this very special occasion. Our lifelong friends were elderly and some were quite ill, so I didn't want to be in an environment where some of my close friends would not be able to attend. After considering a family cruise or trip to Israel, etc., we decided in November 2007 that we would make a special anniversary party on February 15, which happened to fall on a Friday, giving us a full weekend of celebration.

It was now a challenge to reach our goal of creating the kind of event that Jerry and Aviva would never forget. A warm and fuzzy atmosphere with our closest friends and the immediate family with the best food and entertainment possible. We had done some exploratory investigation the prior winter in Florida and had whittled down the number of possibilities. The restaurant venue we finally selected was a beautiful old-world style facility with a room that would comfortably seat 55 people and had its own bar and cocktail reception area. It was run by an old-world European gentleman who still wore business suits and ties. He walked us through an extraordinary experience with almost unlimited food selection.

Also, during the previous winter, Aviva and I had enjoyed an entertainer named Scott Ringersen, a retired police officer in his forties who was fulfilling his life's dream and had become an Elvis impersonator. Every Thursday, at a local biker bar, Scott entertained a full house of Elvis lovers, singing the crowd's favorite songs and wearing unique Elvis costumes. We thoroughly enjoyed that evening, and decided to try to get Scott to be our entertainment for our fiftieth anniversary party. We negotiated, and Elvis agreed to join Jerry and Aviva on February 15th. It was to be a surprise for everyone but my immediate family, and it was something that I had always dreamed of doing.

The tables were placed just right in an intimate setting. At approximately 8:00 when my guests were seated, I announced, "Ladies and gentlemen, I'm proud to announce that Elvis is now in the building." Then our Elvis entered with great fanfare. The great thing about Scott was his willingness to perform any of our favorite songs; he even rehearsed a skit that my children and grandchildren had prepared in our honor.

Scott also agreed (without even the knowledge of my immediate family) that I would do one song with him, to honor my darling wife. It was one of Elvis's most famous songs, "Viva Las Vegas." I grabbed a microphone and Scott started singing the melody, and when he got to the "Viva Las Vegas" part, I sang my favorite words, *"Aviva, where are you? Aviva, I need you!"* and this continued throughout the song. Everyone in that room knew GL so well that even though I was considered a self-reliant, competent individual, that particular chant was my crutch that made me a whole person: the fact that Aviva was always there for me was crucial. Everybody laughed so hard because this was a truly humorous moment, which only my closest loved ones could share.

Everybody was either laughing or crying, as my bride and I hugged and kissed.

The skit that my children performed was fabulous: it included many songs and dances that followed the story line of our 50 years of marriage. This was about us, but it was also about everyone in that room, and it made them feel that they were truly a special part of our lives and that evening.

It was amazing that of the 55 close friends and relatives we invited, all but 3 attended. This in itself made the evening special: there was not a person in that room that we had not shared a special moment in our lives with. But probably the most important two tables were made up of my childhood friends—the members of the Arverne Demons. There were 21 people at that table, with 12 of my friends from the time I was 8 years old, some 70 years ago.

Two of my dearest friends, Harvey and Paul, were both extremely ill. Harvey had a sense of humor matched by none. There was no way that he was going to miss our party, even with his prior cancer and recent stroke, which caused him to be wheelchair-bound. But it was my friend Paul's appearance that overwhelmed me. Aviva and I had met at Paul and Lilly's wedding. Paul was in the later stages of cancer and was in tremendous pain and losing weight at a rapid pace. His wife Lilly had explained to us how much they wanted to attend, but she said it would be impossible for Paul to leave his New York hospital bed and fly to Florida. So it was much to our amazement that Paul showed up that evening! He told us there was no question in his mind that he would join Jerry and Aviva. I cry while writing about this, knowing that obviously Paul agreed with me that *"Can't is not an option."*

It is now almost five years since Paul died. Harvey is also gone, as are a few others. I think I knew, when I looked at those two tables that evening, that this would probably be the last meeting of many of the gang, which I called *the boys of summer*. I am writing this story during the week after Hurricane Sandy, which devastated the great place we all grew up in, Rockaway Beach. It is also interesting to me that the name *Sandy* was a very prevalent name for girls of my generation.

Someone who never had a chance to attend our celebration was my younger sister, Freya. She had suffered for almost two years with terminal cancer and died when she was only fifty-seven. We were not on good terms when she got sick; she was mad at me because she felt I hadn't treated her well at the wedding of our daughter, Michelle. To this day, I don't know what I did that upset her so much.

Freya had an unhappy life. Her first marriage to her children's father had ended in divorce, but she had met and married a wonderful man and was very happy for a short period of time. One night her husband Al was coming home from work. He was stopped at a stop sign when another driver plowed into him, leaving Al paralyzed from the neck down for the rest of his life. His accident and resulting paralysis ended this wonderful but short period of my sister's life. Freya was dealt a lousy hand.

When she got sick, I called her many times to reinstate and repair our relationship, which we both really wanted. I'm glad we were able to spend quality time together before she died. I went to the doctor with her many times because her husband was really unable to accompany her. Spending time with Freya made me feel good; regardless of who's wrong or who's right, it's never right to be mad for the rest of your life. I truly believe people should take the steps necessary to try to make things better. I'll always be comforted that at the end of Freya's life, she knew that I loved her.

Let's end this part on a high note. When you feel sorry for yourself, just think what could be, and count your blessings. Sharing your life with others who care is one of the most important things you can do to keep yourself young at heart. Spending time on things that matter always pays off. You never know the last time you will ever see a good friend again—so don't waste any opportunity.

Planning the Future

So you just read my thoughts on my last 15 years of full retirement, and you must be thinking, *What is he complaining about? He seems to be very busy and a generally happy person.* This is generally an accurate statement, but there have been many hours in this retirement scenario that have left me unfulfilled. I'm not a paranoid person, and I love to converse with people of all ages, but that's not always possible. Sometimes, I can see on younger faces that I'm an annoying old man and they can't wait for me to stop talking and go away.

I have so much knowledge and experience, but no one wants it. This was a statement I heard from a wonderful elderly gentleman, Abe Steinhorn, who was my neighbor at Pine Lake Park. Abe just passed on, at age 92. He was a successful businessman and a highly decorated World War II hero, a man who wanted no more than to be treated respectfully as a person and not an old man. Unlike some other cultures, Americans seem to tolerate their seniors, but not to embrace them in a way they deserve.

Most of us will stay quiet, because we're needy and do not want to make waves that may detach us from whatever connections we have in our world. This may sound depressing, but the only reason I bring it up is because if you don't talk about things, most people remain oblivious to our feelings. In my own case, I give the impression of a complete, independent, and capable human being, able to do just about anything I want to do.

Obviously, though, this is not true. I am somewhat debilitated by my myasthenia gravis and other medical conditions, but, on the surface, I'm treated as if I'm still the same person I was 20 years ago. That's because of my demeanor. As we get older, people need love, affection, and attention like anybody else, regardless of how much money they have. So I ask any younger person who is reading this book that the next time you get involved with a much older person, try to put on blinders. Give all of your time to listen, and perhaps learn.

JERRY'S LAW #12:
"You learn much more by listening than by talking."

I'd like to conclude this chapter with some of the things I do to make my so-called golden years better. I follow a strict schedule on a variety of things that I'm convinced make my quality of life in my senior years better. I work out three times a week in the fitness center, for a minimum of 90 minutes, and I do stretching on the alternative days. I talk a lot when I'm in the fitness center: it's social therapy for me.

I have one alcoholic drink a day and make mostly healthy food choices, and I continue my daily use of vitamins. The most important foods in my life at present are prunes (for obvious reasons) and sardines, for they're a great source of Omega-3 fatty acids, which are recommended for a healthy heart.

Reducing stress is perhaps the most important element in one's quality of life. Also a happy marriage, and keeping close relations with your dear friends and family. I always knew that stress reduction was the most important, but that fact was confirmed to me when I was introduced to Dr. Sarno, a practicing neurosurgeon, who decided one day that 90% of back operations were not needed, and he developed a program to identify what was causing the stress in our lives, which is the main cause of back pain.

He was treated by his profession as some sort of a quack. Most geniuses on the edge of something controversial are usually disparaged. He just recently retired, but he wrote three books, and I recommend any of them to anyone who is having back pain. I can personally vouch for three loving relatives who have been cured of back pain by Dr. Sarno without a medical operation or treatment of any kind, and they have maintained this pain-free condition over the last 20 years. It's amazing.

Keeping active within your ability and certainly challenging your brain is also important. My ability to memorize far exceeds my expectations. These are simple tasks, but I promise if you have the control to do these few things daily, you'll be a much happier person.

On the lighter side, I have a few additional suggestions. Start a car trip with your gas tank totally filled and your bladder totally empty. Driving on main highways with your GPS set to indicate the next available rest stop does wonders to reduce stress. When you do stop, use the first stall on the far right of the restroom: scientific studies have proven this stall is typically much cleaner than all others. If that fails, look on the floor to examine the cleanliness conditions, and keep your shoes on.

When leaving home to do some chores, try to do at least three separate errands on your to-do list. It's always worked out for me, and it saves all-important time and energy. If I want to go to the bagel shop, I'll go get some light bulbs, and I'll go to the bank. I always do three things, so I don't waste time. Try it next time, it works!

Never be concerned about speaking about your feelings, and share your experiences and good humor with loved ones. Most people are very busy with their own lives, so don't stand on principle and wait for somebody to figure out what you're upset about. It's a self-defeating policy. If somebody loves you, tell them the way you feel. You may not always be right, but you're always entitled to your feelings.

So this chapter about retirement was probably a rollercoaster of emotions and information that might be somewhat confusing as to what direction I'm taking my life. I know I have to find a new project, something that will enrich my life and keep me active for the remainder of my days, and I think I've found it. Within a few months, I will finish this memoir and move on to my next major project.

I got this idea while working out in my fitness center. I've met several people who have similar needs as I, all highly successful and inquisitive people, frustrated by their lack of involvement with other interesting people. So I'm forming a group called the Senior Boys' Club (and we may admit girls), to introduce ourselves to each other, to meet weekly, and to share our life's experiences and good humor. This idea was clear in my mind since people live longer and stay healthy longer. They need the companionship of others who share many of their interests. The basic idea is to bring together compatible people for companionship. Anyone can join; we won't discriminate.

I plan to advertise this with a notice on our building's bulletin board. I'll start in my building, which has some 320 apartments, from which I expect participation of at least 20 boys and girls over 65 years old. We'll meet once a week, and then we'll start developing ideas together and then expand it beyond just my building.

I meet people who are 10 to 20 years younger than me who are recently retired. They have experienced success in life, but their regular daily activities have been curtailed by their retirement. They need new challenges, and my Senior Boy Club Manual will get their innovative engines churning again. It's going to be wonderful to meet all these interesting, fabulous people, and to hear parts of their life stories. We'll start a website to connect people with similar interests—like a dating service, like Christian Mingle or J-date.

Once it takes off we'll expand it. Then I'll bring in the troops, some young person who wants to put in the time and energy. Remember, when forming a business, you always have to find a niche that no big company wants to explore or develop it into a successful venture. When GL gets an idea and all the research is positive and the vibes are good,

I will find the energy and ambition deep down to make it a success. So wish me luck and look for the announcement: the National Senior Boys' Club of America.

JERRY'S LAW #17:
"The faster you move, the slower time passes,
the longer you live."

Another great Rockaway Reunion.

Arverne Demons 65th Reunion cruising Florida's Intracoastal Waterway, 1999.

Our 50th wedding anniversary celebration with "Elvis" Scott Ringersen, 2008.

The Whitney and Leberfeld families celebrating our
50th wedding anniversaries, 2008.

Find Jerry . . .
Pine Lake Park
celebration,
July 4, 2011.

The Family:
Happy
Hannukah
2012.

PLP Players
performing
*Prisoner of
Second
Avenue,*
summer 2012.

19

Reflections

So here we are in March of 2013, at the beginning of the end of Benny the Book's book. It's been difficult to piece together my thoughts and reflections of my almost 80 years on earth. If you've stuck with me to this point, you might as well continue since here is where I let it all hang out with no holds barred.

JERRY'S LAW #5: "Do it by the book, but be the author."

Although I haven't mentioned it before, an important thread in my life has been lyrics—words that link our lives to music. I was 10 years old when I wrote the first of many lyrics to popular music that defined my life's experiences. Those lyrics were to the tune of "So Long, It's Been Good To Know You" by Woody Guthrie. It describes my experience when my parents were called to the principal's office because of my misbehaving. My version goes something like this:

The telephone rang in my home one day
The Dean to my mother had something to say
Your son is in trouble, believe it or not,
So come here to my office or he will be shot.
(And the song goes on from there.)

From that time forward, my childhood dream was to become a popular music lyricist. I wrote numerous songs in my lifetime, mainly about dealing with my own important life experiences. This brings me to the point of how music lyrics affected my learning and motivated my thinking.

Perhaps the most influential lyrics were produced by two important music poets of my generation. One was Johnny Mercer, whose song "Accentuate the Positive" was the #1 Billboard song in 1945. The other was Jacques Brel, who produced a musical review in the 1960s called *Jacques Brel Is Alive and Well and Living In Paris*. Aviva and I visited this off-Broadway play of folk songs about many of the sad complexities of life. Brell was a brilliant musical poet whose lyrics will live forever. The words of both these wonderful lyricists have stayed with me, and I refer to them frequently during my thought process.

Johnny Mercer's *Accentuate the Positive* goes like this:

You've got to accentuate the positive
Eliminate the negative
Latch on to the affirmative
Don't mess with Mister In-Between
You've got to spread joy up to the maximum
Bring gloom down to the minimum
Have faith or pandemonium's
Liable to walk upon the scene

This is a simple message that I've tried to live with all my life. It says positive thinking and actions motivate one's successes and happiness. And there is no good side to negative thoughts. If there only one message to make one's life happy and fulfilled, it's *accentuate the positive.*

The Jacques Brel lyrics that mean the most to me are from the song "Carousel." These lyrics have given me a better understanding of how to live my life in the present. The song was presented by the cast in this way. They begin singing slowly and continue the verses in each cycle, going a little faster and then a little faster and then faster and faster and suddenly they stop.

Carnivals and cotton candy
Carousels and calliopes

Fortune-tellers in glass cases
We will always remember these
Merry-go-rounds quickly turning
Quickly turning for you and me
And the whole world madly turning
Turning, turning 'till you can't see
We're on a carousel
A crazy carousel
And now we go around
Again we go around
And now we spin around
We're high above the ground
And down again around
And up again around
So high above the ground
We feel we've got to yell
We're on a carousel
A crazy carousel

This is a story of human life; it speeds up as you get older and suddenly stops, ending one's life on Earth. This message has motivated me to keep going, to keep creating new challenges, proving that GL's not ready to get off the carousel yet. This song was probably the motivation for me to take up acting later in life.

Recently I saw a movie called *Quartet*. It's about retired, former musicians living together in an English nursing home and the difficulties faced by famous people who retire and have to adjust to their circumstances. Once a year they put on a performance, displaying their former musical talents to raise funds to keep the nursing home open. At the end of the movie I realized that the most important message was how much the audience—young and old—appreciated and was motivated by those older people who were still able to perform at a high level, giving hope and pleasure to all the age groups in the audience. So I thought about my acting group, which also gives one major performance a year. Their ages range from 60 to 95, and they are always concerned about the level of their performances. Every year some consider dropping out for fear that the audience will not enjoy their performance.

As I watched this movie, I realized that the audience that we perform to is receiving as much benefit as the performers being encouraged that the show can go on at any age.

And of course, there is my latest adventure of writing my memoirs. It's been just over a year, and I can finally see the finish line. It's been a difficult journey going through one's life, trying to be truthful and thoughtful on the way, and this led to the title of my book: *Can't Is Not an Option*.

In the next few pages, I will try to encompass the influential people in my life as well as those experiences that affected my opinions for the last 80 years.

Big Government Doesn't Seem to Work

From the time I started thinking about politics in my 20s to today, the subject of bigger government has always been in the forefront of American's minds. The intellectuals and the liberals will argue that we are a very rich country and that we have to take care of those in need. Also, it puts more people to work in government jobs, thus reducing our unemployment rate. And their most passionate point is that it is the most practical way of redistributing the wealth of our country to those in need. The fact is the bigger our government, the less efficient, more expensive, and more uncontrollable. It used to be that a government job was for more security and less pay and benefits, and if you wanted more you would have to compete in the open job market. That circumstance has totally been turned around in my lifetime. Once there are more people working for the government and/or receiving government assistance, the less competitive we will be as a nation in this global economy.

It is my strong conviction that this country grew to its greatness through smaller government, more individual freedoms, less regulation, and more opportunities through entrepreneurship and personal effort. It is the major factor that separates our great country from all the rest. We should not allow our oversized and overpaid government to change that factor. I believe that government is way too large and has forgotten what has made us the greatest country in the history of the world. Our appeasement of China, Russia, OPEC, and other foreign influences is turning out to be our Achilles' heel that has caused six years of stagnation with no immediate improvement in sight. Let the government give a free hand of all those who desire to build their futures. Let's renew the policy of encouraging foreign students with special skills to quickly enter our economic system by giving them legal status upon graduation.

Over the years, many famous people I admire had similar thoughts. Here are some of the quotes that I think you will find interesting:

"In general, the art of government consists of taking as much money as possible from one party of citizens to give it to the other."
—VOLTAIRE

"A government big enough to give you everything you want, is strong enough to take everything you have."
—THOMAS JEFFERSON

"No man's life, liberty, or property is safe while the legislature is in session."
—MARK TWAIN

"I don't make jokes. I just watch the government and report the facts."
—WILL ROGERS

"A government which robs Peter to pay Paul can always depend on the support of Paul."
—GEORGE BERNARD SHAW

"I contend that for a nation to try to tax itself into prosperity is like a man standing in a bucket and trying to lift himself up by the handle."
—WINSTON CHURCHILL

"The government's view of the economy could be summed up in a few short phrases. If it moves, tax it. If it keeps moving, regulate it. And if it stops moving, subsidize it."
—RONALD REAGAN

Fellow citizens, I rest my case.

Political Correctness 2013

The current claims about racism and anti-feminism are way out of whack and effectively splitting apart the good citizens of our country. Today we are honored to have the first black president in the history of our country. Black men and women hold very important positions in both our government and the corporate world. All minorities have much greater opportunities today than I had as a young Jewish boy trying to make it in the corporate world. In the 1950s, it would be very uncomfortable to walk side-by-side with a black or even a Hispanic woman. The prejudices we grew up with affected our thought processes. Today most of our preconceived prejudices are long gone; mixed races and all religions are very much accepted by most Americans. The minorities in the next 50 years will probably become the majorities of the future, and it is essential that we live side-by-side as equals without discrimination for our great country to stay great. So those politicians, academic intellectuals, and even religious leaders: shame on you for perpetuating and overstating these wrongdoings. The idea of dividing the citizens of this nation through exaggerated claims of racism, anti-gay and anti-feminism feelings is sinful, to say the least, and should not be tolerated. To stop this we must have the strength to speak up without threat of being called a racist.

I could write a full chapter alone on this awful restrictive policy of political correctness. I wish we could all feel free to judge people only by their actions, since (as we all know) there are good and bad in all segments of our society. There are too many examples of political correctness that I could write about, so I'll just mention a few examples.

I grew up in a Christian country where I felt grateful that I was accepted as an American and able to practice my Jewish religion whenever and wherever I desired. Although we didn't celebrate the Christmas holiday, I've always loved the idea that it was the time of year where people would help one another and families would come together with joy in the spirit of giving. There are groups today that want to eliminate many of the Christmas symbols and songs from our schools and public places. Those might be technically against the freedom of religion amendment in our Constitution, but they are harmless events that are part of our great history. To accentuate this point, let us not forget that Christmas is a national holiday, and until that changes, let us not diminish the best part of the year for most Americans.

Present Immigration Policy = Insanity

Incidentally, we do have immigration laws. We are a country of laws, and that being said, we have 10 to 15 million illegal immigrants in our country today. We love immigrants; most of our parents were immigrants. But the politicians of today are not solving the problem but dividing our country as if you are either for or against any form of immigration. That is ridiculous. The great majority of Americans would like to find a fair way of resolving this problem. First of all, many of the highly educated foreigners who study much-needed professions such as science, math, engineering, etc. in our universities are not given a special path to citizenship that encourages them to stay in this country. On the other hand, illegal immigrants are ignored in some ways and encouraged to stay without permission and receive benefits that are not afforded to our own citizens. For example: at present, 13 states are giving illegal immigrants the right to enter state universities and be subsidized as if they are state residents, whereas students from out of state are charged double the tuition. This is not fair and creates anger between young people. Our borders are not properly maintained; arrested foreigners are set free and encouraged to continue their illegal stays. This causes hard-working legal employees in this category to skip their responsibilities to pay taxes. We accept all human beings in our emergency rooms without cost, and we force people such as domestics to risk embarrassment by paying them off the books. We don't make them legal, so they don't pay taxes. I could go on with these examples forever, but most Americans want most of these immigrants to stay within a fair and equitable new policy. The icing on the cake for me was the mayor of New Haven Connecticut recently declared that all illegal immigrants must be given the right to vote. Wow! And the federal government still subsidizes sanctuary cities (those cities that don't enforce any immigration laws) even when illegals break all laws. This is political correctness gone wild.

Let's resolve this problem. It's very doable. The only ones who perpetuate it are all the politicians who use this issue to enhance their votes and their pocketbook. Vote them out—it's the American way.

Financial Conditions in America Today

As of March 2013, we have a deficit—in other words, a debt of over 16.5 trillion dollars and rising. This is a number well in excess of anything anyone could ever imagine. With some exceptions, Americans, including our politicians and media, seem little concerned of its potential devastation of our society as we know it. Putting one's head in the sand never concludes with good results. The sound, basic financial policies of starting and operating my businesses were obtained at New York University in my Basic Finance 101 course. You need not be a famous economist to know that our present course will lead us, and certainly our children, into a awful place that we have have never experienced.

Here are some of my thoughts on this subject. We simply can't keep borrowing with no plan to repay our debt. The Chinese and the Arabs who own a good part of this debt may become a commanding force that control our economic independence. Remember, one of my most important business rules: you must control at least 51% of your business to be successful.

Our present government, with the Federal Reserve's complicity, has held our interest rates to virtually zero for the last number of years. It is inevitable that eventually inflation will force rising interest rates that will raise our debt to an inconceivable level. A government that continues to spend significantly more than it takes in will fail, and perhaps in the near future. They will be forced to print even more money, thus diminishing any savings or assets you may have.

Remember what the former Prime Minister of Great Britain Margaret Thatcher said:

"Socialism is great until you run out of other people's money."

The strength of our economic system has always been based on supply and demand, thus creating the best product for the least amount of money, making us very competitive on the world markets. What kind of a system is it when all the U.S. banks offer the same uncompetitive, low-interest rates on our savings and certificates of deposit, all of which are presently well under 1%? The banks, with a government wink, protect their weak balance sheets and are able to charge credit card holders with interest in excess of 20% on your unpaid credit card balances.

Even more important is that we have more credit card debt than could ever be imagined, held by middle- and lower-income people who have limited ability to ever pay off those balances. So what do they do? They keep spending and making the minimum payments of maybe $50 a month, thus increasing their balance due to these outrageous interest charges, and allowing them to somewhat falsely maintain their spending habits. We will come to a time when the banks will never be able to collect the majority of this debt without putting the whole country into bankruptcy.

The second most devastating condition in our country is the government-run student loan program. Again, this is giving money to people who probably will never be able to repay it, just kicking the can down the road. Within the foreseeable future the default rate on these loans will reach the point where the entire program will come tumbling down. How can we ask our students to pay back these amounts of money that will negatively affect their lives forever?

What plans will our bloated government develop to spend more money in the near future? The last month we received three robocalls saying something like this: "If you're not getting government assistance, call this number to see if you qualify." How about doing more to create jobs? The great majority of the Congress, including our president, are lawyers by profession; they may be good at being attorneys, but they sure stink at being sound business people and administrators.

Remember when they gave mortgages with no down payments to people who had no ability to pay? This government giveaway to obtain votes could someday bring our country down. So add together the student loans, the unlimited credit cards, the still-defaulting home mortgages, plus all the government entitlements, and you'll see what will lead us down a path to our demise as a great nation. Remember, the Soviet Union went down from its own weight, and presently the socialist European nations such as Greece, Spain, and Portugal are close to following suit.

Oh, did I forget to mention our new healthcare program affectionately called Obamacare? Remember what the Democrats majority leader Nancy Pelosi said: We have to pass it and we can read it and learn more about it. Well, we learned more about it, and we know that it will be much more expensive than originally promised. More government spending that we can't afford. There was a great quote recently from P. J. O'Rourke:

> "If you think health care is expensive now, wait until
> you see what it will cost when it's free."

I think you get the message, which is clear to anyone who wants to take their heads out of the sand. In my lifetime, Americans have been asked at times to sacrifice, which we did proudly. If our present government would give us a clear plan to reduce our deficit and create new jobs, most Americans would be first in line to assist. We don't want to give our money to a government that lies to us while wasting that money on inflated government duplicate programs, grants, and subsidies to the lobbyists who finance their campaigns while they give their friends and relatives high-paying jobs. It may sound cynical, but sadly, we all know its true. Our only option is to stay aware of the facts. Hold our representatives accountable, and if necessary, vote them out of office, no matter their political affiliation.

The Now Generation

I'd like to reflect on how this generation reacts differently from those growing up in the 40s and 50s. You might think that the definition of the Now Generation would be people wanting to take care of their responsibilities immediately, not putting them off for some future time. My observation is that it's the opposite, meaning "I want to enjoy myself now," which leads to the definition of instant gratification. In this segment I will attempt to explain what's wrong with the Now Generation. Apologies to anyone, including my own family members, who might take this personally.

It's obvious to me that most parents and children of this decade believe it's imperative to get a college education to land an interesting job with a decent salary. The idea of starting in the mailroom and working your way up is no longer considered attractive (and not really an option, since there's a diminishing need for a mailroom). When graduates start out with a higher-level job than they are qualified for, it usually it does not end well. The experience young people gain from starting at the so-called bottom rung and working their way up gives them the background and maturity to succeed, even in the economy we are living through today. These thoughts remind me of a quote by a friend of mine, which really hits the mark:

> "This young generation is trained and groomed as house pets and must still learn to survive in the wild."

This quotation perhaps is a little bit strong, but it makes its point. This generation is enjoying special benefits above and beyond my comprehension. That in itself is not bad, but if you've done almost everything by the time you reach 30, what do you have to look forward to? Most children, including those who are less advantaged, enjoy a cell phone, a computer, HD television, plus numerous other objects. Travel, eating out at restaurants, going to concerts, etc., etc. are a part of their normal lifestyles. Experiencing the pleasures of success at an early age takes away the greatest motivation that I experienced: dreaming, dreaming of someday living the American Dream. Don't get me wrong, there is still many motivated young people succeeding today as defined in the following quote:

> *"You can't put a limit on anything.*
> *The more you dream, the further you get."*
> —MICHAEL PHELPS

I don't want to belabor this, so I'll move on and list some short points on this subject, just to get it out of my system. Don't misunderstand me: I get my greatest satisfaction and enjoyment from talking to young people. They are generally interested and open, saying what's on their mind without filtering it through the political correctness of our society.

Role Models?

- The strong influence of TV shows like *Jersey Shore* and the Kardashians on our children.

- Rap music is presently the most popular music to this generation. As explained in my memoir, musical lyrics have been an important motivational part of my life. In rap, I have no idea what the heck anybody is saying. When I asked my grandchildren, they tell me they don't understand most of the words themselves; it's about the music. A few words I do pick up are usually the F word or words about killing cops, and raping or beating women. Whatever happened to "God Bless America" or perhaps "The Impossible Dream"?

- Young celebrities having babies without spouses not concerning themselves with the importance and difficulty raising a child and setting a poor example for their young fans.

- Comedians who find no difficulty in poking fun at specific people that they perhaps don't agree with. We used to make fun of the broad aspects of someone's cultural background, perhaps, but we never insulted any other human being directly. In my mind, this is nasty and borders on bullying, an unfortunate situation that is growing within our present society of young people.

- Teachers who befriend some students but don't command the respect that good educators have to achieve to get our children's attention. It almost impossible to fire an unqualified teacher after tenure, thus discouraging the good teachers. Teachers from my generation are still remembered and loved.

Of course, there are many more, but I hope you get my drift.

And finally, an activity that most of my generation can't stand is the total computerization of our grandchildren, including cell phones. Text - ing that says very little but diverts their attention from anything else, including their grandparents. The posting of their personal thoughts and silliness to their so-called hundreds of best friends, which I explained to them becomes a permanent record, perhaps someday to be used against them.

The ability to watch certain programming well beyond their age and maturity, which parents—no matter how hard they try—can never control. They are inclined to speak in short, abbreviated sign language to each other, thus affecting grammar and other important aspects needed in their adult life. Getting news and other information from unverifiable sources and very rarely taking the time to follow *Jerry's Law #19: Always verify to clarify*. And my personal pet peeves: Using cell phones in public places such as restaurants and sporting events, thus limiting their ability to absorb what's going on around them. And the *pièce de résistance* is talking on the cell phone during family dinners. This is where GL will always draw the line.

These new habits may be all well and good, but it is as true today as it was in my generation that those children who do extra activities above and beyond the normal have the greater chance to be happy and to succeed with their dreams. Those children who write for the school newspapers, participate in music and arts and sports, and volunteer for charitable work will separate themselves from others whose primary achievements are being great texters and having thousands of "friends" on Facebook.

Okay, I got it out of my system. I feel better so I'm canceling my shrink appointment and moving on.

Although some of my comments in this final chapter may not seem to follow my creed to "accentuate the positive," like many things in life, we have to overcome the roadblocks that may stand in our way. Over my lifetime, I've called myself a strange combination: a Cynical Optimist. Perhaps inspecting what you expect will give you some clarification, meaning good things don't always happen immediately, and clearing the path may be necessary.

It's my strong opinion that people should tell their rags-to-riches stories. For our country to maintain its standing in the world, we must keep the American Dream a reality. In today's America, with over-expanded entitlements and a country being divided by our media and politicians into categories of rich or poor, this seems to be a much less real hope. Our middle class is dwindling, which is an indication that the dream is fading. It should be noted that everyone still has the opportunity to succeed, but only with the right, positive mindset. When I first entered the real world and started looking for a job, I was petrified about the millions of people I had to compete with, but soon found out that less than 10% of our population had the desire to achieve to the next level of success. Those 10% were enough to move our country forward and enabled those who were committed a greater place to start building their American Dream. Even though 10 percent sounds small, it's way above the world's average. Virtually every one of my childhood friends had that mentality and moved their needle upwards. We must encourage our young generation and remind them that America is still the land of opportunity and that through their own efforts, fulfilling their dreams can be achieved.

When ideological thinking leaves college classrooms and becomes federal government policy, we are doomed to fail. Theory cannot replace reality, thus you can't change the things that historically made America great. I utilized the real American principles, including a strong work ethic, and I was rewarded by living the American Dream.

Listening is perhaps the most important aspect of learning for me. It started with sitting around our family dinner table when I was very young. Listening is something that is dying in today's society. It came to me that you learn much more by listening than by talking. Most people do not listen with the intent to understand; they listen with the intent to reply. This is why the written word is so important toward our ability to learn from others. I don't always have the answers, but I always have the questions, and then I usually can get the answers. This was one of my most important keys to success.

I'm proud to believe that I have a little Don Quixote in me, in his words, "Fight for the right without question or pause," etc. Many times in my life I've fought for things on principle. The three co-op boards I served on are perhaps my best examples. People always think that if you fight hard for something there's some personal benefit involved. I can state with a clear conscience that I never got any special benefits for those efforts—just a great feeling of doing the right thing even though it might rub some people the wrong way. Never accept these words from others: "Why do you care? It doesn't affect you personally." Stand up for what you believe, even if you lose some acquaintances on the way. Those so-called friends will never, ever understand where you're coming from. Those who stand up for principle and the good of others have to be encouraged and not put down as somebody annoying

354

because they are different from the crowd. Crowds very rarely accomplish anything important, wherein the individual and entrepreneurs are the brave ones who make our lives and country better.

Learning our history is perhaps the most important way to maintain civility and peace around the world. It's amazing to me that in many school districts our young generations of students learn very little history, namely about World War I and II, and specifically about the Holocaust. Also, I don't believe geography, one of my favorite subjects, is taught at all. History does repeat itself. In questioning young people, as I do often regarding subjects such as the Holocaust and World War II in general, the most common answers seem to be, "I think we learned about it or are going to learn about it" many are unable to discuss the issues in any depth. This is scary, to say the least. There are radicals all over the world who would love to destroy our way of life, and so the term "forewarned is forearmed." A recent Florida article advised that an organization called Holocaust Remembered had closed down. These were Holocaust survivors who went to classrooms and other venues to tell their stories of Hitler's death camps. When they started their Florida organization, there were 15,000 members and now barely 150 remain, too frail to continue. We have a tendency to either forget or disregard over time. The Holocaust was not just a blip in our lifetime. Just like our tragedy of 3,000 Americans being murdered by Muslim fanatics on September 11, 2001, there are those who will kill innocent people. These subjects must be discussed in depth with the next generation of leaders—namely our children and grandchildren—because nothing else but the facts can protect us from our enemies. Israel today stands pretty much alone in an area surrounded by their enemies. The world's leaders stand silent while Iran develops its bomb, the bomb that might first kill the six million Jews in Israel but for sure will reach many more of the hated Jews and Christians around the world in a short time. Israel stands between us and possibly the next war and the destruction of the free world as we know it. When I was 12 years old and a member of the Boy Scouts, their motto was (and still is) "Be Prepared." The so-called intellectual approach we are now using is no replacement for the practical approach we learn through history. If the schools don't teach our children, we must. Don't assume they fully understand or are intelligent or interested enough that they pick it up on their own.

On a recent cruise, Aviva and I met a wonderful couple from Texas named Dale and Rita Brown. They are devout Christians, and they live in rural America. We are Jewish and live in urban America. We discussed so many subjects, and even though we come from two different worlds, we had so many things in common. Human rights, believing in America, the right to practice religion as we see fit, and the great importance of individualism, to name a few. I truly believe that if I would write down the ten most important factors in my life and asked Americans from all across our country—political far left or right, rich or poor, well-educated or not—to list theirs, that 70 to 80% of their lists would match mine. Yet we are all bogged down by politically inflamed rhetoric that leads us to concentrating on issues that have mostly been resolved by law or practically resolved by our society, such as abortion, gay marriage, and racism. All well and good, and these should be discussed, but the truth is most Americans believe in family, work, and country. So a good start would be to agree to this: Let's converse on the items we agree on, which will probably be the most important, and work from there. Our good friends, the Browns, I know would agree.

As you can tell by this chapter, this man is very concerned about the future of our country. Many of the things that I grew up with and made me the success I am are changing before my eyes. This cynical optimist still believes that America will wake up and right the course. In the words of a man who lived the American Dream and who most positively affected my life and thinking, one of our greatest presidents:

"Freedom is never more than one generation away from extinction. We didn't pass it to our children in the bloodstream. It must be fought for, protected, and handed on for them to do the same, or one day we will spend our sunset years telling our children and our children's children what it was once like in the United States where men were free."
—Ronald Reagan

My Secrets to Starting Your Own Business

The greatest high you can receive during your working life is being successful in your own business. So I now offer for your review Jerry's guidelines in starting your own small business.

1. Find a niche too small for the big guys.

2. Look for a new popular trend.

3. Prepare a financial and marketing plan.

4. Timing is important, so prepare to be in the right place at the right time.

5. Control at least 51% of the business and all partners must have skin in the game, meaning making a financial investment.

6. Always be hands-on and have more knowledge of your business than your employees.

7. Try to enter a business with the least government regulations.

8. Give yourself enough working capital to get you through one full year.

9. If you proceed, give yourself at least three years to make a decent profit.

10. Follow Jerry's Laws: Inspect what you expect, you cannot do the minimum and reach the maximum, and verify to clarify.

As a very successful businessman and my good friend Bob Bellantoni likes to say, "It seems the harder I worked, the luckier I got."

And to quote my dear departed friend and one of the most successful men I had the good fortune to be with, Bob Edgell, "Nothing in the world could take the place of persistence. Talent will not, nothing is more common than unsuccessful men with talent. Keep it simple, touch all bases, and eliminate surprises. But be persistent."

So this is my formula for a word I love: entrepreneurship. With hard work and some luck, you could be the next Steve Jobs, whose words will end this segment:

"Time is limited, so don't waste it living someone else's life."

How I Would Like to Be Remembered

1. By the substance of my words, not my tone.

2. As a man who stood up for what he believed in regardless of the potential cost.

3. As a man who appreciates the American way and what it has given him; something that he would give his life to defend.

4. As a man who could never be intimidated by threats and always would speak up for what he believed in.

5. As a man who would not accept the words "What do you care about that problem? It won't affect you personally."

6. As a man who liked to make money but never was obsessed with it.

7. As a man who was a friend to his children, but even more important, a good parent.

8. As a man who wrote his memoirs for the right reasons.

9. As a man who always tried new things but learned from his past experiences.

10. As a man unique in dress as well as actions, often hard to read, always taking chances, and who would never back away from a challenge.

11. As a man who dealt with problems quickly and didn't let them fester out of control, even if he had to swallow his pride.

12. As a man who did it by the book, but was the author.

13. As a man who loved his wife so much and always realized how lucky he was.

Now that you've finished Benny the Book's Book, you should know me almost as well as I know myself. I can sum up the story of my life, the experiences I've learned from, and my philosophy after almost 80 years of living, into one sentence:

If you accentuate the positive, and never give up and never give in, you will find that . . .

Can't Is Not an Option.

Made in the USA
Lexington, KY
21 May 2013